A Guide to
Manuscript Collections
in the
History of Psychology
and Related Areas

Bibliographies
in the
History of Psychology and Psychiatry
A Series

Robert H. Wozniak, General Editor

A Guide to
Manuscript Collections
in the
History of Psychology
and Related Areas

COMPILED BY

Michael M. Sokal

AND

Patrice A. Rafail

KRAUS INTERNATIONAL PUBLICATIONS
A Division of Kraus-Thomson Organization Limited

Millwood, New York / London, England / Nendeln, Liechtenstein

Copyright © 1982 Michael M. Sokal and Patrice A. Rafail

First Printing

Printed in the United States of America

Library of Congress Cataloging in Publication Data

Sokal, Michael M.
  A guide to manuscript collections in the
history of psychology and related areas.

(Bibliographies in the history
of psychology and psychiatry)

  Bibliography: p.
  Includes index.
  1. Psychology—History—Archival resources.
2. Psychology—History—Manuscripts. I. Rafail,
Patrice A.   II. Title. [DNLM: 1. Psychology—
History—MANU CATA. Z 6611.P9 S683g]
BF81.S58   016.15'09   81-17189
ISBN 0-527-84420-9   AACR2

Contents

Introduction

"Historians of psychology have long preached to each other about the importance of manuscript collections for their work . . . but until now have lacked a guide to such collections." This was the stated motivation for the compilation of the original version of this guide published informally in December 1977 by the Wellesley College Colloquium on the History of Psychology. That edition, consisting of 100 multilithed 8½ x 14″ copies, was designed to address this problem and did much to stimulate extensive archival research in the field. Despite the awkwardness of its format, historians and others apparently found the *Guide* useful and its first printing was exhausted by November 1978. A second printing was prepared and it too is now (August 1981) almost exhausted.

Despite the success of this version, it was understood from its inception that it was limited in various ways. It included only entries published in the *National Union Catalog of Manuscript Collections (NUCMC)*. It did not contain a name index, and it gave only the addresses of important repositories of major manuscript collections without describing their contents. This second, greatly expanded version was prepared in an attempt to remedy the limitations of the earlier one.

In order to help scholars further their archival work and to stimulate research on a wide variety of topics in the field, one characteristic of the original version of the *Guide* has been retained. The scope of this volume is as broad as that of the first. The subject index gives a good idea of the range of material included in this *Guide*. Here it is perhaps appropriate to note simply that the volume presents descriptions of manuscript collections relating to all types of psychology, psychiatry, psychoanalysis, child development, parapsychology, phrenology, neurology, physiology, mental health, hygiene, and deficiency; and anthropology, social work, and university administration as they relate to psychology.

This version includes more than five hundred entries on individual manuscript collections, while the original included only about 230. In expanding the *Guide*, many sources were used. The 1976, 1977, 1978 and 1979 volumes of *NUCMC*—those issued since the last *Guide* was published—were all consulted and relevant descriptions were copied for inclusion here. In addition, in going beyond *NUCMC*, the compilers consulted many other directories and bibliographies, received the help of several distinguished scholars, corresponded with dozens of archivists and librarians, and visited many manuscript repositories themselves. This *Guide*, then, includes many different types of entries. Some of the descriptions are, as with the original version, taken straight from *NUCMC*. Many more entries printed here are based upon the *NUCMC* description as supplemented by additional information, often based upon the compilers' own research or upon correspondence with the appropriate archivist. Quite often the added material includes a list of major correspondents represented in the collection in question, so that researchers interested in particular individuals can trace them through the name and institution index. Other entries included here are drawn from descriptions published in articles, library newsletters, and similar sources, again often supplemented by the compilers' research or by correspondence. Finally, some collections are described in print for the first time ever in this *Guide*.

The *Guide* is divided into two main sections. The first and larger section covers individual manuscript collections, while the second describes the most important manuscript repositories in the U.S. and other countries. All entries are accessible through a name and institution index, a repository index and a subject index, designed to make the use of this volume as easy as possible.

Despite the *Guide*'s scope and the compilers' extensive search, users of this volume will undoubtedly find flaws in its pages. The compilers hope that they can remedy these errors in future editions, and would appreciate being informed of any omissions or corrections.

Acknowledgments

The two of us could not have compiled this volume without the extensive help of many others, only some of whom can be mentioned here. It is a pleasure to thank these men and women for all that they did to aid us in our work.

Three individuals in particular—Ludy T. Benjamin, Jr., of Texas A & M University, and John A. Popplestone and Marion White McPherson of the Archives of the History of American Psychology—deserve special thanks. Ben had compiled a list of many collections within the scope of this *Guide* which he kindly allowed us to use; this eased our work load considerably. He also prepared descriptions of several important repositories that contributed greatly to the second section of this volume. In fact, many of its strengths are the result of his work. Since the Archives was established in 1965, John and Marion have kept a "locator file" of collections important for the history of psychology which they kindly allowed us to consult. Though admittedly imperfect—it is based upon rumor and hearsay and gossip as well as on accurate reports—this file proved extremely useful in our work. In fact, any statement of what this book owes to Ben and John and Marion is bound to understate the debt many times.

In trying to locate as many collections as possible, we asked those scholars who have worked extensively within the area of this *Guide* for information about sets of papers and archives that the first edition missed. Several responded, and these individuals—Mitchell G. Ash, Wolfgang G. Bringmann, David E. Leary, Jacques Quen, Eugene Taylor, Michael Wertheimer, and William R. Woodward—have done much to make this edition as inclusive as it is. We have undoubtedly missed many other important collections, but we would have missed many more without the help of these seven men.

Once we located the collections that we wanted to include in this volume, we had to get the information that we needed to prepare the descriptions of them. We were not able to visit many of the most relevant repositories, so we had to rely primarily on the efforts of archivists and manuscript librarians for this information. Most of these men and women were extremely helpful. But 19 in particular did so much and went so far out of their way to help us that they deserve special mention. These individuals are: Mary B. Blessing, Stanford University Archives; Deborah Cozort, MIT Archives; Bernard R. Crystal, Columbia University Libraries; Clark A. Elliott, Harvard University Archives; Lilace Hatayama, University of California at Los Angeles Library; Paul T. Heffron and Paul G. Sifton, Library of Congress; Kathleen Jacklin, Cornell University Libraries; David Klaassen, Social Welfare History Archives; Kathleen McIntyre, University of Missouri Western Historical Manuscript Collection; Irene Moran, University of California, Berkeley, Bancroft Library; Patrick M. Quinn, Northwestern University Archives; Michael T. Ryan, University of Chicago Libraries; G. Edwin Southern, Jr., and Robert L. Byrd, Duke University Libraries; Ann L. S. Southwell, University of Virginia Library; Joseph G. Svoboda, University of Nebraska Archives; Manfred Waserman, National Library of Medicine History of Medicine Division; and Connie Wolf, Missouri Institute of Psychiatry Library. Again, their contribution to this volume can only be underestimated.

Other archivists and manuscript librarians who helped us in our work are: Miriam F. Aarons, Los Angeles Psychoanalytic Society and Institute; Gary J. Arnold, Ohio Historical Society; Marguerite K. Ashford, Bernice P. Bishop Museum; W. E. Bigglestone, Oberlin College Archives; Judith Bohnan, Canadian Mental Health Association; Y. Boynton, Galesburg State Research Hospital; A. W. Buckingham, Morningside College; Emmett D. Chisum and Gene M. Gressley, University of Wyoming American Heritage Center; Maxine B. Clapp, University of Minnesota Archives; John M. Clayton, Jr., University of Delaware Archives; Bruce C. Compton, Historical Society of Pennsylvania; Jean M. Converse, University of Michigan Institute for Social Research; Hilary Cummings, Southern Illinois University Libraries; Farila David, Foundation for Research on the Nature of Man; Carolyn A. Davis and Amy Doherty, Syracuse University Libraries; Anne P. Diffendal, Nebraska State Historical Society; John Dobson, University of Tennessee Library; Jeanne Miller Eaton, Institute of Gerontology; John S. Ezell and Teresa O'Guin, University of Oklahoma Western History Collections; Alice K. Garren, Gracewood State School and Hospital Library; Neil W. Gerdes, Chicago Theological Seminary Library; Alex Gildzen, Kent State University Libraries; Peter Gottlieb, West Virginia University Libraries; Frances Goudy, Vassar College Library; Jane Haase, Austen Riggs Center; Nancy Harney, Hartford Seminary Foundation; J. William Hess, Rockefeller Archive Center; Judith Hollenberg, Illinois Department of Health and Developmental Disabilities; Toma Iglehart, University of Texas Perry-Castenada Library; Glen Jenkins, Cleveland Medical Library; Nellie Johns, Yerkes Regional Primate Center Library; Karl Kabelac, University of Rochester Library; Nathan M. Kaganoff, American Jewish Historical Society; Marilyn Katz, Child Welfare League of America; Helen R. Lansberg, The Institute of Living Library; Albert C. Lewis, University of Texas Humanities Research Center; Susan Longenecker, Vermont State Hospital Library; Michael Lordi, The New School; Nancy McCall, Johns Hopkins

ACKNOWLEDGMENTS

University Medical Archives; Joyce Marson, White Memorial Medical Center Library; Alexandra Mason, University of Kansas Libraries; Glenn Miller, Institute for Psychoanalysis of Chicago; Christine M. Missoff, New York State Library; Julia C. Morgan and M. C. Beecheno, Johns Hopkins University Library and Archives; Mary Mylenki, Payne-Whitney Psychiatric Clinic Library; Charles Niles, Jr., Boston University Libraries; Sylvia Nissenoff, American Personnel and Guidance Center; Wayne Norman, Parapsychology Foundation Library; Jean F. Preston, Princeton University Library; Ruth M. Reynolds, New York Psychoanalytic Institute; William H. Richter, University of Texas Barker Texas History Center; Mary Rider, Vanderbilt University Library; Marvin Rosen, Elwyn Institutes; Elizabeth Shenton, Schlesinger Library on the History of Women, Radcliffe College; Richard A. Shrader, University of North Carolina Southern Historical Collection; Leonard Skonecki, Dayton Mental Health and Developmental Center Library; Bonnie Stecher, Massachusetts Department of Public Health; John D. Stinson and Paul R. Rugen, New York Public Library; Jeanette M. Thomas, Association for Research and Enlightenment; A. Ronald Tonks, Southern Baptist Convention Historical Commission; Carolyn Waller, Bradley Hospital Medical Library; Eleanor Wash, Lanterman State Hospital; Alison Wilson, National Archives Center for Polar and Scientific Archives; and Anthony Zito, Catholic University Archives.

Several of the entries and some of the materials in the appendices are reprinted here with the very kind permission of the owners of their copyrights. For this permission, it is a pleasure to thank: Dr. C. J. Hogrefe, of the Verlag für Psychologie, Gottingen, and C. J. Hogrefe, Inc., Toronto; Ms. Kathleen Jacklin, of the Department of Manuscripts and University Archives, Cornell University Libraries; David Klaassen, of the Social Welfare History Archives, University of Minnesota; and Dr. Arnold Thackray, of the University of Pennsylvania, and editor of *Isis*.

Two college work-study students at Worcester Polytechnic Institute, Robert Baker and Richard Wilson, also helped us greatly in all sorts of ways and earned our thanks many times over.

Finally, thanks are due to three individuals connected with the publisher of this volume, who helped make it possible. Marion Sader, editor-in-chief of Kraus International Publications, gave us aid and assistance—particularly moral support—when we were swamped with what seemed like thousands of "sorry, no information available" letters. Steven L. Goulden, Kraus's managing editor, helped us turn what we collected into what we hope is a useful and informative volume. And Robert Wozniak, who edits the series in which this volume appears, deserves thanks for talking us into doing this second edition after we swore up and down that, after the first edition, we would never do another *Guide*.

Guide to
Manuscript Collections

1. *Adams, Donald Keith, 1902-1971.*
Papers, 1924-70. ca. 6 ft.
In University of Akron, Archives of the History of American Psychology (Akron, Ohio).

   Psychologist. Class notes (1924-25) taken by Adams as a graduate student at Harvard University, and material relating to his associations with members of the Gestalt school of psychology, work with government agencies, and career on the faculty of Duke University. Major correspondents include Urie Bronfenbrenner, Julius F. Brown, J. F. Dashiell, Tamara Dembo, R. L. Flowers, James Q. Holsopple, Peter H. Klopfer, Wolfgang Köhler, David Krech, Robert Leeper, Kurt Lewin, Konrad Lorenz, William McDougall, Robert B. MacLeod, Florence Miale, James G. Miller, Henry Allen Moe, H. A. Murray, Joseph B. Rhine, Wolfgang Schleidt, John B. Schooland, Edward C. Tolman, Alex Waite, Hans Wallach, W. H. Wannamaker, Herbert F. Wright, Robert M. Yerkes, and Karl Zener.

2. *Allen, Doris Twitchell, 1901-   .*
Papers, 1944-66. 3¾ ft.
In University of Akron, Archives of the History of American Psychology (Akron, Ohio).

   Psychologist. Minutes, correspondence, committee reports, and directories of the International Council of Psychologists and the International Council of Women Psychologists.

   Unpublished guide available.

   Access restricted.

3. *Allen, Doris Twitchell, 1901-   .*
Papers. ca. 130 ft.
In University of Cincinnati Library, Special Collections (Cincinnati, Ohio).

   Correspondence, reports, publications, and other material relating to Allen's personal and professional activities.

3

4. *Allport, Floyd H., 1890-   .*
Papers, 1927-67.
In Syracuse University Library (Syracuse, New York).
   Professor of psychology at Syracuse University. Class and lecture notes, newspaper clippings, thesis materials, manuscripts, research notes, and collected professional and personal correspondence. A copy of Allport's Ph.D. thesis (1919, Harvard) is included, along with manuscripts of unpublished books.
   A guide is available at the repository.

5. *Allport, Gordon Willard, 1897-1967.*
Papers, 1930-67. 20 ft.
In Harvard University Archives (Cambridge, Massachusetts).
   Professor of social ethics and psychology. Correspondence, manuscripts of lectures, reviews, research notes, material relating to teaching, reprints, and other material.
   Finding-aid for major correspondence series available in the repository.
   Access restricted.
   Information on literary rights available in the repository.

6. *Almack, John Conrad, 1883-1953.*
Papers, 1920-49. 10 ft. (ca. 150 items).
In Stanford University Archives, Green Library (Stanford, California).
   Professor of education at Stanford University. Manuscripts and published copies of articles and other writings by Dr. Almack. Subjects covered include history, education, psychology, sociology, health, medicine, child growth and development, poetry, short story and mystery story writing, and handwriting. Includes articles for the *American School Board Journal* and the *Stanford Spellers.*
   Unpublished guide and register in the repository.
   Information on literary rights available in the repository.
   Gift of Dr. Almack's widow, Mrs. Lowell Turrentine, 1968.

7. *American Association of Psychiatric Social Workers, New York.*
Papers, 1921-58. 33 folders and 1 legal-size folder.
In University of Minnesota, Social Welfare History Archives (Minneapolis, Minnesota).
   The collection is arranged in three basic sections. Annual material includes minutes of the annual meetings, secretary's reports, and presidential addresses. The committees are divided by functions, whether administrative or study. Not all the committees are covered for all the years of the association's existence. Association publications include the serial publications, which are the *News-Letter,* the *Journal of Psychiatric Social Work,* and the *Bulletin;* pamphlets and reprints. The Social Welfare History Archives holdings of the *News-Letter,* the *Journal,* and the *Bulletin* are nearly complete, and these publications contain much important information on the work of the association.

8. *American Education Fellowship.*
Records, 1924-61. 21 ft.
In University of Illinois Archives (Urbana, Illinois).

Correspondence, financial statements, audit reports, journals, ledgers, directors' and treasurers' reports, promotional material, galley and page proofs, back issues, reprints, and other records of the American Education Fellowship (before 1944 the Progressive Education Association) and its magazine, *Progressive Education*. Includes material relating to local chapters, academic freedom, the status of the progressive education movement, the New Education Fellowship of London; the fellowship's commissions on educational freedom, Indian affairs, human relations, the relationship of the school to the college, separation of church and state, the Institute for the Study of Personality Development, the General Education Board, and the National Commission on Cooperative Curriculum Planning.
Received 1964-65.

9. *American Orthopsychiatric Association.*
Records, 1962-78. 10 ft.
In University of Minnesota, Social Welfare History Archives (Minneapolis, Minnesota).

The collection contains copies of papers presented at the association's annual conferences, reflecting a multidisciplinary approach to a broad range of issues affecting children, adolescents, and their families, schools, and communities. The association brings together psychiatrists, psychologists, psychiatric social workers, and related professionals who share a concern for mental health and the study of human behavior. A reel of microfilm within the collection contains minutes of executive committee meetings (1923-1963).

10. *American Psychological Association.*
Records, 1920-66. 60 ft. (ca. 50,000 items).
In Library of Congress, Manuscript Division (Washington, D.C.).

Correspondence, reports, administrators' records, minutes, congressional testimony, financial data, printed matter, and other papers, largely administrative, reflecting problems associated with the organization and management of the association's boards, committees, and publications. Includes papers of Willard Olson, executive secretary; and correspondence of John Darley, Thelma Hunt, Fillmore Sanford, Dael Wolfle, and Robert M. Yerkes; and material relating to gerontology, mental health, insurance problems of psychologists, the relationship between psychologists and the clergy, loyalty oaths, ethical standards, and the relationship between the association and government agencies.
Unpublished finding-aid in the library.
Information on literary rights available in the library.
Gift of the association, 1967-68.

11. *American Psychological Association.*
Addition, 1912-72. ca. 30,000 items.
In Library of Congress, Manuscript Division (Washington, D.C.).

11. *(Continued)*

Correspondence, reports, minutes of meetings, testimonies of congressional hearings, ballots, financial papers, and other records of various groups within the association, including the Council of Representatives, the Board of Directors, lesser boards and committees, and executive officers. Includes papers of Arthur H. Brayfield, executive officer, and material relating to the Conference of State Psychological Associations (1952-67), American Association of Applied Psychologists (1938-44) which merged with the association in 1946, and the *Journal of Abnormal and Social Psychology* (1949-55). Topics covered include civil rights and minority groups, information exchanged with the U.S.S.R., and Medicare. Correspondents include George W. Albee, Isador Chein, Kenneth E. Clark, Dorothy Clendenen, Erasmus Hoch, J. McVicker Hunt, and Leona Tyler.

Finding-aid in the repository.

Information on literary rights available in the repository.

Gift of the association, 1973.

12. *American Psychological Association. Division (16) of School Psychology.*

Records, 1946-71. ca. 8 ft.

In University of Akron, Archives of the History of American Psychology (Akron, Ohio).

Convention plans and evaluations, membership applications, election procedures, and brochures. Major correspondents include Jane Hildreth, Boyd McCandless, Harriet O'Shea, Keith Perkins, and George A. Stouffer.

Unpublished finding-aids in the repository.

In part, restricted.

Information on literary rights available in the repository.

Gift of the division, 1967 and after.

Additions to the collection are expected.

13. *Ames, Louise (Bates), 1908-* .

Papers, 1939-64. 4 ft. (3000 items).

In Library of Congress, Manuscript Division (Washington, D.C.).

Child psychologist and educator. Correspondence; bibliography of Dr. Ames (articles, monographs, reviews, films, and TV series) 1933-65; statement of Dr. Ames's work, 1939-49; correspondence, clippings, printed matter, and memorabilia relating to the work of Dr. Ames and her collaborator, Frances Lillian Ilg, as columnists and doctors, and to the Gesell Institute of Child Development.

Unpublished finding-aid in the library.

14. *Anderson, Archibald Watson, 1905-65.*

Papers, 1938-65. 4 ft.

In University of Illinois Archives (Urbana, Illinois).

Professor of history and philosophy of education at the University of Illinois. Correspondence, reports, and other papers relating to: the history of education, the University of Illinois College of Education, students, publications, and the life of Anderson; policies and meetings of the Progressive Education Association, the American Education Fellowship, the John Dewey Society and its yearbooks; and Anderson's work in editing and securing contributions for *Educational Administration and Supervision, Educational Theory, History of Education Journal, Journal of Educational Psychology,* and *Progressive Education.* Correspondents include Theodore Brameld, H. C. Buchnolz, Orin B. Graff, H. Gordon Hullfish, Harold Rugg, Ordway Tead, Isaak N. Thut, and William Van Til.

Unpublished finding-aid in the repository.

Received 1965.

15. *Angell, James Rowland, 1869-1949.*
Papers, 1874-1950. 13 ft.

In Yale University Library (New Haven, Connecticut).

Educator and psychologist. Professional and personal correspondence, biographical sketches, two diaries written as a boy in China, notes, lectures and speeches, manuscripts of writings, book reviews in French and English, printed material, awards, itineraries, memorabilia, and family and academic photos. Many papers relate to Angell's presidency of Yale University. Includes records relating to Angell's education at Harvard and membership in the Old Colonial Historical Association and Harvard Graduate Club, and two record albums concerning his career as educational consultant for the National Broadcasting Company. Most of the family correspondence is from Angell's father, James Burrill Angell (1829-1916), educator and diplomat; his mother, Sarah Swoope (Caswell) Angell (1831-1903); and his wife, Marion Isabel (Watrous) Angell. Other correspondents include Charles Bakewell, Harriet B. Caswell, Thomas Thompson Caswell, John Dewey, Alfred S. Hadden, William James, Lois Angell McLaughlin, A. H. Pierce, E. A. Shepard, Phillip Watrous, and other members of the Angell family.

Unpublished register in the library.

Information on literary rights available in the library.

Gift of Mrs. Angell, 1949-67.

16. *Association for Jewish Children of Philadelphia.*
Records, 1855-1974. 28 vols. and 45 boxes.

In Philadelphia Jewish Archives Center (Philadelphia, Pennsylvania).

Correspondence, minutes, reports, case files, registers, rollbooks, publicity material, and photos, of a community child-care agency and its predecessors, Jewish Foster Home and Orphan Asylum, Home for Hebrew Orphans, Foster Home for Hebrew Orphans, Juvenile Aid Society, Homewood School, Bureau for Jewish Children, and Northeastern Orphan Home. Includes information about children in the homes, adoption and foster home committees, and foster or adoptive parents; and records of the German-Jewish Children's Aid Committee (later European Jewish Children's Aid Committee), which helped bring European refugees to this country from 1934 until after World War II.

Unpublished inventory in the repository.

Gift of Joseph Taylor for the association.

17. *Association for the Aid of Crippled Children: oral history collection.*
Oral histories. 10 items.
In Columbia University Libraries (New York, New York).

Transcripts of tape-recorded interviews with members of the board and staff of the Association for the Aid of Crippled Children, later known as the Foundation for Child Development, focusing on the transition of the organization from a service agency to a foundation, which was made possible by the bequests of Milo Belding. Relates to the association's support of research in prenatal and perinatal problems, genetics, and embryology; conferences on prematurity, the placenta, limb morphology, and teratology; and studies of learning disabilities, mental retardation, and accident prevention. Describes international collaborative studies with the University of Aberdeen, the Karolinska Institute (Stockholm), and the University of Kyoto, as well as staff cooperation with the National Institutes of Health and the background of President Kennedy's Panel on Mental Retardation. Includes personal recollections of Dugald Baird, John Lind, William McPeak, Clement Reid, Laurence Rockefeller, and Howard Rusk. Persons interviewed include Herbert Birch, Lewis Cuyler, Charles Dollard, Mrs. Richard Emmet, Alice Fitz-Gerald, Mrs. Ross McFarland, Leonard Mayo, Stephen Richardson, Milton Senn, Robert Slater, and Chester Swinyard.

Described in *The Oral History Collection of Columbia University* (1973), pp. 18-19.

Access restricted.

Underwritten by the association.

18. *Audio Cassette Collection.*
Oral history, 1960- . ca. 1000 tapes and 12 manuscripts.
In Lewis Audiovisual Research and Teaching Archive (Tucson, Arizona).

Interview with Erika Freeman, psychologist, author, and protégé of Theodore Reich; and an interview with Margaret Mead, anthropologist. Recollections of Ann and Leon Steinberg, who sought healing through psychic surgery, are included.

Unpublished guide available.

19. *Augusta Mental Health Institute.*
Records, 1836-1941. 363 vols.
In Maine State Archives (Augusta, Maine).

Records of the hospital, established in 1834, for mentally ill persons. Includes financial records, data on women and men who worked with patients, register of patients, records showing the allowances of patients, and town clerk records on patients who had formerly resided in the town and later died in the institute. Minutes of the Board of Trustees meetings include notes on discussions of hospital policy regarding the condition of the patients and the physical surroundings of the institute.

Access restricted.

20. *Austen Riggs Center, Inc.*
Records. 1 box.
In Austen Riggs Library, Austen Riggs Center, Inc. (Stockbridge, Massachusetts).
Early financial negotiations and records of the center. Includes lectures delivered by Austen Fox Riggs, M.D., at Harvard Medical School and Williams College. Includes a history of the center, a list of staff members, and minutes of staff meetings, 1940-47.
Donated by Miss Alice Riggs.

21. *Axtelle, George Edward, 1893-1974.*
Papers, 1959-66. 8 ft.
In Southern Illinois University Archives (Carbondale, Illinois).
Professor of education and philosophy at Southern Illinois University. Correspondence relating to the publication of *The Collected Works of John Dewey*, which Axtelle edited, Axtelle's activities as president of the executive committee of the John Dewey Society, and the American Humanist Association, of which he was president.
Inventory in the repository.
Gift of George E. Axtelle, 1968.

22. *Baer, Jean Hitchcock, 1918-1974.*
Papers, 1946-75. 4½ ft.
In University of Illinois at Chicago Circle Library (Chicago, Illinois).
Researcher and authority in the field of student counseling and guidance, and professor of education. Papers include information on vocational counseling for the Social Security Disability Program, mental health, and educational psychology.

23. *Baldwin, James Mark, 1861-1934.*
Papers, 2 boxes.
In Princeton University Library (Princeton, New Jersey).
Psychologist. Correspondence, a scrapbook, and many press clippings.

24. *Barnard, Frederick Augustus Porter, 1809-1889.*
Papers, 1853-89. 8 vols. and 1 box.
In Columbia University Libraries (New York, New York).
Educator. Correspondence, sermons, miscellaneous addresses, reminiscences and memoirs. Most of the correspondence is addressed to Eugene and Julius Hilgard and relates to the University of Mississippi, of which Barnard was president from 1856 to 1858.

25. *Barnes, Earl, 1861-1935.*
Scrapbooks, 1882-1912. 2 ft.
In Stanford University Archives (Stanford, California).
Professor of education at Stanford University. Chiefly research notes and case

25. *(Continued)*

histories, together with correspondence and reprints of scholarly articles (1882-97), relating to Barnes's interest in child psychology and development; correspondence, clippings, and programs (1894-96) relating to his affiliation with the California Teachers Association; articles (1907-08) clipped from the *London Daily News* about British personalities; and articles, reviews, bibliographies, and clippings (1892-1912), pertaining to race relations, status of Blacks in the United States, and to Haiti and South Africa.

Unpublished finding-aid in the repository.

Gift of Mr. Barnes's son, Joseph Barnes, 1957.

26. *Bartholomew, Jacob, 1818-1863.*

Papers, 1836-86. 581 items.

In Indiana University, Lilly Library (Bloomington, Indiana).

Granville College faculty member (Granville, Ohio) and justice of the peace in Butte County, California. Papers from the Ohio period (1838-49) include letters from f iends and relatives, letters and papers on phrenology from Orson Squire Fowler, material from Granville College, and letters from Abraham Bartholomew, a Lutheran minister, relating to his work and to meetings of the Lutheran Synod in Ohio. California papers include overland diary (1850), official papers of Bartholomew's term as justice of the peace, household account book (1859-63), and letters and papers relating to South Feather Water Company in Forbestown, California, owned by Bartholomew and D.W.C. Gaskill. Other papers are Bartholomew's wife's, Emily (Ebersole) Bartholomew, including diaries (1859-61), letters, and his estate papers. Correspondents include Bartholomew's father, George Bartholomew.

Card index in the repository.

27. *Beard, George Miller, 1839-1883.*

Papers, 1853-1923. ca. 2 ft.

In Yale University Library (New Haven, Connecticut).

Physician of New York City. Correspondence, writings, biographical material, newspaper clippings, photos, and other papers, relating to Beard's work on the medicinal uses of electricity, the definition of criminal insanity, and his interest in spiritualism. Includes letters received by his daughter, Grace Alden Beard, relating to a biographical study of her father.

Unpublished register in the library.

Information on literary rights available in the library.

Gift of Mr. and Mrs. George Beard Walker, 1971.

28. *Beaver, James Addams, 1837-1914.*

Papers, 1855-1914. 20,000 items.

In Pennsylvania State University Library (University Park, Pennsylvania).

Lawyer, judge, and governor of Pennsylvania. Business and personal correspondence, pamphlets, circulars, clippings, and photos, chiefly covering Beaver's campaigns and term as governor. Includes material relating to his Civil War service with the 45th Pennsylvania Regiment, his business enterprises in the

Bellefonte, Pennsylvania, area; his term as justice of the Superior Court of Pennsylvania, his service as trustee and board president of Pennsylvania State College, the Curtin Memorial Monument, Camp Curtin in Harrisburg, Pennsylvania, and the State Hospital for the Insane in Warren, Pennsylvania.
Unpublished guide in the library.
Information on literary rights available in the library.
Gift of Thomas Beaver and Benjamin J. Gryctko.

29. *Beers, Clifford Whittingham, 1876-1943.*
Papers, 1905-18, 1966. ca. 4 ft.
In Yale University Library (New Haven, Connecticut).
Founder of the mental hygiene movement. Drafts and notes for Beers's book *A Mind That Found Itself* (1908); printed material, pamphlets, and clippings, relating to Beers's work in the field of mental hygiene.
Unpublished register in the library.
Information on literary rights available in the library.
Gift of Mrs. Beers and Emily L. Martin.

30. *Bender, Lauretta, 1897-   .*
Papers, 1926-73. 3 drawers.
In Brooklyn College Library, Special Collections (Brooklyn, New York).
Psychiatrist and author. Correspondence, a scrapbook, and photos of Bender, whose interests were in child psychiatry and visual motor gestalten. Major correspondents include Karl Menninger and various state officials.

31. *Bentley, Arthur Fisher, 1870-1957.*
Papers, 1891-1960. 14,774 items.
In Indiana University, Lilly Library (Bloomington, Indiana).
Philosopher. Correspondence and manuscripts of Bentley's writings, together with correspondence of his wife, Imogene Shaw Bentley. Major correspondents are John Dewey, Felix Kaufmann, Count Alfred Korzybski, and Orland Otway Norris. Other correspondents include Richard Philip Baker, Percy Williams Bridgman, Morris Raphael Cohen, Harold Thayer Davis, Stuart Carter Dodd, Seba Eldridge, Horace Snyder Fries, Bertram Myron Gross, Charles Banner Hagen, Jerome Hall, William Powers Hapgood, Ralph Stayner Lillie, George Andrew Lundberg, Ernest Nagel, Charles K. Ogden, Nicholas Henry Pronko, Joseph Ratnor, Merrill Flagg Roff, Leslie Evan Schlytter, Richard Wirth Taylor, Solomon Weinstock, and Kenneth Powers Williams.
Card index in the repository.
Access restricted.
Gifts of Arthur F. Bentley, 1953; Mrs. Bentley, 1958-60; and Julius Altman, 1960; additions from Mrs. Bentley's estate, 1972.

32. *Berdie, Ralph F., 1916-1974.*
Data. 8 boxes.
In University of Minnesota Archives, Walter Library (Minneapolis, Minnesota).
Two boxes contain his Minnesota Dropout Study Data, which are mostly questionnaires and blueprints.

33. *Bernfeld, Siegfried, 1892-1953.*
Papers, 1854-1970. 6000 items.
In Library of Congress, Manuscript Division (Washington, D.C.).

Psychoanalyst. General and family correspondence, manuscripts and type-scripts of writings, reports, minutes of meetings; and printed material, in German and English, chiefly 1930-53, relating to Bernfeld's professional activities in Europe and America, and to educational reform, psychoanalytic theory and the theory cf consciousness expressed in point-set topology, the Wiener Psycho-analytischer Vereinigung, Jewish youth movements, and the San Francisco Psychoanalytic Study Group. Approximately half of the collection consists of correspondence, writings, articles, biographical data, bibliographies, and other research material on Sigmund Freud, compiled by Bernfeld and his wife, Suzanne Aimee (Cassirer) Paret Bernfeld. Freud's correspondents include Wilhelm Fliess, Ludwig Jekels, Theodor Reik, Hanns Sachs, Ernst Simmel, and George Sylvester Viereck. Other material includes drafts of writings by Paul Federn, Otto Fenichel, Ernest Jones, Herbert Silberer, and Gustav Wyneken, on such topics as dreams, projection, education, Marxism, and socialism, as they relate to psychoanalytic theory. Bernfeld's correspondents include Leslie Adams, Franz Alexander, William G. Barrett, Manfred Bernfeld, Sergi Feitelberg, Otto Fenichel, Hilda Geiringer, Josef Gicklhorn, Fritz Goldmann, Willi Hoffer, Ernest Jones, Bernard Kamm, Ernst Kris, Hans Lampl, Rudolf Olden, Helen F. Puner, Otto Rank, Theodor Reik, Erwin Rohm, Hanns Sachs, Ernst Simmel, Rene Spitz, William Stern, Ernst Waldinger, and Gustav Wyneken.

Unpublished finding-aid in the repository.

Information on literary rights available in the repository.

Gift of Mr. Bernfeld's daughters, Rosemarie Ostwald and Ruth Goldberg, 1970.

Additions to the collection are expected.

34. *Bill, Fred Adelbert, and Family.*
Papers, 1793-1957. 10 boxes and 3 cases.
In Minnesota Historical Society, Archives and Manuscripts (St. Paul, Minnesota).

Includes pamphlets by phrenologists describing the character of Clara and Fred Bill.

Unpublished guide available.

35. *Billings, John Shaw, 1838-1913.*
Papers, 1861-1918. 44 ft.
In New York Public Library (New York, New York).

Librarian and surgeon. Correspondence and papers relating to Billings's work with the U.S. Army Medical Department (1861-95), Johns Hopkins Hospital (1873-90), National Board of Health (1879-81), the 10th and 11th Census, University of Pennsylvania Hospital and Laboratory of Hygiene (1890-95), New York Public Library (1895-1913), Committee of Fifty on the liquor problem (1893-1904), Carnegie Institution (1902-13), etc.; family correspondence, including letters from Billings to his wife regarding his Civil War experiences; lectures, addresses, notes, and miscellaneous papers. Correspondents include Alexander Agassiz, Alexander G. Bell, John Bigelow, Henry P. Bowditch, Henry C. Burdett,

John L. Cadwalader, Andrew Carnegie, Melvil Dewey, Robert Fletcher, Francis Galton, Daniel C. Gilman, Silas W. Mitchell, William Pepper, Stephen Smith, and George Sternberg.

Inventory in the library.

36. *Bingham, Walter Van Dyke, 1880-1952.*

Papers, 1852-1965. ca. 60 ft.

In Carnegie-Mellon University, Hunt Library (Pittsburgh, Pennsylvania).

Professor, researcher, and consultant in applied psychology. Mainly correspondence, together with speeches, articles, reports, minutes, financial records and other papers, relating to Bingham's interests in accident prevention, aptitude and intelligence testing, personnel selection, guidance and placement, industrial relations, interviewing, and occupational studies. Material also relates to other aspects of psychology applied to the problems of education, business, government, and individuals; and to his association with the American Association for Applied Psychology and its *Journal of Consulting Psychology;* the American Psychological Association; the Boston Elevated Railway; the Carnegie Institute of Technology, Division of Applied Psychology (later the Division of Cooperative Research); the Civil Service Assembly of the United States and Canada; the Thomas A. Edison Company (Orange, New Jersey), for which Bingham directed research on the emotional influence and practical effects of music; the National Occupational Conference, the New York State Association of Applied Psychology, the Personnel Research Federation of New York City, the Psychological Corporation, the Scott Company of Philadelphia, committees on army personnel classification in World Wars I and II, the Adjutant General's Office, the U.S. Employment Service, the U.S. Indian Service, and the U.S. Office of Education's Occupational Information and Guidance Service. Includes a manuscript and notes of his *Aptitudes and Aptitude Testing* (1937); items from his student days at Beloit College, Harvard University, and the University of Chicago; his teaching (1908-15) at Teachers College of Columbia University, at Dartmouth, at Stevens Institute of Technology, and at the Harvard Summer School; family correspondence, including that of his wife, Millicent Todd Bingham; and material on the establishment and performance (1954-65) of twelve annual Bingham Memorial Lectures. Correspondents include James R. Angell, J. W. Baird, J. Carleton Bell, Edwin G. Boring, Oscar K. Buros, J. McKeen Cattell, J. Crosby Chapman, R.C. Clothier, Knight Dunlap, Shepherd I. Franz, Frank B. Gilbreth, Erich von Hornbostel, Charles H. Judd, Harry D. Kitson, Arthur W. Kornhauser, H. S. Langfeld, J. B. Miner, B. V. Moore, C. S. Myers, Johnson O'Connor, Donald G. Paterson, P. J. Rulon, Beardsley Ruml, Walter Dill Scott, Carl E. Seashore, Percival Symonds, Lewis M. Terman, E. L. Thorndike, L. L. Thurstone, E. B. Titchener, Morris S. Viteles, J. B. Watson, Harry P. Weld, F. L. Wells, Guy M. Whipple, Clark Wissler, Dael Wolfle, R. S. Woodworth, Robert M. Yerkes, Clarence Yoakum, and others.

Gift of Mrs. Bingham, 1969.

37. *Blanton, Margaret (Gray), 1887-1972.*

Papers, 1845-1972. 13 boxes, 1 tape, and 1 package.

In State Historical Society of Wisconsin (Madison, Wisconsin).

37. *(Continued)*
Correspondence, diaries, biographical material, genealogical notes and documents, and other items. Includes correspondence of Margaret Blanton and her husband, Smiley Jordan Blanton, psychiatrist.
Partially restricted.

38. *Blanton, Margaret (Gray), 1887-1972.*
Papers of Margaret Gray and Smiley Blanton, 1897-1972. 12 ft. (ca. 6300 items).
In University of Tennessee Library (Knoxville, Tennessee).
Author. Personal correspondence, research material; manuscript of Mrs. Blanton's novel, *The White Unicorn* (1961); unpublished manuscripts of short stories, poetry, articles, and essays; recipes, and scrapbooks; and correspondence, speeches, manuscript of *My Analysis with Sigmund Freud* (1971), articles, columns, publications, diplomas, citations, and photos, of her husband, psychoanalyst Smiley Blanton (1882-1966). Includes Mrs. Blanton's research material on St. Thomas à Becket, St. Bernadette, Sam Davis, George Hughes, Eliza Johnson, and Dick Whittington.
Unpublished finding-aid in the repository.
Access restricted.
Gift of Mrs. Blanton, 1973.

39. *Board of Charities and Reform.*
Records, 1873-1969. ca. 10 cubic ft.
In Wyoming State Archives and Historical Department (Cheyenne, Wyoming).
Minutes of board meetings, correspondence, reports, and prison records regarding the Children's Home, State Penitentiary, State Mental Hospital, and State Tuberculosis Sanitorium.

40. *Boas, Franz, 1858-1942.*
Papers, ca. 1858-1942. ca. 50,000 items.
In American Philosophical Society Library (Philadelphia, Pennsylvania).
Anthropologist and linguist. Personal and professional correspondence, diaries, and family papers, including material on anthropology and linguistics in the United States, and the development of their study; and anthropology in Latin America; science, academic freedom, race, and similar subjects.
Unpublished calendar in the library.
Open to investigators under library restrictions.
Gift of the Boas family.

41. *Boder, David Pablo, 1886-1961.*
Papers, 1927-56. 8 ft.
In University of Akron, Archives of the History of American Psychology (Akron, Ohio).
Psychologist and professor at the Illinois Institute of Technology. Personal correspondence, lecture notes, prepublished and unpublished manuscripts, tests, photos, slides, film laboratory equipment, sound recordings, case records of patients, and tapes of interviews with displaced Europeans in 1946 and with

victims of the Kansas City flood of 1951. Includes material relating to the Psychological Museum, Chicago, which Boder founded. Major correspondent is Arnold Gesell.

Unpublished description and index in the repository.

Open to investigators under restrictions of the repository.

Information on literary rights available in the repository.

Gift of the Illinois Institute of Technology and Mrs. Boder, 1967.

42. *Bollingen Foundation.*

Records, 1939-73. ca. 78,000 items.

In Library of Congress, Manuscript Division (Washington, D.C.).

Correspondence, grant applications and reports, legal papers, minutes, clippings, printed material, and other records (chiefly 1953-68), relating to the history of philanthropy founded by Paul and Mary Conover Mellon to fund scholarly research and publication in the general area of the humanities, and to the foundation's fellowship and contribution programs. Includes files relating to the awarding of the Bollingen Prize in Poetry, publication of the Bollingen Series by Princeton University Press, and the publication of the collected works of Carl Jung and Paul Valéry. Correspondents include John D. Barrett, Huntington Cairns, Malcolm Cowley, T. S. Eliot, Abraham Flexner, Raymond B. Fosdick, Donald Gallup, Vaun Gillmor, Gotthard Gunther, Irving Howe, Carl Jung, Erich Kahler, Siegfried Kracauer, Joseph W. Krutch, Jacques Maritain, Paul Mellon, Erich Neumann, Maud Oakes, Paul Radin, Herbert Read, Mary Ritter, Allen Tate, Mark Van Doren, Stanley Young, and Heinrich Zimmer.

Unpublished finding-aid in the repository.

Access restricted.

Gift of the foundation's trustees, 1973.

43. *Boring, Edward Garrigues, 1886-1968.*

Papers, 1919-69. 45 ft.

In Harvard University Archives (Cambridge, Massachusetts).

Teacher of psychology at Harvard University, and editor. Correspondence, including some as editor of the journal *Contemporary Psychology*; lecture notes; manuscripts of publications; and subject files, including notes, processed and printed material, and other papers. Much of the material in the subject files relates to research in psychology.

Information on literary rights available in the repository.

Gift of Mr. Boring, 1964 and 1969.

44. *Boston Insane Hospital, Austin Farm.*

Records, 1896-1903. 4 vols.

In Harvard University, Countway Library of Medicine (Boston, Massachusetts).

Housing for the psychiatric care of men and women until 1898 when men were transferred to Pierce Farm. Records consist of patients' registers, including admission and discharge dates, cause of illness, and patient data such as date of birth, age, religion, occupation, and marital status.

Access restricted.

45. *Boston Insane Hospital, Pierce Farm.*
Records. 2 vols.
In Harvard University, Countway Library of Medicine (Boston, Massachusetts).
Housing for the psychiatric care of men and women until 1898 when the women were transferred to Austin Farm. Records include a daily register of patients, with name, occupation, marital status, and medical history for the time spent at the farm.
Access restricted.

46. *Boston Parents' Council.*
Records, 1930-38. 3 boxes.
In Radcliffe College, Schlesinger Library on the History of Women in America (Cambridge, Massachusetts).
Records of an organization created to bridge the gap between scientists studying child development and parents seeking information about normal child growth. Includes material on child study, parent and child, social service agencies, Massachusetts Council for Parent Education, Massachusetts Society for Mental Hygiene, National Council of Parent Education, Spelman Fund, U.S. Office of Education Emergency Education Program, and White House Conference on Child Health and Protection, 1930. Persons represented include Dr. E. Stanley Abbot, Josephine D. Abbott, T. Grafton Abbott, Ralph P. Bridgeman, Dr. Augusta F. Bronner, Clifford K. Brown, Dr. Linwood W. Chase, Marie L. Donahoe, Abigail A. Eliot, Dr. Henry B. Elkind, Sybil Foster, Mrs. Robert F. Herrick, Ann C. Hoague, Gladys B. Jones, Edward C. Lindeman, Mrs. Douglas Mercer, Mrs. H. A. Skilton, Dr. Douglas A. Thom, and Alfred Whitman.
Unpublished finding-aid in the repository.
Deposited by Mercy Fogg, archivist of Garland Junior College (Boston, Massachusetts), 1973.

47. *Boston State Hospital.*
Records, 1839-1954. 63 vols.
In Harvard University, Countway Library of Medicine (Boston, Massachusetts).
Institution for the psychiatric care of men and women founded in 1837, later changed in 1896 to the Boston Insane Hospital, and then in 1908 to Boston State Hospital. Volumes include case histories, admissions records, records of restraints and seclusions, recorded deaths, and attempts at escape.
Access restricted.

48. *Bouck, William C., 1786-1859.*
Papers, 1727-1866. ca. 2 ft. and 1 reel of microfilm.
In Cornell University Library, Department of Manuscripts and University Archives (Ithaca, New York).
Governor of New York State. In part, photocopies (15 items). Correspondence, appointment papers, official documents, and other papers chiefly relating to Bouck's political career and concerning his service as sheriff of Schoharie County, New York; member of the New York State Assembly, postmaster of West Middlebury, New York; member of the New York State Canal Commis-

sion, and Assistant U.S. Treasurer at New York City. Papers relating to Bouck's governorship and to his later public life include material on the national subtreasury plan, the direct tax, the antirent movement and resultant civil disturbances (mainly in Schoharie and Rensselaer counties), prisons in New York State, the Barnburner-Hunker factionalism in the Democratic Party, and pre-Civil War tensions. Considerable material (bills of seizure, deeds, indentures, and other papers) pertains to the sale of lands (1727-1858) in Schoharie County and adjacent areas. Miscellaneous items include New York State Militia commissions; copies of wills and probate papers, and other legal documents (1771-1859) of Bouck, his father, Christian, and his grandfather, William; papers relating to Bouck's Wisconsin land investments, his rental incomes, and other personal and family business; estate inventory of Cornelius Feeck; and business papers of Benjamin and Juliet Best and John Ferguson.

Unpublished guides available in the library.

Also described in the *Report of the Curator and Archivist, Collection of Regional History, Cornell University Library* (1958-62), pp. 29-31.

Gift of Mrs. William B. Cornell, 1962.

49. *Bouck, William C., 1786-1859.*

Papers, 1727-1866.

Addition, 1798-1859. ca. 2 ft.

In Cornell University Library, Department of Manuscripts and University Archives (Ithaca, New York).

Governor of New York. Correspondence, petitions, statements, and other documents and papers, chiefly relating to Bouck's career as sheriff of Schoharie County, New York; member of the New York State Assembly; postmaster of West Middlebury, New York; member of the New York State Canal Commission; Assistant U.S. Treasurer at New York City; and governor. Topics include state and national politics, internal improvements, canal construction, railroad construction and finance, state prison and insane asylum conditions, temperance, antirent disturbances, abolitionism, and mail contracts. Bouck's personal papers include leases, surveys, deeds, accounts, and other papers, including those of his father, Christian, and his sons, concerning land interests in Schoharie County, New York, and Milwaukee, Wisconsin; and papers relating to Bouck's service as a Lutheran layman, particularly as treasurer of the Foreign Missionary Society, and also pertaining to Hartwick Seminary.

Unpublished guide in the library.

Gift of Mrs. William B. Cornell, 1963.

50. *Bowman, Lillie Lewis, 1899-1968.*

Papers, 1915-66. 1¼ ft.

In University of Akron, Archives of the History of American Psychology (Akron, Ohio).

Psychologist whose primary interest was in educational research, primarily gifted children. Professional papers, course outlines, and conference programs are included in the collection.

Unpublished guide available.

Access restricted.

51. *Bregman, Elsie Oschrin, 1896-1969.*
Papers, 1918-69. 4 ft.
In University of Akron, Archives of the History of American Psychology (Akron, Ohio).

Psychologist and professor at Teachers College, Columbia University, New York. Clinical records (1922-36), reprints of journal articles, various selection and placement tests used primarily at R. H. Macy Company, New York City (1919-21); and published tests including *Bregman Revision of the Army Alpha Examination* and the *Bregman Language Completion Scales.* Major correspondents include Paul S. Achilles, George K. Bennett, Phyllis Blanchard, Dean R. Brimhall, James McKeen Cattell, Harold E. Jones, Truman L. Kelley, H. C. Link, Carl Murchison, Donald G. Paterson, Harold Seashore, Percy S. Straus, Robert L. Thorndike, and Dael Wolfle.

Unpublished inventory in the repository.

Permanent deposit by Judith Bregman, 1971.

52. *Breitwieser, Joseph Valentine, 1885-1950.*
Papers, 1935-42. 10 items.
In University of North Dakota Library (Grand Forks, North Dakota).

Dean of School of Education and director of Graduate Division, University of North Dakota. Transcripts of radio interviews and other material relating to psychology and education, including bibliography (1930) of educational publications of the university.

53. *Bressler Family.*
Papers, 1881-1961. ca. 1200 items.
In Nebraska State Historical Society Collections (Lincoln, Nebraska).

Correspondence relating to state mental hospitals in Nebraska and experience in World War II defense plant work, together with manuscripts of poems and songs by Julia Bressler, and financial records of a Genoa, Nebraska, family.

Gift of Allan Bressler (Grand Island, Nebraska), 1965.

54. *Brill, Abraham Arden, 1874-1948.*
Papers, 1889-1964. ca. 1800 items.
In Library of Congress, Manuscript Division (Washington, D.C.).

Psychoanalyst, translator-author, and lecturer. Correspondence (1908-57), manuscripts of articles and lectures, reviews of Brill's translations of various books by Sigmund Freud, psychoanalytic writings of other authors, certificates and diplomas, and other papers, chiefly 1907-48, relating to Brill's career and his role in the development of psychoanalytic thought in the American medical community. Includes papers of Brill's wife, Kittie Rose Owen Brill, Brill family papers, records of the New York Psychoanalytic Society which Brill founded, bulletins and rosters of the American Psychoanalytic Association, and other material on Esperanto, obscenity, and birdwatching, in which Brill expressed interest. Correspondents include Eugen Bleuler, Manfred Bleuler, Anna Freud, Sigmund Freud, Smith Ely Jelliffe, and Clinton Preston McCord.

Unpublished finding-aid in the repository.
Access restricted.
Gift of Mr. Brill's son, Edmund Rogers Brill, 1967-71.

55. *Brimhall, Dean R. 1886-1972.*

Papers, 1881-1972. 30 ft.
In University of Utah Libraries, Special Collections Department (Salt Lake City, Utah).

Government official, editor, and aviation executive. Personal papers, including general and family correspondence, diaries and daybooks, financial records, biographical material, and Brimhall family records, particularly diary (1881-1932) and other papers of Brimhall's father, George H. Brimhall, president of Brigham Young University; correspondence, charter and bylaws, minutes of meetings, interim and annual reports, and articles and publications, of the Psychological Corporation, which conducted human engineering research, and of which Brimhall was executive secretary; material relating to *American Men of Science* (3d. ed., 1921), of which he was co-editor; correspondence and other business records (1931-45) of Utah Pacific Airways, of which he was president; correspondence, speeches, news releases, and articles relating to his career with the Works Progress Administration (1935-39) and Civil Aeronautics Administration (1939-51); material on the Mormon Church Relief Program; correspondence, speeches, theater scripts, awards, newspaper clippings, and scrapbooks, of Brimhall's wife, Lila (Eccles) Brimhall (b. 1891), actress and professor of speech and theater at the University of Utah; and subject files on Brimhall's writings, politics, education, mining, electric power, and petroglyphs.
Register published by the repository in 1978.
Gift of Mr. and Mrs. Brimhall, 1972-74.

56. *British Sexological Society.*

Archives. Minute books and correspondence, 1897-1940. 28 ft. plus books and journals.
In University of Texas, Humanities Research Center (Austin, Texas).

Business and personal correspondence of the founding members of the society, formerly known as the British Society for the Study of Sex Psychology. Correspondents include Edward Carpenter, Magnus Hirschfield, Laurence Housman, and George Ives. Later members included E. M. Forster, Edward Garnett, and George Bernard Shaw.

57. *Brown, John, 1821-1895.*

Papers, 1830-1932. 382 items.
In Ohio Historical Society (Columbus, Ohio).

Farmer and soldier, son of John Brown the abolitionist. Correspondence, diaries (1858, 1861), notes, newspaper clippings, and other papers. Subjects mentioned include the raid on Harpers Ferry (1859), farming in Ohio, sheep raising, tanning, phrenology, and spiritualism. Many of the letters are addressed to Brown's wife, Wealthy C. Hotchkiss. A letter book (1847-49) of the firm of Perkins and Brown, wool dealers of Springfield, Massachusetts, contains 632

57. (Continued)

letters of John Brown, Sr. Other correspondents include Brown's granddaughter, Owen Brown; his stepmother, Mary Ann Day Brown; his brothers, Jason, Owen, Salmon, and Frederick; his sisters, Ruth Brown Thompson, Ellen Brown Fablinger, and Annie Brown Adams; his mother-in-law, Maria P. Hotchkiss Wellman; his son-in-law, T. B. Alexander; other members of the Brown family; his school friend, George B. Delamater; fugitive slave Thomas Thomas, Orson S. Fowler, Franklin B. Sanborn, Nelson Sizer, Samuel Roberts Wells, and Jarvis J. Jefferson (regarding the remains of Watson Brown, who was killed at Harpers Ferry).

Inventory and calendar published in 1962 by the Ohio Historical Society.

Gift of Mr. and Mrs. T. B. Alexander, 1925-36.

58. Bruner, Jerome Seymour, 1915- .

Papers, 1915-1971. 90 ft.

In Harvard University Archives (Cambridge, Massachusetts).

Teacher of psychology at Harvard University. Personal and professional correspondence, including some relating to activities of various professional societies and Bruner's research; appointment books and financial records; autobiographical papers; notes, reports, and publications, relating to research projects; and material relating to teaching.

Access restricted.

Information on literary rights available in the repository.

Acquired from Mr. Bruner.

59. Bryant, Louise Frances (Stevens), 1885-1956.

Papers, ca. 1908-56. 5 ft.

In Smith College Library, Sophia Smith Collection (Northhampton, Massachusetts).

Social welfare and public health worker. Correspondence, documents, reports, articles, and printed records relating to Mrs. Bryant's work in child health and school feeding programs for the Russell Sage Foundation, as a lecturer in the psychology of social work at the University of Pennsylvania, as a criminal probation officer, as a caseworker dealing with retarded children, as a medical editor, and in other projects involving the Girl Scouts, the United Hospital Fund, the National Committee on Maternal Health, and the American Association of University Women. Includes papers relating to her personal life and a typescript and privately printed copy of *Bequest from a Life: A Biography of Louise Stevens Bryant* (1963) by Lura Beam.

Card catalog and unpublished inventory in the library.

Open to investigators under restrictions accepted by the library.

Information on literary rights available in the library.

Gift of Miss Lura Beam (Bronxville, New York), 1962.

60. Bullowa, Margaret, 1909-1978.

Papers, 1933-78. 7 boxes.

In Institute Archives and Special Collections, Massachusetts Institute of Technology (Cambridge, Massachusetts).

Neurologist, psychiatrist, and researcher on the development of language in children. Collection consists chiefly of professional papers, correspondence with colleagues, grant proposals and reports, conference notes and programs, student notes, speeches, and drafts of publications, all dating primarily from the 1960s and 1970s.

Access unrestricted.

Container list available in archives.

61. *Bunts Family.*
Papers.

In Cleveland Medical Library, Howard Dittrick Museum of Historical Medicine (Cleveland, Ohio).

Includes papers of Alexander T. Bunts, neurosurgeon at the Cleveland Clinic and the Lakeside Hospital, Cleveland. This collection includes correspondence, operative notes, and consultation records.

62. *Bureau of Indian Affairs: Canton Asylum for Insane Indians.*
Records, 1910-34. 4 ft.

In Federal Archives and Records Center, Kansas City Archives Branch (Kansas City, Missouri).

Employee data, ledgers, and correspondence of the asylum, established in 1901 in Canton, South Dakota. Patient data and YWCA work with the asylum is included.

63. *Bureau of Social Hygiene.*
Records, 1911-40. 32 ft.

In Rockefeller Archive Center (Pocantico Hills, North Tarrytown, New York).

Annual reports, minutes, dockets, history, budgets, treasurer's reports, pledges, commitments, project files, and other records. Includes material on prostitution, vice, narcotics, police corruption, criminology, crime reporting, juvenile delinquency, birth control, eugenics, maternal health, police training, population, public administration, sex education, and venereal disease. Organizations and projects presented include the American Birth Control League, American Social Hygiene Association, American White Cross Association on Drug Addiction, Associates for Government Service, Association of Grand Jurors, British Social Hygiene Council, Brooklyn Continuation School, Canadian Social Hygiene Council, Crew Study (Detroit), European Police Systems, Harvard Crime Survey, 1926-35, Institute of Criminology, Laboratory of Social Hygiene, League of Nations, Massachusetts Narcotics Survey, Massachusetts State Prison Colony, National Research Council Committee on Drug Addiction, National Research Council Committee on Sex Research, New York Boys' Club, New York Police Psychopathic Laboratory, Policewoman's Handbook, and Uniform Criminal Statistics. Correspondents include Lawrence Dunham, Abraham Flexner, Raymond B. Fosdick, Felix Frankfurter, Leonard V. Harrison, J. Edgar Hoover, Starr Murphy, John D. Rockefeller III, Franklin D. Roosevelt, Alfred E. Smith, George Wickersham, and Arthur Woods.

Unpublished inventory in the repository.

64. *Burkes, DeWitt C.*
Papers, 1940-57. 1 ft.
In University of Oregon Library (Eugene, Oregon).
Psychiatrist. Correspondence (1954-57) relating to the Central Inspection Board, American Psychiatric Association; minutes (1955-58) of staff meetings of the Morningside Hospital in Portland, Oregon; correspondence (1940-50) concerning the North Pacific Society of Neurology and Psychiatry, organization papers (1955-57) of the Portland Psychiatrists in Private Practice, and correspondence (1947-49) relating to the beginnings of the Portland Chamber Orchestra Association.

65. *Burrow, Trigant, 1875-1950.*
Papers, 1909-50. ca. 50,000 items.
In Lifwynn Foundation Collections (Westport, Connecticut).
Phylobiologist and psychiatrist. Correspondence, memoranda, manuscripts of published and unpublished works; reports, laboratory notes, references to and reviews of Burrow's writings; and other papers. Includes material relating to the development of group analysis and phylobiology and of the American Psychoanalytic Association, of which Burrow was a founder and president. Correspondents include Sherwood Anderson, Abraham A. Brill, Walter B. Cannon, A. J. Carlson, G. E. Coghill, Havelock Ellis, Paul Federn, Sigmund Freud, Kurt Goldstein, C. Judson Herrick, Smith Ely Jelliffe, Carl G. Jung, Clyde Kluckhohn, Alfred Korzybski, D. H. Lawrence, John T. MacCurdy, Adolf Meyer, Gardner Murphy, Clarence P. Oberndorf, Herbert Read, Harry Stack Sullivan, William Alanson White, and Lance Whyte.
Some of the correspondence has been published in *Science and Man's Behavior* (1953), and *A Search for Man's Sanity: The Selected Letters of Trigant Burrow with Biographical Notes* (1958).
Access restricted.
Information on literary rights available in the repository.
The repository also has microfilm of the collection.

66. *Butler, Nicholas Murray, 1862-1947.*
Papers, 1891-1947. 1479 items and 180 file drawers.
In Columbia University Libraries (New York, New York).
President of Columbia University. Correspondence, drafts of Butler's writings, miscellaneous private papers, memorabilia, clippings (some mounted), and other printed matter relating to his life and career. Includes Butler's correspondence with the following presidents of the United States: William McKinley, Theodore Roosevelt, William Howard Taft, Woodrow Wilson, Warren G. Harding, Calvin Coolidge, Herbert Hoover, Franklin D. Roosevelt, and Harry S. Truman.
Gift and bequest of Dr. Butler, 1946-47.

67. *Calbreath Family.*
Papers, 1843-1939. 3 ft.
In University of Oregon Library, Special Collections (Eugene, Oregon).

Physician and superintendent of the Oregon Insane Asylum, 1899-1908. Includes correspondence, diaries, manuscripts, and financial records of the Calbreath family.

68. *Camden, Thomas Bland, 1829- .*
Papers, 1862-1907. 1 box and 1 reel of microfilm.
In West Virginia University Library, (Morgantown, West Virginia).
Physician. Correspondence ledgers and other papers of T. B. Camden; appraisement and account book of the estate of John S. Camden; diary entries of Thomas L. Feamster, a Confederate soldier, noting troop movements in Greenbrier County in 1861 and 1864-65. The Feamster material is on microfilm. T. B. Camden's correspondence, on his professional and political activities, includes letters from friends regarding his dismissal as superintendent of the State Hospital for the Insane at Weston.
Gift of Roy Bird Cook, 1954.

69. *Camden County, New Jersey, Psychiatric Hospital, Lakeland.*
Records, 1886-99. 1000 items.
In Historical Society of Pennsylvania Collections (Philadelphia, Pennsylvania).
Bills paid by the hospital, then called the Camden County Asylum.
Purchase, 1952.

70. *Canadian Mental Health Association.*
Archives.
In Canadian Mental Health Association Archives (Toronto, Ontario).
Minutes, reports, and literature distributed to the public.

71. *Cannon, Walter Bradford, 1871-1945.*
Papers, 1896-1945. 24 ft.
In Harvard University, Countway Library of Medicine (Boston, Massachusetts).
Physiologist. Correspondence (1917-18, 1922-24, 1930-45) including material on the China Medical Board, United China Relief, and the Medical Bureau to Aid Spanish Democracy; notes on the study of alimentation by x-ray (1896); tracings (1901-04); and notes for lectures and articles.
Open to investigators under library restrictions.
Gift of Cannon's family.

72. *Cannon, Walter Bradford, 1871-1945.*
Papers, 1905-28. ca. 800 items.
In American Philosophical Society Library (Philadelphia, Pennsylvania).
Physiologist. Largely correspondence with William Williams Keen, a Philadelphia surgeon.
Gift of Mr. Cannon, 1942.

73. *Carnegie Corporation.*
Oral Histories, 1966-70. 75 items.
In Columbia University Libraries (New York, New York).

73. *(Continued)*

Transcripts of tape-recorded interviews of officers, staff members, and grant recipients of the Carnegie Corporation, discussing its work during the past 58 years in adult education, area studies, art education, cognitive research, education testing, library science, music education, national security, social science research, teacher education, and other areas. Recounts the central corporation's administrative history and its relations with other Carnegie institutions, with other major foundations, and with the federal government; and traces the work of independent agencies which originally received all or part of their funds from the foundation. Persons represented include James R. Angell, James Bertram, Nicholas Murray Butler, Oliver C. Carmichael, Robert Franks, Walter Jessup, Nicholas Kelley, Frederick Paul Keppel, Clyde Kluckhohn, Thomas W. Lamont, William S. Learned, Russell C. Leffingwell, Frederic A. Mosher, Arthur Page, Henry Pritchett, Elihu Root, Jr., Elihu Root, Sr., Beardsley Ruml, James E. Russell, William F. Russell, Whitney H. Shepardson, Irvin Stewart, and Samuel A. Stouffer.

A comprehensive index is available in the Oral History Research Office, Columbia University. Also described, with a complete list of persons interviewed, in *The Oral History Collection of Columbia University* (1973), pp. 68-70.

Access restricted.

74. *Carroll, John Bissell, 1916-*

Papers, 1949-67. ca. 3 ft.

In Harvard University Archives (Cambridge, Massachusetts).

Teacher of education and educational psychology at Harvard University. Correspondence, memos, and material relating to Harvard Graduate School of Education.

Access restricted.

Information on literary rights available at the repository.

75. *Cattell, James McKeen, 1860-1944.*

Papers, 1869-1948. 41 ft. (ca. 15,000 items).

In Library of Congress, Manuscript Division (Washington, D.C.).

Professor of psychology, editor and publisher. Correspondence, childhood diaries, speeches, articles, notes, reports, bulletins, other printed material, page proofs of the book, *James McKeen Cattell . . . Man of Science* (1948), news clippings, certificates, diplomas, photos, and other papers. Includes much correspondence on the preparation of articles for publication in the various journals edited by Cattell, files of material relating to the American Association for the Advancement of Science, the Psychological Corporation, the Science Press, other scientific organizations and the publication, *American Men of Science,* in all of which he was very active; and family correspondence (mostly 1880-1906). The bulk of the papers date after 1896. Correspondents include John Dewey, Asaph Hall, Ellsworth Huntington, William James, Charles Sanders Peirce, and Edward B. Titchener.

Register published in 1962 by the library.

Information on literary rights available in the library.

Gift of Jaques Cattell, 1957.

76. *Cattell, James McKeen, 1860-1944.*
Papers, 1869-1948.
Addition, 1835-1940. ca. 34,000 items.
In Library of Congress, Manuscript Division (Washington, D.C.).

Professor of psychology, editor, and publisher. Chiefly general and family correspondence and manuscripts of books and articles; together with speeches and lecture notes, financial papers, biographical and genealogical material, articles by others, and printed matter (chiefly 1900-30). Includes correspondence relating to articles written for periodicals that Cattell edited or published, including *Science, Popular Science Monthly, School and Society,* and *The American Naturalist;* and material relating to his dismissal from the faculty of Columbia University in 1917, American Association of University Professors, American Association for the Advancement of Science, and his resignation from the Century Club after its refusal to accept Dr. Jacques Loeb into its membership. Correspondents include his mother, Elizabeth McKeen Cattell; his father, William Cassady Cattell, president of Lafayette College; and James R. Angell, Charles E. Bessey, Franz Boas, Edwin G. Boring, Nicholas Murray Butler, Otis W. Caldwell, John Dewey, William J. Humphreys, Joseph Jastrow, David Starr Jordan, Vernon Kellogg, Burton E. Livingston, Jacques Loeb, Arthur O. Lovejoy, Thomas Hunt Morgan, Raymond Pearl, Carl E. Seashore, Edward L. Thorndike, Edward Titchener, and John B. Watson.
Unpublished finding-aid in the repository.
Information on literary rights available in the repository.
Gift of Mr. Cattell's son, McKeen Cattell, 1972.

77. *Cattell, James McKeen, 1860-1944.*
Papers, 1890-1919. ca. 500 items.
In Columbia University Libraries (New York, New York).

Professor of psychology at Columbia University. Correspondence, reports, and court records. Includes material relating to Cattell's interest in academic freedom; and letters written by Cattell to John Dewey, G. Stanley Hall, and George Rives.

78. *Cayce, Edgar, 1877-1945.*
Psychic Readings, 1903-44. 14,000 readings.
In Association for Research and Enlightenment (Virginia Beach, Virginia).

Psychic and seer. Topics covered in the readings include psychology, psychiatry, psychical research, dreams, reincarnation, pre-history, and Atlantis, as well as information outlining Cayce's views on the causes of and treatments for the common cold, psoriasis, cancer, epilepsy, and many other diseases. Also available are supplemental data relating to the readings, including case histories, documentations, and reports.

79. *Cayce [Edgar] Foundation Archives.*
In Association for Research and Enlightenment (Virginia Beach, Virginia).

Collection contains the records of the Foundation, personal correspondence and memorabilia of Cayce, records of some of the earlier organizations that formed around his work, and some correspondence of Andrew Jackson Davis.

80. *Chaloner, John Armstrong, 1862-1935.*
    Papers, 1862-1932. 6471 items and 1 vol.
    In Duke University Library (Durham, North Carolina).
        Lawyer of Cobham, Virginia. Business and personal correspondence, legal briefs and notes concerned with trials and appeals against the state of New York, and against the *Washington Post* for slander; literary manuscripts of treatises on the lunacy laws of various states, and miscellaneous papers, chiefly 1880-1920. The letters (about half the collection) relate to Chaloner's attempts to have himself declared sane, verdicts from psychologists concerning his mental conditions, the fostering of motion pictures for rural areas, the circulation of some of his poems on European politics prior to 1914, and congratulations to Chaloner on obtaining a favorable verdict regarding his sanity in the U.S. Supreme Court. Includes canceled checks, telegrams, invitations, and clippings, the latter largely confined to the career of Chaloner's divorced wife (Amelie Rives, who later married Prince Pierre Troubetskoy) and to the comment caused by the popular phrase coined by Chaloner, "Who's looney now?" Among the correspondents are Arthur Brisbane, Philip Alexander Bruce, Richard Evelyn Byrd, J. H. Choate, Walter Duranty, A. C. Gordon, Joseph Jastrow, Claude Kitchin, L. S. Overman, and W. L. Phelps.
        Card index in the library.
        Acquired 1940, 1954.

81. *Chapin Hall for Children, Chicago.*
    Records, 1857-1964. 15 ft.
    In Chicago Historical Society Library (Chicago, Illinois).
        Correspondence, minutes of meetings (1867-1958), admission and dismissal ledgers, financial records, and other papers, relating to the hall, which provides day-care services for working mothers, and was founded in 1860 as the Chicago Nursery and Half-Orphan Asylum. Includes correspondence and reports (1946-64) relating to the Chapin Hall Ridge Farm Preventorium (Lake Forest, Illinois), an organization seeking to assist dependent and neglected children with behavior problems.
        Information on literary rights available in the library.
        Gift of the hall, 1967-68.

82. *Chicago Area Project.*
    Records, 1920-72. 77 ft.
    In Chicago Historical Society Library (Chicago, Illinois).
        Correspondence, minutes, reports, and other working papers, of a community-oriented program for delinquency prevention and research, administered by Clifford Robe Shaw (1896-1957), Anthony Sorrentino (1913-   ), and Henry Donald McKay (1899-   ). Includes related papers of the Institute for Juvenile Research (formerly the Juvenile Psychopathic Institute) with which Shaw and McKay were associated, and routing correspondence, position papers, and mimeographed material relating to Sorrentino's work with the Illinois Youth Commission.
        Unpublished guide in the library.

Access restricted.
Information on literary rights available in the library.
Gifts of Mrs. Sorrentino, 1972, and the Institute for Juvenile Research, 1973.

83. *Child Study Association of America.*
Records, 1907-65. 17½ ft.
In University of Minnesota, Social Welfare History Archives (Minneapolis, Minnesota).

The records include correspondence, annual reports, financial records, reports, committee records, pamphlets, guest books, notebooks, photographs, and scrapbooks. In addition to organizational records, the collection also includes records of two semi-autonomous organizations, the Inter-Community Child Study Committee, 1929-35, and the National Council of Parent Education, 1930-48; and the personal papers of two individuals, Sidonie Gruenberg, 1904-50, and Josette Frank, 1930-65. Heaviest concentration for the records as a whole is in the period 1930-65. Subjects include children's literature, effect of radio and television on children and adolescents, art, sex education, mental health, family relationships, child development, parents' study groups, training in values, race relations, and the impact of war on families. Individuals and organizations represented in the correspondence include Lyman Bryson, Eleanor Roosevelt, Eduard C. Lindeman, Society for Ethical Culture, Anti-Defamation League of B'nai B'rith, Family Service Association of America, National Conference of Christians and Jews, National Congress of Colored Parents and Teachers, and the Progressive Education Association. One reel of microfilm contains minute books of the Society for the Study of Child Nature, 1890-1900, a predecessor of CSAA.

An unpublished inventory is available in the repository.
The collection is open to all qualified scholars under library guidelines.
Gift of CSAA Board of Directors, 1967.

84. *Child Study Association of America. Supplement.*
Records, 1908-72. 45 ft.
In University of Minnesota, Social Welfare History Archives (Minneapolis, Minnesota).

The bulk of the supplement covers the period 1955-70 and documents the association's shift toward training staff members of other agencies who work with parents and children.

85. *Clevenger, Shobal Vail, 1843-1920.*
Papers, 1864-1924. 2 boxes.
In National Library of Medicine (Bethesda, Maryland).

Surveyer, editor, reformer, and psychiatrist. Correspondence, photos, articles, notes, memoranda, documents, clippings, and printed matter. Many letters relate to Clevenger's association with the Illinois Eastern Hospital for the Insane, America reminiscences and opinions on various subjects, including scientists and physicians.
Gift of S. R. Shapiro, 1956.

86. *Clippings.*
Collection, 1953- . ca. 5 cabinets.
In Menninger Foundation Archives (Topeka, Kansas).
Clippings from state and national newspapers concerning psychiatry and persons involved in the field.

87. *Clothier, Florence, 1903-*
Papers. 2 boxes and 1 carton.
In Radcliffe College, Schlesinger Library on the History of Women in America (Cambridge, Massachusetts).
Psychiatrist and author. Collection contains correspondence, a journal, and professional material regarding information on euthanasia, abortion, and birth control.
Partially restricted.

88. *Coad, Pauline Corson.*
Oral history, 1958. 3 tapes.
In Cornell University Library, Department of Manuscripts and University Archives (Ithaca, New York).
Recollections concerning Hiram Corson and various Cornell faculty members. Remarks regarding Corson's practice of spiritualism and a reference to a visit by Madame Helena Petrovna Blavatsky, a noted spiritualist.
Published guide available.

89. *Coblentz, William Weber, 1873-1962.*
Papers, 1884-1960. 4 ft. (ca. 350 items).
In Library of Congress, Manuscript Division (Washington, D.C.).
Physicist and author. Correspondence (1893-1960), journal kept on the solar eclipse expedition to Sumatra and the return through Europe (1926), manuscripts and annotated printed copies of two books, *Man's Place in a Super Physical World* (1954), and *From the Life of a Researcher* (1951); biographical material, memorabilia, financial records (1884-1905), scientfic notebooks concerning stellar and planetary radiation (1914-26) and psychic phenomena (1910-15), photos, and printed copies of Coblentz's works, frequently annotated (1903-53). Most of the material relates to Coblentz's pioneer work in the fields of infrared spectroscopy, and to the application of radiometry to astronomical problems. Correspondents include Cleveland Abbe, Charles G. Abbot, George E. Hale, Dayton C. Miller, August H. Pfund, and William R. Whitney.
Information on literary rights available in the library.
Gifts of Mr. Coblentz, 1952-60.

90. *Coe, George Albert, 1862-1951.*
Papers, 1893-1952. 3 ft.
In Yale University, Divinity School Library (New Haven, Connecticut).
Professor at Union Theological Seminary, New York, New York. Correspondence, writings, memorabilia, printed material, and other papers, relating to Coe's writings and work in the fields of religious education and psychology of

religion, and his affiliation with the Committee on Militarism in Education, of which he was chairman, and the Religious Education Association, of which he was honorary president. Correspondents include William Clayton Bower, Emil Brunner, Adelaide Case, Harrison Elliott, and A.J.W. Myers.
    Unpublished register in the repository.
    Information on literary rights available in the repository.
    Permanent deposit.

91. *Conger, George Perrigo, 1884-1960.*
Papers, 1623-1957. ca. 11 ft.
In University of Minnesota Library, Manuscripts Division (Minneapolis, Minnesota).
    Professor of philosophy at the University of Minnesota. Correspondence with colleagues and friends, autographs of noteworthy philosophers and others, and notes and drafts of Conger's book, *Epitomization* (1949). Correspondents include W. F. Albright, Lew Ayres, Joseph H. Ball, James Ford Bell, George Boas, Solon J. Buck, Rudolf Carnap, Merle Curti, John Dewey, Will Durant, Orville Freeman, Lord Halifax, Sidney Hook, Hubert H. Humphrey, Y. P. Mei, Karl Menninger, David Saville Muzzey, Eugene Ormandy, Henry Fairfield Osborn, Bertrand Russell, Margaret Sanger, George Santayana, and Jan Christian Smuts.
    Unpublished inventory in the repository.
    Information on literary rights available in the repository.

92. *Conklin, Edwin Grant, 1863-1952.*
Papers. 57 cartons.
In Princeton University Library (Princeton, New Jersey).
    Biologist. Correspondence, working papers, lecture notes, drawings, and seventeen drawers of glass slides.

93. *Cooke, Alice Rebecca, 1861-1956.*
Papers, 1884-1956. ca. 50 items.
In Sandwich Historical Commission (Sandwich, Massachusetts).
    Owner and matron of the Locust Grove Asylum, a mental health facility, 1907-38. Cooke was one of the first female operators of such a facility.

94. *Coolidge, Oliver S.*
Papers, 1861-64. 43 items.
In Duke University Library (Durham, North Carolina).
    Union soldier, of Massachusetts. Correspondence between Coolidge and his sister, chiefly while serving with Maj. Gen. Ambrose E. Burnside's coast division, and in Burnside's bodyguard and at headquarters, Department of the Ohio. Includes description of battles at Roanoke Island and New Bern, North Carolina, and Fredericksburg, Virginia, military life, and the cities of Annapolis, Maryland, New Bern, North Carolina, and Cincinnati, Ohio. Includes references to Burnside, Elias Howe, and Edward Stanly, and marital problems, alcoholism, spiritualism, and racial and nativist attitudes.
    Unpublished finding aid in the repository.
    Acquired, 1975.

95. *Copeland, William R., 1909-*
Papers, 1965-69. ca. 6 ft.
In Wayne State University, Archives of Labor History and Urban Affairs (Detroit, Michigan).

Union official and Michigan legislator. Correspondence, office files, and reports, concerning state tuition grants, osteopathic colleges, the Grandmere Conservation Bill, air and water pollution problems in Michigan, water resources planning, and mental health problems. Correspondents include William Broomfield, Mayor Jerome Cavanagh, John Dingell, Philip A. Hart, John Lesinski, Ernest Mazey, and Walter P. Reuther.

Unpublished finding-aid in the repository.
Information on literary rights available in the repository.
Deposited by Mr. Copeland, 1968.

96. *Cornell, Ethel Letitia, 1892-1963.*
Papers, 1906-64. 4 ft.
In Cornell University Library, Department of Manuscripts and University Archives (Ithaca, New York).

Psychologist, associated with the New York State Education Department. Correspondence, articles, reports, proceedings of meetings, bibliographies, and other papers, pertaining to intelligence testing and the nature of intelligence, exceptional children, growth studies, the characteristics and language usage of high school students, early secondary education in New York State, mental health, the school psychologist, the New York State Psychological Intern Training Program, the activities of the American Psychological Association and the New York State and American Associations for Applied Psychology; examination books and notes from courses at Cornell and Columbia Universities; creative writing and other non-scientific manuscripts; certificates and diplomas; and various blocks and drawings used in psychological testing.

Gift of Miss Cornell's estate, 1965.

Cornell University (cf. Student Notebooks).

97. *Corson, Hiram, 1828-1911.*
Papers, 1852-1946. 7 ft.
In Cornell University Library, Department of Manuscripts and University Archives (Ithaca, New York).

University professor. Correspondence, reviews of books and articles by Corson and other scholars, drafts of lectures and articles; anatomical, physiological and surgical drawings; scrapbooks, clippings, printed matter, and photos, relating to Corson's travels, life, and career as professor of English literature at Girard College in Philadelphia, St. John's College in Annapolis, Maryland, and Cornell University; to Shakespeare, Chaucer, Tennyson, Browning, and other figures of English literature; to the medical career of Corson's son Eugene; to spiritualism; and to personal affairs. Correspondents include Mathew Arnold,

Henry Ward Beecher, Helena Petrovna Blavatsky, Edwin Booth, Robert Browning, Francis James Child, Mary Cowden Clarke, George William Curtis, Edward Everett, Willard Fiske, Jessie Fothergill, Horace Howard Furness, Frederick J. Furnivall, Daniel Coit Gilman, Samuel Steman Haldeman, Edward Everett Hale, James Orchard Halliwell-Phillipps, Bret Harte, Nathaniel Hawthorne, Oliver Wendell Holmes, William Dean Howells, Charles Mansfield Ingley, William James, Pierre Janet, Henry Wadsworth Longfellow, James Russell Lowell, John D. Meiklejohn, J. Parker Norris, Goldwin Smith, Andrew Dickson White, Walt Whitman, John Greenleaf Whittier, and Woodrow Wilson.

98. *Coston, Isaac Newton, 1832-1910.*

Papers, 1886-89. 1 ft.
In Idaho State Historical Society Collections (Boise, Idaho).

Lawyer of Idaho City, representative in the Territorial Council, member of the Board of Trustees of the Idaho Insane Asylum, and member of the Idaho Constitutional Convention (1889). Correspondence, director's reports, requisitions, and bids dealing with the Insane Asylum at Blackfoot, Idaho; calendars and resolutions of the Idaho Constitutional Convention; miscellaneous business correspondence; and ledgers.

Unpublished description in the repository.
Gift, 1960.

99. *Coues, Elliott, 1842-1899.*

Papers, 1820-98. 1 box.
In State Historical Society of Wisconsin Collections (Madison, Wisconsin).

Ornithologist, author, and founder of the American branch of the Gnostic Theosophical Society. Correspondence (1863-98) relating to Coues's activities as a member of the Gnostic Theosophical Society; correspondence (1820-29) of Coues's mother, Charlotte Ladd Coues, and (1832-60) of his father, Samuel Elliott Coues, relating to efforts to establish the New Hampshire Asylum for the Insane and to his work as president of the American Peace Society; and other papers.

100. *Craddock, Ida C., 1857-1902.*

Papers, 1877-1923. 4 ft.
In Southern Illinois University Archives (Carbondale, Illinois).

Author and lecturer on religious eroticism. Correspondence and literary manuscripts (some edited for publication by Theodore Albert Schroeder), relating to Miss Craddock's study of religious eroticism; together with manuscripts by Schroeder entitled *The Philosophy and Moral Theology of an Erotomaniac* (ca. 1917). Titles include *Diary of Psychical Experiences* (1894-1902), by Mrs. Soph (her spiritual name), *Heavenly Bridegrooms* (ca. 1894), and *Lunar and Sex Worship* (1902). The correspondence is between Miss Craddock and mutual friends of hers and of Schroeder and between Schroeder and those friends.

Inventory in the repository.
Acquired as part of the Theodore Schroeder papers, 1969.

101. *Creswell, Cordelia, 1868?-1950.*
Correspondence, 1886-1932. 1300 items.
In University of Michigan, Michigan Historical Collections (Ann Arbor, Michigan).
Public school teacher and supervisor of special education at Grand Rapids, Michigan. Correspondence relating mainly to education, particularly the public schools of Grand Rapids and the education of retarded children.
Gift of Mrs. Charles Rawley, 1952.

102. *Crozier, William John, 1892-1955.*
Correspondence 1918-55. 5 ft.
In Harvard University Archives (Cambridge, Massachusetts).
Professor of general physiology. Includes correspondence in chronological, alphabetical, and subject series; the collection contains notes for teaching and for other lectures (1912-55).
Open to investigators only upon prior application.
Information on literary rights available in the repository.

103. *Culler, Elmer A., 1889-1961.*
Papers, 1921-46. 1 ft.
In University of Rochester Library (Rochester, New York).
Collection contains correspondence, research notes, drafts, and final copies of articles. Includes lab data and articles relating to Culler's interest in hearing sensitivity in animals; material relating to programs of the Midwest Psychological Association, 1936-37; and background material and a review article on William Ellery Leonard's autobiography, *The Locomotive God* (1927).

104. *Curti, Margaret, 1891-1961.*
Papers, 1921-64. 5 in.
In University of Akron, Archives of the History of American Psychology (Akron, Ohio).
Psychologist. Correspondence and notes concerning experiments of Pavlov and reflecting Curti's work with preschool play, racial difference, and intelligence tests; and laboratory experiments concerning conditioned reflexes.
Unpublished guide available.

105. *Curtis, John Green, 1844-1913.*
Letters. ca. 500 items.
In Columbia University Libraries (New York, New York).
Professor of physiology at Columbia University. Letters relating to the history of medicine, psychology and vivisection.

106. *Cushing, Harvey W., 1869-1939.*
Papers.
In Cleveland Medical Library, Howard Dittrick Museum of Historical Medicine (Cleveland, Ohio).

Surgeon and neurologist, educated at Yale and Harvard Universities. Engaged in private practice and taught at Johns Hopkins, Harvard, and Yale. Collection includes correspondence, biographical material, obituaries, and family records.

107. *Dallenbach, Karl M., 1887-1971.*

Papers, 1895-1969. 17 ft.

In Cornell University Library, Department of Manuscripts and University Archives (Ithaca, New York).

Psychologist; professor at Ohio State University, 1915-16; Cornell University, 1916-48; and University of Texas, 1948-69; and editor of the *American Journal of Psychology*, 1926-67. Documenting his research in psychology, particularly in attention, sensation and memory, and his other professional activities is correspondence with Harold J. Bachmann, Madison Bentley, Morton E. Bitterman, C. P. Boner, Edwin G. Boring, Albert P. Brogan, Forrest Lee Dimmick, Isidore S. Finkelstein, Goldwin Goldsmith, J. Stanley Gray, G. Stanley Hall, Margaret C. McGrade, Max F. Meyer, Robert B. Morton, Edwin B. Newman, Theophilus S. Painter, Leo J. Postman, Harry H. Ranson, Thomas A. Ryan, E. C. Sanford, Maryvenice E. Stewart, Edward B. Titchener, Walter S. Turner, Harry P. Weld, Logan Wilson, and others. Administrative records produced while he was head of the Department of Psychology at the University of Texas, Austin, include reports on buildings and budgets, research papers, staff and annual reports, minutes of staff meetings, and correspondence with academic organizations. Records concerning his editorship of the *American Journal of Psychology* include statements on editorial policy decisions, correspondence on printing and advertising, financial and subscription records, and manuscripts and galley proofs. Other professional papers include reprints of colleagues' articles, notes and articles on perception and facial vision, published biographical articles on Edwin C. Boring and Edward B. Titchener, and photographs of colleagues. His personal correspondence with members of his family concerns property settlements and management, the establishment of a John W. Dallenbach fellowship, and his genealogical research on the Dillenbach-Dillenbeck-Dallenbach family.

Unpublished guide available.

Restricted in part.

[This entry is reprinted with permission from the *Documentation Newsletter*, Department of Manuscripts and University Archives, Cornell University Libraries, vol. 2, no. 2 (Fall 1976).]

108. *Dandy, Walter Edward, 1886-1946.*

Papers, 1920s and 1930s. 6 ft.

In Johns Hopkins University, Alan Mason Chesney Medical Archives (Baltimore, Maryland).

Professor of neurosurgery at Johns Hopkins University. Correspondence and case reports of neurosurgical patients.

Access permitted to accredited scholars upon written application.

Gift, ca. 1960.

109. *Danvers State Hospital.*
Records, 1870-90 (scattered).
In MacDonald Medical Library, Danvers State Hospital, administered by the Charles V. Hogan Regional Center (Hathorne, Massachusetts).
Handwritten case books, day books, and ledgers, including a record of the Therapeutic Bath Room.
Uncatalogued and not available for circulation.

110. *Davidson, Thomas, 1840-1900.*
Papers, 1860-1900. 18 ft. (23,000 items).
In Yale University Library (New Haven, Connecticut).
Philosopher. Correspondence, lectures, articles, printed matter, and clippings, pertaining to the career of Davidson, who came to the United States in 1867 and was associated with the St. Louis and Concord schools of philosophy, the founding of the Fellowship of New Life, the establishment of a branch of the Fellowship of New Life in New York City, and the establishment of the Breadwinners' College. He was also associated with the establishment of a summer school for the cultural sciences in St. Cloud, New Jersey, Farmington, Connecticut, and Keene, New York. From 1878 to 1884, Davidson lived in Domodossola, Italy, in contact with the Rosminian order. Papers include a section of material of Edward Endelman, one of Davidson's students. Correspondents include Henry Adams, John Dewey, Oliver Wendell Holmes, William James, Henry Cabot Lodge, John Stuart Mill, and Stephen Samuel Wise.
Unpublished register in the library.
Information on literary rights available in the library.
Gift of Charles M. Bakewell, William H. Kuclane, and Mrs. Edward Endelman, 1932-61.

111. *Davis, Andrew Jackson, 1826-1910.*
Papers, 1848-81. ca. 165 items.
In Yale University Library (New Haven, Connecticut).
Spiritualist. Letters to Davis's benefactor, William Green, Jr., relating to his work with spiritualism and healing; and to personal, family, and financial matters.
Unpublished register in the library.
Information on literary rights available in the library.
Gift of Esther A. Tiffany, 1973.

112. *Davis, Noah Knowles, 1830-1910.*
Lecture notes.
In University of Virginia Library (Charlottesville, Virginia).
Professor of psychology.

113. *Dean, Emily (Washburn), 1870-1958.*
Papers, 1902-57. ca. 430 items.
In Chicago Historical Society Library (Chicago, Illinois).
Social worker. Correspondence, printed ,natter, and other papers reflecting

Mrs. Dean's activities in the fields of social service and politics. The bulk of the papers relates to the Juvenile Protective Association of Chicago, mental hygiene societies in Illinois, and the Illinois Republican Women's Clubs. The material is related to the library's Mary McDowell papers and Agnes Nestor papers.

Unpublished guide in the library.

Gift of Ada B. Huncke, 1959.

114. *De Jong, Russell Nelson, 1907-*

Papers, 1920-60. 4 ft.

In University of Michigan, Michigan Historical Collections (Ann Arbor, Michigan).

Professor of neurology at the University of Michigan. Correspondence (1940-56) regarding resident physicians, and minutes (1947-60) of the executive faculty of the University of Michigan Medical School; financial records of the Department of Neurology; and correspondence (1950-59) regarding the *Journal of Neurology.*

Gift of Dr. De Jong, 1962.

115. *Delabarre, Edmund Burke, 1863-1945.*

Papers, 1890-1938. ca. 2 ft.

In University of Akron, Archives of the History of American Psychology (Akron, Ohio).

Professor of psychology and founder of the Psychological Laboratory, Brown University (Providence, Rhode Island). Protocols (1890-1938) for formal laboratory experiments on discrimination, thresholds, and illusions; a scientific manuscript entitled "Tetralogic Monism"; and notes (1892-1914) concerning the influence of *Cannabis indica* and *Cannabis sativa* on mood, muscular steadiness, reaction time, memory, and other psychological responses.

Unpublished inventory in the repository.

Information on literary rights available in the repository.

Gift of Mrs. Delabarre, 1970.

116. *Delabarre, Edmund Burke, 1863-1945.*

Papers, 1900. 4 items.

In U.S. National Archives and Records Service, Center for Polar Archives, (Washington, D.C.).

Professor of psychology at Brown University (Providence, Rhode Island). Journal, narrative, annotated map, and photo album, relating to the Brown-Harvard Expedition to Labrador, 1900, of which Delabarre was a member.

Unpublished finding-aid in the repository.

Information on literary rights available in the repository.

Gift of Mrs. Dorcas D. Crary, 1973.

117. *Denny, Bishop Collins, 1854-1943.*

Papers, 1873-90.

In University of Virginia Library (Charlottesville, Virginia).

An analysis of University of Virginia professor Noah Knowles Davis's lectures on psychology.

118. *Department of Correctional Services and Department of Mental Hygiene. New York.*
Records, 1840-1971. 500 cubic ft.
In New York State Archives (Albany, New York).
Contains material about the Western House of Refuge in Albion, New York, established in 1893 as a reformitory for women. Information about inmates and the administration of state institutions for the insane and criminal is included.
Partially restricted.

119. *Dewey, John, 1859-1952.*
Collected papers, 1891-1973. ca. 450 items.
In Southern Illinois University Library (Carbondale, Illinois).
Philosopher and educator. Papers written by, to, or about Dewey.
Information on literary rights available in the repository.
Gifts and purchases from various donors and sellers, 1965 and after.
Additions to the collection are expected.

120. *Dewey, John, 1859-1952.*
Correspondence, 1930-50. 151 items.
In Columbia University Libraries (New York, New York).
Educator and philosopher. Letters and postcards from Dewey to Corinne Chesholm Frost, largely devoted to philosophical problems.
Gift of Corinne Chesholm Frost.

121. *Dewey, John, 1859-1952.*
Letters, 1894-1906. ca. 100 items.
In University of Chicago Library (Chicago, Illinois).
Philosopher and educator. Letters covering Dewey's years at the University of Chicago as head professor of the Department of Philosophy and the Department of Pedagogy, and as director of the School of Education. The material reflects the evolution of his educational ideas, and deals with his administrative activities. It also reflects his thinking on pedagogy as a university discipline; teacher training as a university function; the proper role of an organizational unit devoted to educational study, teaching, and research within an embracing university framework; and the purpose, operation, and financing of the Dewey School.
Described in "A Preliminary Listing of Dewey Letters, 1894-1904," by Robert L. McCaul in *School and Society* (October 1959).

122. *Dewey, Sabino L., 1899-1973.*
Papers, 1924-39. ca. 60 items.
In Southern Illinois University Library (Carbondale, Illinois).
Forms part of the repository's John Dewey collection.
Correspondence, photos, broadsides, and pamphlets, by, to, or about Dewey's father, John Dewey (1859-1952), philosopher and educator.
Information on literary rights available in the repository.
Gift of Mr. Dewey, 1967.

123. *Dimmick, Forrest Lee, 1893-1968.*
Papers, 1911-68. 6 ft.
In Cornell University Library, Department of Manuscripts and University Archives (Ithaca, New York).
Psychologist and professor of psychology at the University of Michigan, 1921-25, and Hobart College, 1925-47. Documents his research in vision, particularly color vision, night vision, visual acuity, and color aptitude testing. Includes correspondence with Karl M. Dallenbach, Edwin G. Boring, and fellow participants in the Inter-Society Color Council, Kenneth L. Kelly, Deane B. Judd, Carl Foss, and Faber Birren; numerous publications written and edited by Dimmick; newsletters, color swatches, and testing materials concerning his work on the Color Aptitude Test; correspondence, notes, and reports concerning his retirement activities as consultant for the Biological Science Communications Project. Also includes papers concerning his biographical research on his former professor, Edward Bradford Titchener, which include copies of two letters written by Titchener from Oxford (1889-90), one letter written from Cornell (1912), lists of classes Titchener took while he was a student in Leipzig under Wilhelm Wundt, an archival listing of other Titchener material, a recorded interview (1967) with a colleague of Titchener, Harry P. Weld, and genealogical tables of the Titchener family from England.
Unpublished guide available in the repository.

[This entry is reprinted with permission from the *Documentation Newsletter*, Department of Manuscripts and University Archives, Cornell University Libraries, vol. 2 no. 1 (Spring 1976).]

124. *Dix, Dorothea, 1802-1889.*
Papers, ca. 1826-86. 2 boxes.
In Menninger Foundation Archives (Topeka, Kansas).
Correspondence and speeches concerning improvements in nursing care, prisons, and hospitals for the insane.

125. *Doll, Edgar Arnold, 1889-1969.*
Papers, 1915-58. 23 ft.
In University of Akron, Archives of the History of American Psychology (Akron, Ohio).
Psychologist at the Vineland Training School (Vineland, New Jersey) and the Devereux Foundation (Devan, Pennsylvania). Correspondence, tests, raw and normative data, calculation sheets, and prepublication manuscripts, chiefly relating to the "Vineland Social Maturity Scale," of which Doll was the author. Includes correspondence pertaining to personnel, patients, and research; and permission to translate the scale and plans for its foreign adaptations. Correspondents include Edwin G. Boring, Henry H. Goddard, William Healy, Clark Hull, Grace Kent, Alfred C. Kinsey, Samuel C. Kohs, Stanley D. Porteus, Lewis M. Terman, and Marion Traube.
Information on literary rights available in the repository.
Gift of Eugene and Geraldine Doll, 1969.

126. *Donahue, Wilma Thompson, 1900-* .
Papers, 1946-70. 26 cubic ft.
In Institute of Gerontology Archives, University of Michigan (Ann Arbor, Michigan).
Psychologist, researcher in gerontology, and founding Director of the Institute of Gerontology, 1965-70. Collection includes correspondence, speeches, lectures and research materials, especially relating to Institute research, the Michigan Commission on Aging, and federal government committees.
Unpublished register available in archives.

127. *Donaldson, Henry Herbert, 1857-1938.*
Papers, 1890-1938. ca. 100 items and 49 vols.
In American Philosophical Society Library (Philadelphia, Pennsylvania).
Neurologist. Includes diaries and an unpublished typewritten autobiography: "Memories for My Boys," (1931).
Gift of Mrs. Donaldson, 1939-40.

128. *Doren, Gustavus A., 1838-1905.*
Papers, 1854-1905. ca. 3 ft.
In Ohio Historical Society Collections, (Columbus, Ohio).
Superintendent of the Ohio Institution for Feebleminded Youth (Columbus, Ohio). Correspondence and business records relating to family expenditures, city real estate holdings, farms, newspaper interests, and the Ohio Institution for Feebleminded Youth. Correspondents include trustees of the institution, Ohio political figures, and superintendents of other institutions.
Inventory in the repository.
Gift of Mr. Doren's grandson, Doren Mitchell (Martinsville, New Jersey), 1965.

129. *Dreikurs, Rudolf, 1897-1972.*
Papers, 1911-73. ca. 5000 items.
In Library of Congress, Manuscript Division (Washington, D.C.).
Psychiatrist and educator. Correspondence, journals (1915-23); manuscripts of books, articles, speeches, and television lectures; transcripts of counseling and therapy sessions, case studies from classroom situations, notes, printed matter, photos, memorabilia, and other papers, chiefly 1937-72. Correspondence documents Dreikurs's private psychiatric practice in Chicago, his role in creating the Community Child Guidance Centers of Chicago, his professorship of psychiatry at Chicago Medical School, his directorship of the Alfred Adler Institute, and his editorship of *Individual Psychology Bulletin* (1941-51). Correspondents include Alfred Adler, Victor Frankl, John Haynes Holmes, George Kelley, Abraham Maslow, Jacob Moreno, Hans Morgenthau, Carleton Washburne, and Sumner Welles.
Finding-aid in the repository.
Information on literary rights available in the repository.
Gifts of Dr. and Mrs. Dreikurs, and various donors, 1971-73.

130. *Druck, Rae.*

Papers, ca. 1917-47. 5 in.

In Minnesota Historical Society, Archives and Manuscripts (St. Paul, Minnesota).

Minutes, correspondence, and reports of the Child Psychology Study Circle (1924-47).

131. *Dryer Family.*

Correspondence, 1839-1938. 166 items.

In New-York Historical Society Collections (New York, New York).

Correspondence (chiefly 1846-82) of Rev. Horatio N. Dryer and other members of the Dryer family of Stockport and Stuyvesant, New York. Includes letters (1856) from Utica, New York, where Rev. Dryer served as a steward of the State Lunatic Asylum; letters from his daughter, Harriet L. Dryer, while a student at the Friend's Boarding School (Washington, New York); letters from his son, Dr. Robert Dryer, while serving with the U.S. Army at Richmond and Petersburg, Virginia, and later from New Orleans and Texas; and letters (1867-80) from another son, George W. Dryer, steward at the Minnesota Hospital for the Insane in St. Peter, Minnesota.

Unpublished guide available in the repository.

Gift of the Oregon Historical Society, 1968.

132. *Duke University.*

Professors' papers, 1773-1954. 451 items and 16 vols.

In Duke University Library (Durham, North Carolina).

Chiefly nineteenth century papers. Includes volumes relating to the work of Clara and William Stern and P. Eugen Berthold in child psychology; volumes of Robert Galt concerning his lectures in medicine and chemistry at the University of Pennsylvania; and papers of William Hooper, North Carolina educator, of Nathaniel Beverley Tucker and Lawrence Washington, professors at the College of William and Mary, and of William B. Yonce, professor at Roanoke College.

Card index in the library.

Acquired, 1930- .

133. *Dummer, Ethel (Sturges), 1866-1954.*

Papers, 1766-1954. 8 file drawers.

In Radcliffe College, Schlesinger Library on the History of Women in America, (Cambridge, Massachusetts).

Philanthropist and social welfare leader of Chicago. Correspondence, reports, minutes of meetings, photos, speeches and articles by and about Mrs. Dummer, documenting her efforts on behalf of the juvenile delinquent, the prostitute, and the illegitimate child; her interest in progressive education and public schools in Chicago; and her work with leaders in the mental hygiene movement. Includes papers of the Sturges and Dummer families as well as Mrs. Dummer's correspondence with prominent sociologists, psychiatrists, social workers, and educators of the first half of the twentieth century. Persons represented include Jane Addams, Herman Morris Adler, C. Anderson Aldrich, Katharine Susan Anthony,

133. *(Continued)*
Mary Bartelme, Jessie Binford, Louise deKoven Bowen, Sophonisba Preston Breckinridge, Scott Buchanan, Edward Burchard, Ernst W. Burgess, Charles M. Child, Charles L. Chute, Flora J. Cooke, William E. Dodd, Thomas D. Eliot, Havelock Ellis, Lucy R. Flower, Ernst R. Groves, Alice Hamilton, William Healy, Charles J. Herrick, Robert M. Hutchins, Marion E. Kenworthy, Samuel H. Kraines, Julia Lathrop, Mary E. McDowell, Karl A. Menninger, Adolf Meyer, Winfred Overholser, George T. W. Patrick, Allen B. Pond, Oliver Reiser, Azile B. Reynolds, William E. Ritter, Margaret Dreier Robins, Virginia Robinson, Milton Singer, Jessie Taft, Graham Taylor, William Isaac Thomas, Miriam Van Waters, Margaret Wagenhals, Carleton Washburne, John Broadus Watson, Dora Wells, Marguerite Wells, William A. White, Mary H. Wilmarth, and Elizabeth L. Woods.

134. *Dunlap, Knight, 1875-1949.*
Papers. 10 letters.
In Johns Hopkins University, Milton S. Eisenhower Library (Baltimore, Maryland).
Psychologist and professor of psychology at Johns Hopkins University. Major correspondents include John C. French, Arthur O. Lovejoy, and C.W.E. Miller.

135. *Dunton, William Rush, 1868-   .*
Scrapbook of Harlem Lodge, 1891-1938. 1 vol.
In Maryland Historical Society Library, (Baltimore, Maryland).
Correspondence, photos, bulletins, menus, and pamphlets relating to Harlem Lodge, a private sanitarium for the mentally ill. The scrapbook was put together by Dr. Dunton, head of the sanitarium.

136. *Earle, Pliny, 1809-1892.*
Papers, 1837-91. 1 vol. and 9 boxes.
In American Antiquarian Society Collections (Worcester, Massachusetts).
Physician and psychiatrist. Correspondence, diaries, medical and travel notes, lectures, case notes, and articles on insanity. Includes Earle's letters (1837-64) to his family from Europe, Cuba, and Washington.

137. *Earl Warren and the State Department of Mental Hygiene.*
Oral history, 1970-71. 246 pages.
In University of California at Berkeley, Bancroft Library, Manuscripts Division (Berkeley, California).
Interview with Portia (Bell) Hume concerning her work in mental health services and the development of the Langley Porter Neuropsychiatric Institute.

138. *Edgett-Burnham Company.*
Records, 1854-1930. 102 ft.
In Cornell University Library, Department of Manuscripts and University Archives (Ithaca, New York).
Correspondence (ca. 1883-1920) with the Federal Trade Commission, the New York State College of Agriculture at Cornell, the New York State Canned Good

Packers Association, the New York State Factory Investigating Commission, the U.S. Department of Agriculture, and the U.S. Navy Department; brokerage accounts, cashbooks, daybooks, ledgers, check registers, company farm accounts, corn accounts, daily reports of the packing and canning department, ensilage records, inventories, labor and time books, merchandise books, payroll records, sales books, and other purchasing, production, and fiscal records of a canning company and its pioneering predecessors, Edgett and Totten and the Wayne County Preserving Company. Includes correspondence (ca. 1885-1910) of Edwin G. Burnham, president of the company, discussing the Democratic Party in Wayne County, New York, the area crop situation, and the State Custodial Asylum for Feeble-Minded Women at Newark, New York; and early photos of company personnel.

Unpublished guide in the library.

Gift of Glenn E. Finch, in memory of George A. Burnham, 1965.

139. *Edwards, Frederick, 1863-1948.*
Papers, 1883-1945. 213 items and 79 vols.

In Duke University Library (Durham, North Carolina).

Episcopal clergyman and president of the American Society for Psychical Research. Correspondence, journal (1884-1945, 52 vols.), sermons, meditations, and poems, chiefly relating to psychical phenomena and Edwards's views on theology and spiritualism. Includes World War I letters from his son, Frederick Trevenen Edwards.

Card index in the library.

Gifts, 1956-58.

140. *Eliot, Charles William, 1834-1926.*
Papers, 1869-1924. 199 ft.

In Harvard University Archives (Cambridge, Massachusetts).

President of Harvard College. Personal and official correspondence, copies of speeches, photos, and other items relating to Harvard and its presidency.

Shelf list in the repository, and indexes in correspondence.

Information on literary rights available in the repository.

141. *Elliot, Richard Maurice, 1887-1969.*
Papers, 1914-66. 10 ft.

In University of Minnesota Archives, Walter Library (Minneapolis, Minnesota).

Psychologist. Professor of psychology, University of Minnesota, 1919-56. Long-time editor, Century Psychology Series.

142. *Ellis, Alexander Caswell, 1871-1948.*
Papers, 1871-1960. ca. 67 ft.

In University of Texas Library, Texas Archives (Austin, Texas).

In part, photocopies.

Educator. Correspondence, notes, maps, leases, deeds, speeches, writings, examinations, class records, pamphlets, books, financial records, farm records, and college administration records, concerning family affairs, Ellis's cultural and

142. *(Continued)*

conservation activities, his work with mental and physical health groups, his work as a professor of philosophy of education and educational psychology, his work in adult education, sports and physical exercises, establishment and maintenance of institutions for the care and treatment of people with mental health problems, and the Hogg Mental Health Foundation. Includes farm records and data for a book Ellis wrote with E. J. Kyle. Persons represented include Eunice Aden, Newton D. Baker, William J. Battle, R. L. Batts, Mr. and Mrs. Roy Bedichek, H. Y. Benedict, Annie W. Blanton, H. B. Chadwick, J. Y. Chadwick, G.O. Clough, Tom Connally, Minnie F. Cunningham, J. Frank Dobie, Frederick Eby, Mary Heard Ellis, Mary L. Ellis, Orren L. Ellis, H. F. Estill, James E. Ferguson, Miriam Ferguson, Benjamin Fine, S. R. Fulmore, G. Stanley Hall, Edmund Heinsohn, W. P. Hobby, Ima Hogg, Will C. Hogg, Dwight L. Hoopingarner, Newman L. Hoopingarner, J. Edgar Hoover, D. F. Houston, E. J. Kyle, William G. Leutner, John H. Lomax, A. N. McCallum, Albert Mansbridge, S.M.N. Marrs, Rebecca Masterson, S. E. Mezes, Dan Moody, W. L. Moody, Frank M. Morrison, Pat M. Neff, Ella C. Porter, Homer P. Rainey, T. H. Shelby, Morris Sheppard, W.M.W. Splawn, Lutcher Stark, Robert Sutherland, W. S. Sutton, Olin E. Teague, R. E. Vinson, and Robert Yerkes.

143. *Ellis, Havelock, 1859-1939.*

Papers, ca. 1874-1951. 10 vols.

In University of California at Los Angeles Library (Los Angeles, California).

British psychologist. Typescripts and annotated copies of published works, including: original typescript of *Sex and Marriage*, with earlier chapters revised in Ellis's hand and later chapters corrected by François Roussel Delisle, and including four chapters which were suppressed in the printed work; first and fourth editions of *Man and Woman*, with extensive holograph corrections; interleaved copy, with holograph notes of *Man of Genius* (1891) by Cesare Lombroso, which was translated by Ellis; *The New Generation* (1930) by Victor Francis Calverton and Samuel Daniel Schmalhausen, which contains a chapter by Ellis with his marginal, holograph corrections; and proofs of an unpublished work on marriage law reforms, with Ellis's signature and marginal notes.

Unpublished description in the library.

Purchased from Elin Mathews, bookseller, 1950.

144. *Ellis, Havelock, 1859-1939.*

Correspondence, 1894-1950. 105 items.

In Columbia University Libraries (New York, New York).

British psychologist. Letters to Ellis, several drafts of his replies, and a few letters to his executor, Mrs. Françoise Lafitte-Cyon, chiefly relating to Ellis's writings and their influence, as well as to the work of his correspondents in sex studies, pornography, birth control, and pacifism. Correspondents include Henri Barbusse, André Breton, Elie Faure, Robert J. Gibbins, Julian Huxley, Desmond MacCarthy, Bonislaw Malinowski, Naomi Mitchison, John Middleton Murray, Henry S. Salt, and Marie Stopes.

145. *Elwyn Institutes.*
Historical archives, 1852- .
In Elwyn Institutes (Elwyn, Pennsylvania).
   Early records of the institutes, including annual reports, minutes of the board of directors, stray documents, and the like. There is also a small collection of materials relating to the American Association on Mental Deficiency, which consisted primarily of personal papers of Edgar Doll.

146. *Emergency Committee in Aid of Displaced Foreign Scholars.*
Records, 1933-36. 1 box.
In Cornell University Library, Department of Manuscripts and University Archives (Ithaca, New York).
   Correspondence and reports. Largely correspondence from the assistant secretary of the committee, Edward R. Murrow, to the chairman of its executive committee. Includes correspondence of or about Livingston Farrand and Kurt Lewin.

147. *Emergency Committee in Aid of Displaced Foreign Scholars.*
Records, 1933-45. 13 vols. and 195 boxes.
In New York Public Library (New York, New York).
   Correspondence with scholars, colleges, universities, learned societies, and refugee organizations; minutes and papers of the executive committee and the committee on applications; annual reports, financial papers, and other general correspondence and papers relating to the granting of financial and other aid to German, Jewish, and other European scholars and professionals seeking refuge in the United States during and prior to World War II. Most of the correspondence is with Stephen Duggan, secretary of the committee. Includes papers of the American Committee for the Guidance of Professional Personnel, David Riesman, secretary, and Carl J. Friedrich, chairman.
   Unpublished inventory in the repository.
   Gift of the committee, 1946.

148. *Emerson, Louville Eugene, 1873-1939.*
Papers. 16 ft.
In Harvard University, Countway Library of Medicine (Boston, Massachusetts).
   Clinical psychologist at Boston Psychopathic Hospital (1911-19) and Massachusetts General Hospital. Student of William James, Emerson began the practice of psychotherapy in the tradition of Jung and Freud under J. J. Putnam at Massachusetts General. The collection contains family and professional correspondence, patient records, photographs, and memorabilia. Small cache of professional correspondence includes, A. A. Brill, G. Stanley Hall, Smith Ely Jelliffe, Morton Prince, J. J. Putnam, E. E. Southard, and W. A. White. Letters to his fiancé (1904-07) give details of Emerson's classes with James, Royce, Palmer, Münsterberg, and Holt, and letters (1912) from New York describe his meeting with Jung, and the content of Jung's Fordham University lectures.
   Family letters restricted.

149. *Ewer, Mary Anita, 1892-1961.*
Papers, 1922-36. 1 ft.
In Cornell University Libraries, Department of Manuscripts and University Archives (Ithaca, New York).
Correspondence, charts, notes, reports, printed and mimeographed items, and drafts and outlines of writings, relating to Miss Ewer's work in preparing physics research for publication, theosophy, the work of the Theosophical World-University, and mystic symbolism. Included a typewritten draft of "The Medieval Mass in the West" by H. Flanders Dunbar. Correspondents include Ernest Merritt, Edward L. Nichols, Julia K. Sommer, Tutomu Tanaka, and D. T. Wilbur.
Partially restricted.
Gift of Grace St. John, 1966.

150. *Farrand, Livingston, 1867-1939.*
Papers, 1917-39. 1 ft., 25 storage cases, and 7 boxes.
In Cornell University Library, Department of Manuscripts and University Archives (Ithaca, New York).
Psychologist, anthropologist, public health administrator, and president of Cornell University. Correspondence, speeches, clippings, printed matter and other papers, including both personal material and Farrand's official papers as president of Cornell. Correspondents include James H. Hyde, John Campbell Merriam, Josiah Penniman, and Harlow Shapley.
Described in *Reports of the Curator and Archivist: Collection of Regional History, Cornell University* (1948-50), pp. 36-37 and (1958-62), p. 93.

151. *Farrand, Livingston, 1867-1939.*
Additional papers, 1920-34. 1 ft.
In Cornell University Library, Department of Manuscripts and the University Archives (Ithaca, New York).
Psychologist, anthropologist, public health administrator, and university president. Correspondence and printed reports (1926-33) concerning the abolition of compulsory R.O.T.C. Major correspondents include John Campbell Merriam, Josiah Penniman, Harlow Shapley, and other university committee members.

152. *Farrar, Clarence B., 1874-1970.*
Papers, 1902-70. 4 ft.
In American Psychiatric Association Archives (Washington, D.C.).
Psychiatrist, and editor of the *American Journal of Psychiatry* (1931-65), of Toronto, Canada. Correspondence, manuscripts of articles, notes, subject files, clippings, and printed material, relating principally to the *American Journal of Psychiatry*, and the American Psychiatric Association. Correspondents include A. A. Brill, Edward N. Brush, S. E. Jelliffe, Adolf Meyer, and Harry Stack Sullivan.
Unpublished inventory in the repository.
Gift of Mrs. Joan J. Farrar, 1975.

153. *Fear Family.*
Papers, 1865-1931. 3 ft.
In University of Oregon Library (Eugene, Oregon).
Bulk of the collection is of the period 1881-1918, and is mainly correspondence. Letters of William H. Fear, who moved from Burlington, Kansas to Portland, Oregon in 1889, include correspondence pertaining to his courtship of Lucia Drum. From 1905 to 1918, most of the letters are from the Fear children: Lyle, student at Yale University, Sheffield, Scientific School (1905-08); and Lois, student at the University of California (1906-08) and Wellesley College (1908-10). Includes a case of books collected by Lois Fear during her practice of osteopathy in Portland; also, correspondence and other files of Nora B. Green, Portland teacher and spiritualist.

154. *Fein, Leah Gold, 1910-*
Papers, 1959-75. 1¼ ft.
In University of Akron, Archives of the History of American Psychology (Akron, Ohio).
Psychologist. Correspondence and reports regarding her work with the International Council of Psychologists.
Unpublished guide available.
Access restricted.

155. *Fenichel, Otto, 1898-1946.*
Letters, 1920-46.
In Austen Riggs Library, Austen Riggs Center, Inc. (Stockbridge, Massachusetts).
Circular letters, sent among the inner circle of psychoanalysts discussing their stand on current problems and controversies in the field of psychoanalysis.
Presented to the library by Dr. Rapaport.
Edited for publication by Dr. Rapaport.

156. *Fiske, Nathan Welby, 1798-1847.*
Papers, 1824-47. 2 ft.
In Amherst College Library (Amherst, Massachusetts).
Professor of Greek and Latin and of moral philosophy and metaphysics at Amherst College. Notes and manuscripts by Fiske on Greek language and literature, mental and moral philosophy, and American history.
Unpublished finding-aid in the repository.

157. *Flinn, Helen, 1895-*
Papers, 1930-59. 5 in.
In University of Akron, Archives of the History of American Psychology (Akron, Ohio).
Clinical psychologist. Clinic report sheets reflect Flinn's work in psychiatric clinics in Detroit.
Unpublished guide available.
Access restricted.

158. *Folks, Homer, 1867-1963.*
Papers, 1890-1963. ca. 6000 items.
In Columbia University Libraries (New York, New York).
Social worker. Correspondence and papers relating to Folks's activities with the Red Cross after World War I; as a special agent to the military governor of Cuba (1900); as president of the New York State Probation Commission (1907-17); and to his interest in mental hygiene, the care of neglected and delinquent children, tuberculosis, and public health and welfare.
Transferred from the New York School of Social Work, 1970.

159. *Fowler, Lydia Folger, 1822-1897.*
Biographical information.
In Cleveland Medical Library, Howard Dittrick Museum of Historical Medicine (Cleveland, Ohio).
Phrenologist and physician; wife of Lorenzo Niles Fowler, one of the premier phrenologists in nineteenth century America, and the first woman professor of medicine in the United States (at the Central Medical College of New York, in Rochester). Collection includes information collected by F. C. Waites and correspondence from Charles S. Dolley concerning the Fowlers.

160. *Fowler Family.*
Fowler and Wells family papers, 1838-1901.
In Cornell University Library, Department of Manuscripts and University Archives (Ithaca, New York).
Correspondence, articles, lectures, photos, printed matter, and other papers, relating to the practice of phrenology by various members of the Fowler and Wells families, including Orson and Lorenzo N. Fowler, Samuel Roberts Wells, and Charlotte (Fowler) Wells. Includes material relating to *The Phrenological Journal* and *The Practical Phrenologist,* periodicals with which the family was associated. Correspondents include Susan B. Anthony, F.A.P. Barnard, Albert Barnes, Antoinette Brown, William H. Channing, James Freeman Clarke, John W. Edmonds, Frederick W. Evans, O. B. Frothingham, Frances Dana Gage, Sylvester Graham, Sarah Grimké, Bronson Howard, Horace Mann, Eliphalet Nott, Moses Coit Tyler, Benjamin F. Wade, and Elizur Wright.
Described in *Reports of the Curator and Archivist: Collection of Regional History, Cornell University* (1942-45), pp. 21-22; (1948-50), p. 73; (1954-58), p. 43.

161. *Frank, Lawrence Kelso, 1890-1968.*
Papers, 1919-62. 26 containers.
In National Library of Medicine (Washington, D.C.).
Memoranda, papers, and other material on child behavior and development, human welfare, and personality development. Miscellaneous material includes chapters of books, radio scripts, interviews, and reports of conferences on children. Major correspondents include Leona Baumgartner, Bruno Bettleheim, Jacob Bronowski, Mary Bunting, Walter B. Cannon, Alexis Carrel, Barry Commoner, George Corner, Abraham Flexner, Alan Gregg, Karen Horney, Robert

Hutchins, Julian Huxley, Bronislaw Malinowski, Rollo May, Margaret Mead, Karl Menninger, Ashley Montague, Wright Patman, Harold Urey, Mark Van Doren, and Paul Weiss.

162. *Franklin, Christine (Ladd), 1847-1930.*
Papers, ca. 1900-39. ca. 7000 items.
In Columbia University Libraries (New York, New York).
Correspondence, documents, and other papers of Mrs. Franklin and her husband, Fabian Franklin, relating to their work in the fields of psychology and logic. The papers are mainly those of Mrs. Franklin, who lectured at Columbia University (1914-27), and who was well known for her method of reducing all syllogism to a single formula, and for her contributions to knowledge relating to color vision.
Gift of the estate of Margaret Ladd-Franklin through Helen Hotchkiss, 1962.

163. *Freeman, Frank Nugent, 1880-1961.*
Correspondence and papers, 1939-47. 1 box.
In Cornell University Library, Department of Manuscripts and University Archives (Ithaca, New York).
Educator and psychologist. Professor of psychology at Yale University; chairman of the Department of Psychology, University of Chicago; and dean of the School of Education, University of California at Berkeley. Chiefly correspondence and related papers concerning the programs for conferences on junior colleges, and the preparation of the 1947 yearbook for the National Society for the Study of Education. A few manuscripts of articles by Dean Freeman are included. Major correspondents include Grace Bird, Frank B. Lindsay, John L. Lounsbury, Alonzo Franklin Myers, George Dinsmore Stoddard, and Frank Waters Thomas.

164. *Freeman, Frank Nugent, 1880-1961.*
Papers, 1939-47. 1 box.
In University of California at Berkeley, Bancroft Library (Berkeley, California).
Dean of the School of Education, University of California. Correspondence and writings relating to education, junior college conferences, and to the publication of the *National Society for the Study of Education Handbook* (1947).
Key to arrangement in the library.

165. *Freeman, Frank Samuel, 1898-*
Papers, 1927-66. 1 ft. and 2 reels of tape recordings.
In Cornell University Library, Department of Manuscripts and University Archives (Ithaca, New York).
Professor of psychology and education at Cornell University. Chiefly correspondence relating to the psychology of learning, teacher training, intelligence testing, the problem of unqualified practitioners of psychology, and aspects of Freeman's career, including his membership in professional organizations, writings for professional journals and popular magazines, invitations to lecture and teach, and copies of Freeman's articles and book reviews. Includes correspon-

165. *(Continued)*

dence concerning growth and administrative change in Cornell University; American higher education, the history of the Cornell psychology department, Robert M. Ogden's position as the first American Gestalt psychologist, the administration of the psychology and education departments, Freeman's pioneering course in human growth and development, and a proposed course in clinical psychology. Other correspondence and reports pertain to the organization and progress of the University Placement Service (1932-39), administration of the National Youth Administration Student Aid Program at Cornell (1934-37), undergraduate advisory system, and the refusal of the university to cooperate with the German Academic Exchange Service (1939). Correspondents include Julian P. Bretz, Julian E. Butterworth, James B. Conant, Karl M. Dallenbach, Edmund Ezra Day, John Peterson Elder, Livingston Farrand, Joseph McVicker Hunt, Frances L. Ilg, Otto Kinkeldey, Konrad Lorenz, Albert R. Mann, Maud A. Merrill, Howard A. Meyerhoff, Robert M. Ogden, Lewis M. Terman, Vivian T. Thayer; other psychologists, educators, and university officials; and W. Averell Harriman, Herbert H. Lehman, John Taber, Henry A. Wallace, and other political figures.

Open to investigators under restrictions accepted by the library.
Gift of Professor Freeman, 1962-66.

166. *Freud, Sigmund, 1856-1939.*

Correspondence, 1912-36. 43 items.
In American Jewish Archives (Cincinnati, Ohio).
Photocopies.

Austrian physician. Correspondence with Drs. Emil and Mirra Oberholzer, relating to personal matters, medicine, and problems of psychoanalysis. The letters were written from Vienna, Austria, and Zürich, Switzerland. In German.

Open to investigators under restrictions accepted by the repository.
Gift of Dr. Emil Oberholzer, Jr. (New York, New York).

167. *Freud, Sigmund, 1856-1939.*

Letters to Ernst Simmel, 1918-39. 33 items.
In Los Angeles Psychoanalytic Society and Institute (Los Angeles, California).
Translations available.

168. *Freud, Sigmund, 1856-1939.*

Papers, 1926-66. 20 items.
In Leo Baeck Institute Collections (New York, New York).

Austrian psychiatrist. Letters (1927-36) by Freud on personal matters, and newspaper clippings of articles on Freud. In German and English.
Gift and purchase from Dr. Harry Freud (Yonkers, New York), 1959-68.

169. *Fridenberg, Solomon Louis, 1870-*

Papers, 1893-1955. 1 box.
In American Jewish Archives (Cincinnati, Ohio).

Resident of Philadelphia. Manuscripts of plays and of articles on psychology.
Gift of Mrs. Fridenberg (Philadelphia, Pennsylvania).

170. *Friedline, Cora L., 1893-1975.*
Papers, 1894-1948. 1¼ ft.
In University of Akron, Archives of the History of American Psychology (Akron, Ohio).
Psychologist. Correspondence and notes of interviews with E. B. Titchener concerning laboratory experiments.
Unpublished guide available.

171. *Gale, Harlow Stearns, 1862-1945.*
Papers, 1885-1939. 3 ft.
In University of Minnesota Library, University Archives (Minneapolis, Minnesota).
Educator at the University of Minnesota, and municipal employee of Minneapolis. Correspondence, personal diaries, psychological diaries of Gale's children, manuscripts of articles on many subjects, notebooks, and photos intending to debunk spiritualism. Correspondents include Ella Winter Steffens and Joseph Lincoln Steffens.
Unpublished description in the library.
Open to investigators under library restrictions.
Information on literary rights available in the library.

172. *Galt Family.*
Papers, 1756-1894. 5743 items.
In Colonial Williamsburg Manuscript Collections (Williamsburg, Virginia).
Family, personal, and business papers and correspondence of three generations of the Galt family. They center around John Minson Galt I (1744-1808), attending physician at the Lunatick Hospital (later called the Eastern State Hospital) at Williamsburg, Virginia; his son Alexander Dickie Galt (1771-1841), who became attending physician at the hospital upon his father's death; and Alexander Galt's children, John Minson Galt II (1819-62), who was appointed medical superintendent of the hospital when his father died, and Sarah Maria Galt (1822-80). The papers, dating largely from 1820 to 1870, relate to the management of the hospital, to affairs in Williamsburg, to medical education in Philadelphia, and to medical societies in the United States. Includes seven apothecary-surgeon daybooks of John Minson Galt I and Philip Barraud; two saddler and harness maker's account books of Alexander Craig, father-in-law of John Minson Galt I; and letters from William R. Galt, a student at the University of Virginia in the early 1840s, from Alexander Galt (1827-63), sculptor, from Alexander Galt, postmaster of Norfolk, Virginia, from Dorothea L. Dix, a frequent visitor to the hospital and friend of Sarah Maria Galt, and from other members of the Galt family in Williamsburg, Richmond, and Norfolk, Virginia. Also includes poems by Elizabeth Galt, and stories and essays written by various members of the Galt family.

173. *Gardner, Elizabeth F.*
Papers, 1933-59. ca. 1 ft.
In University of Texas Library, Texas Archives (Austin, Texas).

173. *(Continued)*

Teacher and executive secretary of the Texas Society for Mental Hygiene. Correspondence, clippings, pamphlets, and scrapbooks, relating to mental health in Texas and activities of the Texas Society for Mental Hygiene, the Hogg Foundation for Mental Health, and the Texas Society for Mental Health.

Described in *The University of Texas Archives: A Guide to the Historical Manuscripts Collections in the University Library* (1968), p. 133.

174. *Garrett Family.*

Papers, 1811-1930.

In University of Virginia Library (Charlottesville, Virginia).

Contains a petition opposing life appointments to the board of directors of the Eastern Lunatic Asylum in Williamsburg, Virginia, and correspondence of a debate in the Virginia Senate regarding an 1851 insane asylum bill.

175. *Gault, Robert Harvey, 1874-1971.*

Papers, 1909-72. 3 boxes.

In Northwestern University Archives (Evanston, Illinois).

Professor of psychology. The bulk of the papers consists of Gault's various writings, both published and unpublished, including the manuscript of his book, *Social Psychology*. Lecture notes, general correspondence, and miscellaneous writings on juvenile delinquency accompany a biographical file which illuminates Gault's career.

No restrictions.

176. *General Education Board.*

Records, 1902-41. ca. 275 ft.

In Rockefeller Archive Center (Pocantico Hills, North Tarrytown, New York).

Correspondence, surveys, reports, studies, conference proceedings, diaries, minutes of meetings, publications, and administrative and financial records, of a philanthropic organization emphasizing Negro and medical education and education in the South. Organizations represented include the American Association of Junior Colleges, American Council on Education, American Youth Commission, Association of Colleges and Secondary Schools for Negroes, Carnegie Corporation, Commission on Human Relations, Commission on Secondary School Curriculum, Gary Survey, Jeanes Fund, National Council of Parent Education, National Education Association, John F. Slater Fund, Southern Education Board, United Negro College Fund, and U. S. Department of Agriculture. Persons represented include Trevor Arnett, Wallace Buttrick, Robert D. Calkins, Jackson Davis, James H. Dillard, Charles W. Eliot, Leo Favrot, Abraham Flexner, Douglas S. Freeman, Frederick T. Gates, Seaman Knapp, Albert R. Mann, Robert R. Moton, Walter Hines Page, George Foster Peabody, John D. Rockefeller, John D. Rockefeller, Jr., Wickliffe Rose, Anson Phelps Stokes, and Booker T. Washington.

Unpublished inventory and index in the repository.

Also described in *The Rockefeller Archive Center: Open Collections* (1974), pp. 10-12.

177. *Gesell, Arnold Lucius, 1880-1961.*
Papers, 1870-1961. 100 ft. (90,000 items).
In Library of Congress, Manuscript Division (Washington, D.C.).
    Child specialist and director of the Yale Clinic of Child Development. Correspondence, abstracts, addresses, announcements, appointment books, biographical material; books and articles, with galleys; Gesell's reviews of others' books; broadcasts, bulletins, certificates, charts, clinical records, clippings, contracts, diplomas, film scripts, financial papers, genealogical records, illustrations, lectures, legal papers, personnel records, photos, press releases, reports, scrapbooks, and other papers concerning Gesell's professional life. Includes material relating to his work in the Yale School of Medicine; Catherine Amatruda, Louise (Bates) Ames, Burton Castner, Frances L. Ilg, and Helen Thompson; the Connecticut Child Welfare Survey, the Gesell Institute of Child Development, and the Yale Clinic of Child Development; German immigration and assimilation in the United States (1870-1910), the character of Josiah Willard Gibbs (1839-1903), the childhood development of Abraham Lincoln; and the use of motion pictures as educational and scientific research tools (1920-50). Correspondents include James Angell, Roswell Angier, Charlotte Buhler, Glenna Bullis, Leonard Carmichael, Henry Goddard, Walter Miles, Grover Powers, Lewis Terman, Thomas Wingate Todd, and Robert Yerkes.
    Finding-aid in the library.
    Gift of his son and daughter, Gerhard A. Gesell and Mrs. Joseph W. Walden, and Theodore Buehler, 1964.

178. *Gilbert, Wells Smith, 1870-1965.*
Papers, 1897-1965. 3 boxes.
In Oregon Historical Society (Portland, Oregon).
    Includes seven diaries of Page Gilbert; a diary of Wells Gilbert (1902); and information on Page Gilbert's ideas on spiritualism.

179. *Gilbreth, Frank Bunker, 1868-1924.*
Information file, ca. 1910-24. ca. 100 ft.
In Purdue University Library (Lafayette, Indiana).
    In part, transcripts and photocopies.
    Industrial engineer, contractor, and author. Correspondence, research papers, professional reports, case material, lecture notes, charts, data sheets, other papers, slides and photos. This material was accumulated by Gilbreth during his studies in management, time and motion, and new work techniques, in many lines of activity. Includes supplementary material added by his wife, Lillian Gilbreth.
    Finding-aids in the library.
    Open to investigators under library restrictions.
    Information on literary rights available in the library.
    Gift of Mrs. Gilbreth, 1939.

180. *Gilman, Daniel Coit, 1831-1908.*
Papers, 1868-1907. ca. 17,030 items.
In Johns Hopkins University Library (Baltimore, Maryland).

180. *(Continued)*
Author, lecturer, and president of Johns Hopkins University.
Card catalog in the library.
Information on literary rights available in the library.
Gift of Elizabeth Gilman.

181. *Gitelson, Maxwell, 1902-1965.*
Papers, 1930-65. 43 ft. (ca. 25,000 items).
In Library of Congress, Manuscript Division (Washington, D.C.).
Psychiatrist. Correspondence, diaries, college notebooks, medical notes, book reviews, photos, subject files, addresses, lectures, articles, and other papers, relating to psychiatry, psychoanalysis, mental health programs, and education and ethics in the psychiatric profession. The bulk of the papers is records of the American Psychoanalytic Association, of which Gitelson was president; the Center for Advanced Psychoanalytical Studies, the Chicago Institute for Psychoanalysis, the Chicago Psychoanalytic Society, the Sigmund Freud Archives (Inc.); the International Psycho-Analytic Association, of which he was president; the Lionel Blitzsten Memorial (Inc.); and the Psychoanalytic Assistance Fund.
Unpublished finding-aid in the library.
Open to investigators under restrictions accepted by the library.
Deposit of Frances Hannett Gitelson, 1965.

182. *Glazer, Simon, 1878-*
Papers, 1903-48. 1 vol. and 5 boxes.
In American Jewish Archives (Cincinnati, Ohio).
Rabbi. Correspondence, diary (1909, 1922-23), lectures on the Bible, Mishnah, and Talmud; notes on secular common laws, and Hebrew and Yiddish papers. Includes correspondence (1926-48) of Glazer's son, Rabbi B. Benedict Glazer of Detroit, relating to anti-Semitism, Zionism, restrictions, the Lithuanian question, and problems of mental hygiene. Glazer's diary relates to Jewish life in Montreal, Canada, and in New York City; and it contains details of cases in Jewish law, marriage and divorce settlements, and other problems relating to his rabbinical duties. His correspondence relates chiefly to religious and Jewish matters.
Described in *American Jewish Archives*, vol. 7, no. 1 (January 1955), pp. 142-43; and vol. 8, no. 1 (January 1956), p. 49.
Gifts of Rabbi and Mrs. B. Benedict Glazer (Detroit, Michigan).

183. *Gleuck, Sheldon, 1896-   ; and Eleanor (Tournoff) Gleuck, 1898-1972.*
Papers, 1911-72. 50 ft.
In Harvard Law School Library (Cambridge, Massachusetts).
Papers relating to their joint research on juvenile delinquency. Collection also contains data on the Gleucks' work concerning mental illness, mental health, social welfare, child psychiatry, delinquency, crime, and penal law.
Unpublished guide available.

184. *Goddard, Henry Herbert, 1866-1957.*
Papers, 1833-1952. ca. 8 ft.
In University of Akron, Archives of the History of American Psychology (Akron, Ohio).

Psychologist, director of the research department of the Training School, Vineland, New Jersey; and professor at Ohio State University. Correspondence (1906-52), diary-ledger-scrapbook (1833-64) used by Goddard's mother, Sarah Goddard; records of unpublished laboratory data, pamphlets, clippings, scrapbooks, professional and avocational photos, glass slides, films, and personal ephemera. Includes material relating to Goddard's professional activities. Major correspondents include George F. Arps, Earl Barnes, Harold E. Burtt, Walter B. Cannon, George W. Crane, E. A. Doll, Irving Fisher, Florence Fitzgerald, Arnold Gesell, Florence Goodenough, G. Stanley Hall, Willis H. Hazard, C. Judson Herrick, Edith H. Huey, S. E. Jelliffe, Edward R. Johnstone, Elizabeth F. Kite, L. W. Kline, Samuel C. Kohs, Florence Mateer, E. Meumann, M. Newburger, Donald G. Paterson, Winifred Richmond, A. C. Rogers, Edmund C. Sanford, George S. Stevenson, Lewis M. Terman, and Elizabeth L. Woods.
Unpublished guide and index in the repository.
Partially restricted.
Information on literary rights available in the repository.
Gift of Alice M. Whiting, 1962.

185. *Goldman, Emma, 1869-1940.*
Papers, 1902-39. 4 boxes.
In Boston University Library Archives (Boston, Massachusetts).

Lecturer, publicist, and feminist. Personal correspondence, miscellaneous memorabilia, newspaper clippings, and photographs. Major correspondents include Alexander Berkman, Ben L. Reitman, and Almeda Sperry.

186. *Goldsmith, Esther, 1776-1866.*
Papers, 1866-75. 83 items.
In Georgia Historical Society Collections (Savannah, Georgia).

Record of Goldsmith's estate and bills and receipts for payment by it; and letters from the superintendent and resident physician of the State Lunatic Asylum, Milledgeville, Georgia, concerning the treatment and death of her daughter, Henrietta Goldsmith (1820-73).
Unpublished finding-aid in the repository.
Gift of Miss Caroline L. Meldrim, Savannah, Georgia, from the papers of her father, Judge Peter W. Meldrim, 1952.

187. *Goldstein, Kurt, 1878-1965.*
Papers, 1900-65. ca. 3000 items.
In Columbia University Libraries (New York, New York).

Neurologist, psychiatrist, and clinical professor of psychiatry at Columbia University. Correspondence, lecture notes; drafts and manuscripts of articles, essays, and books; and other papers. The material relates to Goldstein's research in psychopathology, schizophrenia, injuries and tumors of the brain, and speech

187. *(Continued)*

and optic disorders. Includes the manuscripts for his books, *The Brain Injured Soldiers: Human Nature in the Light of Psychopathology* (1940); *Language and Language Disturbances* (1948); and *The Organism: A Holistic Approach to Biology Derived from Pathological Data in Man* (1939).

Unpublished calendar in the library.

Gift of Mrs. William E. Haudek, 1968.

188. *Goodenough, Florence, 1886-1959.*

Correspondence. 15 in.

In University of Minnesota Archives, Walter Library (Minneapolis, Minnesota).

Child psychologist and mental tester. Long-time chief psychologist, Institute of Child Welfare, University of Minnesota.

189. *Gould, John Stanton, 1812-1874.*

Papers, 1823-1914. 160 items and 5 vols.

In Cornell University Library, Department of Manuscripts and University Archives (Ithaca, New York).

New York State assemblyman, agriculturalist, and non-resident member of the faculty of Cornell University. Correspondence; diaries (2 volumes, 1823-27); journal (1847-50) kept while a member of the Assembly; geography lecture notes; probate papers, accounts, inventories, and other records relating to Gould's position as administrator of the estates of George Coventry, Joseph Marshall, and Henry W. Reynolds; Gould's estate papers, and legal documents and inventories (1854-1914) pertaining to bank and railroad investments made by him and his second wife, Hannah (Wright) Gould; proposals made by W. S. Leavitt for the curriculum and library at Cornell University; and photos. Journal topics include the Mexican War, antirent troubles, antislavery movement, prison reform, agricultural and medical education, care of the insane, and temperance, with references to Henry Clay, Millard Fillmore, Horace Greeley, William Henry Seward, and Thurlow Weed. Correspondents include Gould's mother, Hannah (Rodman) Gould, and Moses Brown, Cyrus Curtiss, and John B. Hague.

Unpublished description in the library.

Gift of Mrs. Sanford Stoddard and James W. Tyson.

Other papers of John Stanton Gould have been catalogued as part of the library's collection of Gould family papers.

190. *Graham, Clarence Henry, 1906-1971.*

Papers, ca. 1950-65. ca. 1500 items.

In Columbia University Libraries (New York, New York).

Professor of psychology at Columbia University. Manuscripts, typescripts, page and galley proofs, illustrations, and related correspondence, for Graham's book, *Vision and Visual Perception* (1965). Correspondents include Neil R. Bartlett, John Lott Brown, and Lorin A. Riggs.

Deposited by Mrs. Graham, 1972.

191. *Graham, Hazel E., 1906-*
Papers, 1935-70. 1 ft.
In Wayne State University Archives (Detroit, Michigan).
Professor of education in the educational psychology department at Wayne State University. Correspondence and articles concern her work in clinical psychology and with psychological and psychiatric clinics in the Detroit area.
Unpublished guide available.

192. *Greater Philadelphia Federation of Settlements.*
Records, 1939-69. ca. 40 ft.
In Temple University Libraries, Urban Archives (Philadelphia, Pennsylvania).
General files (1939-68); papers (1961-67) of Louise L. Page, president of the federation, 1963-67; papers (1965-69) of the Philadelphia Anti-Poverty Action Committee; study (1966-67) of settlement service in South Philadelphia; Neighborhood Youth Corps records (1965-68); programs for children and teenagers with behavioral problems (1959-68); summer reading camps (1965-68); and training programs for community social workers (1965-66).
Unpublished description in the library.
Deposited by the federation through S. Allen Bacon, Executive Director, 1969.

193. *Griffin-Greenland Collection.*
Papers.
In Canadian Mental Health Association Archives (Toronto, Ontario).
Papers of Dr. John D. Griffin and Cyril Greenland documenting the history of psychiatry in Canada. Archives begin with European contact, pre-institutional attempts to care for the mentally ill, the history of mental hospitals and asylums in Canada, photographs and documents pertaining to mental illness, biographies of people involved in the field, and some unsorted documents.

194. *Griffith, Coleman Roberts, 1893-1966.*
Papers, 1919-63. ca. 17 ft.
In University of Illinois, University Archives (Urbana, Illinois).
Professor and administrator at the University of Illinois, and director of the Bureau of Institutional Research. Correspondence, speeches, curriculum vitae, experiment notes and projects, manuscripts of books and articles; publications, student papers and theses, bulletins, workbooks, scrapbooks, lecture notes, exams, reports, newspaper clippings; and other papers relating to the Bureau of Institutional Research, the University of Illinois Department of Psychology and Division of Humanities, university affairs, the dismissal of Griffith and George Stoddard, Krebiozen; the Defense Research Coordinating Committee, the Council of Ten, the Koch case, the Allerton Conference on Education, Arthur Bestor; American Council on Education's, Office of Statistical Information and Research; academic freedom, Griffith's publications in the field of educational and general psychology, politics, and the University of Illinois Press.
Unpublished finding-aid in the repository.
Received 1965-66.

195. *Gross, Sidney, 1921-1969.*

Papers, ca. 1945-69. 1 reel of microfilm (negative and positive).

In Archives of American Art (Washington, D.C.).

Microfilm of originals loaned for filming by Mrs. Gross in 1970.

Artist and teacher of New York City. Chiefly manuscripts of writings relating to the philosophical and psychological implications of art, aesthetics, theories of color, artistic techniques, and the history of art; together with drawings, exhibition catalogs, clippings, and other papers.

The repository's branches in Boston, Detroit, New York, and San Francisco also have microfilm (positive) of the collection.

196. *Hall, Granville Stanley, 1844-1924.*

Papers, 1850-1970. 8 ft.

In Clark University Archives (Worcester, Massachusetts).

In part, transcripts (typewritten) made in the 1920's by Henry D. Sheldon from originals (some of which have been destroyed) owned by the Hall family.

Psychologist and president of Clark University. Correspondence, notes, manuscripts of writings, Hall family genealogy, material relating to Clark University and educational organizations, and material collected by Dorothy Ross for her biography, *G. Stanley Hall: The Psychologist as Prophet* (1972). Major correspondents include John Wallace Baird, Harry Elmer Barnes, George Hubbard Blakeslee, Franz Boas, Augustus George Bullock, William Henry Burnham, Jonas Gilman Clark, Edward Cowles, Sigmund Freud, Robert Hutchings Goddard, George Frisbie Hoar, Archer Butler Hulbert, William James, Charles Augustus Kraus, Ralph Stayner Lillie, Franklin Paine Mall, Adolf Meyer, Albert Abraham Michelson, James Pertice Porter, Martin Andre Rosanoff, Amy Eliza Tanner, Arthur Gordon Webster, Charles Otis Whitman, Louis Napoleon Wilson, and Carroll Davidson Wright.

Register published in 1972 by the repository.

Information on literary rights available in the repository.

Gifts of the Hall family and Dorothy Ross, 1971; and deposited by various offices of Clark University.

197. *Hall, Granville Stanley, 1844-1924.*

Papers, 1889-1921. 3 ft.

In University of Akron, Archives of the History of American Psychology (Akron, Ohio).

Psychologist, philosopher, and educator. Principally notes from Hall's readings of the professional literature, together with some correspondence, numerous manuscripts and drafts of publications, and minutes (1917) of a few meetings of the Committee on the Examination of Recruits.

Index guide and unpublished register in the repository.

Information on literary rights available in the repository.

Gift of Pennsylvania State University, 1967.

The repository also has microfilm (negative) of the collection.

198. *Hall, Granville Stanley, 1844-1924.*

Sigmund Freud correspondence, 1908-23. 71 items.

In Clark University Library (Worcester, Massachusetts).

Psychologist, philosopher, and educator. Letters concerned with Hall's invitation, as president of Clark University, to Sigmund Freud to give lectures on the nature, origins, and development of psychoanalysis upon the occasion of the twentieth anniversary celebration of the founding of the university. Later letters are concerned with the translation and publication of the lectures, and to some extent with the subsequent history of psychoanalysis as developed by Freud and his contemporaries. Correspondents include Alfred Adler, Franz Boas, A. A. Brill, Leo Burgerstein, Sandor Ferenczi, William James, Ernest Jones, C. G. Jung, James H. Leuba, Jacques Loeb, William Stern, August Weismann, and Wilhelm Wundt.

Described in "Freud Discovers America," by Dr. William A. Koelsch, *Virginia Quarterly Review*, vol. 46, no. 1 (Winter 1970), pp. 115-32.

Information on literary rights available in the library.

Deposit from the papers of Dr. Hall.

199. *Hall, James King, 1875-1948.*

Papers, 1751-1949. 24½ ft., including 15 vols.

In University of North Carolina Library, Southern Historical Collection (Chapel Hill, North Carolina).

Professional correspondence and medical writings (chiefly 1920-48) of Hall, the psychiatrist who founded and directed (1911-48) the Westbrook Sanitorium in Richmond, Virginia. Correspondence includes letters from friends and associates in the medical profession; copies of letters from Hall concerning all phases of medicine, but particularly psychiatry and its institutions and organizations; letters from political leaders concerning state mental institutions; letters pursuing Hall's interest in the relation of crime and mental illness; and letters reflecting his interest in the history of Iredell County, North Carolina, his birthplace. Early papers are of Hall and Nisbet ancestors in Iredell County, including records of the Bethany congregation (Presbyterian), 1775-1872; a physician's day book (1867-71); and records of an academy conducted by Hugh Roddy Hall (1800-56). Also, physicians' pictures, scrapbooks, notebooks, and an inspection report (1864) of a Confederate medical purveyor's depot.

Restricted in part.

200. *Halstead, Ward Campbell, 1908-1969.*

Papers, 1936-68. ca. 11 ft.

In University of Akron, Archives of the History of American Psychology (Akron, Ohio).

Psychologist. Printed material and other papers, documenting Halstead's research on the process of aging, brain function, and the problems of blind children, and his activities in professional organizations; together with correspondence, term papers, and examinations, reflecting the work of his students at the University of Chicago. Includes notices and abstracts of Clark L. Hull's informal seminars, 1935-37. Major correspondents include James Birren, Paul Bucy, James

200. *(Continued)*
W. Crawford, Charles Osgood, Ralph M. Reitan, William B. Rucker, Edwin H. Schludermann, David Symmes, and J. Warren Thiesen.
Unpublished finding-aids in the repository.
Information on literary rights available in the repository.
Gifts of Mrs. Patten, 1967-70.

201. *Hare, Michael Meredith, 1909-1968.*
Papers, 1935-68. 4 ft.
In Yale University Library (New Haven, Connecticut).
Architect, philosopher, and author. Correspondence, diaries, writings, notes, research material, and other papers, relating primarily to Hare's interest in the philosophical, theological, and mystical implications of the creative process, and to his attempts to reconcile the laws of physics and parapsychological phenomena. Correspondents include Hiram Bingham, José M. R. Delgado, Frederic B. Fitch, Quincy Howe, Carl Jung, Henry Margenau, Jacques Maritain, Percival W. Martin, Lewis Mumford, J. B. Rhine, Paul Tillich, Arnold Toynbee, W. Grey Walter, and Paul Weiss.
Unpublished register in the library.
Information on literary rights available in the library.
Gift of Mrs. Hare, 1969.

202. *Harper, William Rainey, 1856-1906.*
Papers, 1886-1906. ca. 10,000 items.
In University of Chicago Library (Chicago, Illinois).
Educator. Official correspondence of Harper as president of the University of Chicago; together with his "red" notebooks, which were diary-type journals of his ideas and activities. Includes some correspondence preceding the establishment of the university.

203. *Harris, Florence R.*
Papers, 1941-71. 2 ft.
University of Washington Libraries, Archives and Manuscripts Division (Seattle, Washington).
Director of the Developmental Psychology Laboratory Preschool, University of Washington. Teaching material, manuscripts, clinical studies, and films, dealing with administrative work in child development and education. Includes information on Head Start and other child development programs.

204. *Harris, William Torrey, 1835-1909.*
Papers, ca. 1855-1909. 4 ft.
In Missouri Historical Society Collections (St. Louis, Missouri).
Educator and philosopher. Correspondence with various philosophers of the St. Louis Movement, including Charles Louis Bernays, Louis J. Block, Benjamin Paul Blood, Henry C. Brockmeyer, Thomas Davidson, Sarah Denman, Ira Divoll, James B. Eads, Samuel H. Emery, Jr., James M. Greenwood, J. Z. Hall, S.

K. Hall, Thomas M. Johnson, Hiram K. Jones, Elizabeth Peabody, Denton Jaques
Snider, and Frank Louis Soldan.
Information on literary rights available in the repository.
Gift.

205. *Harris, William Torrey, 1835-1909.*
Papers, 1866-1908. 20 ft. (ca. 13,500 items).
In Library of Congress, Manuscript Division (Washington, D.C.).
Educator, author, editor, and philosopher. Letters, drafts and printed copies of
Harris's articles, addresses, lectures, and reports, with notes and printed material
used in their preparation; and the manuscripts of his books.
Unpublished finding-aid in the library.
Also described in the library's *Quarterly Journal of Current Acquisitions*, vol.
11, no. 3 (May 1954), p. 161.
Information on literary rights available in the library.
Gift of Edith Davidson Harris, 1953.

206. *Harris, William W., 1816-   .*
Notebook, 1835.
In University of Virginia Library (Charlottesville, Virginia).
Lectures given in the mental philosophy course of Professor George Tucker
(1775-1861).

207. *Hartson, Louis D., 1885-   .*
Papers, 1925-76. ca. 6 in.
In Oberlin College Archives (Oberlin, Ohio).
Assistant professor of psychology (1923-52). His papers consist mainly of his
writings, both manuscripts and printed, and reflect his chief interest in the
development of testing and the administration of intelligence tests. The collection also contains records concerning Raymond H. Stetson and his correspondence with Hartson.

208. *Harvard University Faculty and Other Officers, Deceased before 1940.*
Papers, especially correspondence, 1725-ca. 1940. 10 ft.
In Harvard University Archives (Cambridge, Massachusetts).
    In part, photocopies and transcripts (typewritten).
    Small, separately organized collections, consisting mainly of correspondence,
but including manuscripts of writings and speeches, research and other notes,
reports, biographical and autobiographical papers, and business and other
personal papers. Persons, teaching areas, and offices represented include Alexander Agassiz, zoology, overseer, and fellow; Louis Agassiz, zoology and geology; Emile Arnoult, French; George P. Baker, English, forensics, and dramatic
literature; Ferdinand Bocher, modern languages; Nathaniel Bowditch, fellow
and overseer; Francis Bowen, natural, intellectual, and moral philosophy, natural
religion, and civil polity; LeBaron R. Briggs, English, dean of Harvard College
and Faculty of Arts and Sciences, and overseer; Phillips Brooks, overseer and

208. *(Continued)*

preacher to the university; William E. Byerly, mathematics; Edward Channing, history; William E. Channing, Biblical literature, and fellow; Francis J. Child, rhetoric, oratory, and English; George Derby, hygiene; Ephraim Emerton, history and German; William Everett, Latin and classical literature, and overseer; Williamina P. Fleming, astronomy; Charles T. C. Follen, ethics, history, and German language and literature; Wolcott Gibbs, application of science to the useful arts, and dean of Lawrence Scientific School and School of Mining and Practical Engineering; Asa Gray, natural history and botany; Simon Greenleaf, law; Thaddeus W. Harris, librarian; Frederick H. Hedge, ecclesiastical history and German; Ira N. Hollis, engineering, and overseer; Albert A. Howard, Latin; Frederic D. Huntington, Christian morals, and preacher to the university; Arthur E. Kennelly, electrical engineering; Henry Lee, overseer; John Leverett, president; William C. Loring, law, and overseer; Theodore Lyman, zoology, and overseer; Gordon McKay, benefactor; Amos Main, Harvard graduate; Lawrence S. Mayo, assistant dean of Harvard College and Graduate School of Arts and Sciences; Hugo Münsterberg, psychology; Charles E. Norton, French, fine arts, and overseer; John K. Paine, music; John G. Palfrey, Biblical literature, dean of Divinity School, and overseer; George H. Palmer, philosophy, and overseer; Joel Parker, law; Andrew P. Peabody, Christian morals, overseer, and preacher to the university; Denman W. Ross, theory of design; Truman H. Safford, astronomy; Francis Sales, Spanish and French; Charles S. Sargent, horticulture and arboriculture; William H. Schofield, English and comparative literature; Arthur B. Seymour, botany; Nathaniel S. Shaler, paleontology, geology, and dean of Lawrence Scientific School; Edward S. Sheldon, Italian, Spanish, and modern languages; Evangeline A. Sophocles, Greek; David H. Storer, obstetrics and medical jurisprudence, and dean of the Medical School; Francis H. Storer, agricultural chemistry, and dean of the Bussey Institution; Joseph Story, law, overseer, and fellow; James B. Thayer, law; William Tillinghast, assistant librarian and editor of the *Quinquennial Catalogue;* Dudley A. Tyng, overseer; Henry P. Walcott, overseer and fellow; Samuel B. Walcott, tutor; Samuel Webber, mathematics, natural philosophy, and president; Jens I. Westengard, law; William M. Wheeler, entomology, and dean of Faculty of Bussey Institution (Jamaica Plain, Massachusetts); and William M. Woodworth, microscopical anatomy and zoology.

Unpublished finding-aid in the repository.

Access restricted in part.

Information on literary rights available in the repository.

Acquired from various sources by gift, permanent deposit, and other means.

209. *Harvard University Faculty and Other Officers, Living after 1940.*

Papers consisting mainly of items other than correspondence, ca. 1885-1965. 6 ft.

In Harvard University Archives (Cambridge, Massachusetts).

In part, photocopies and transcripts (typewritten).

Small, separately organized collections, consisting mainly of diaries, manuscripts of writings and speeches, lectures and other teaching material, biographical and autobiographical papers, a scrapbook, and sound recordings of events.

Persons, teaching areas, and offices represented include Comfort Avery Adams, electrical engineering; Weld Arnold, geography and geographical exploration; Walter B. Briggs, librarian; Edwin J. Cohn, physiological, physical, and biological chemistry; Walter F. Dearborn, education; George V. Florovsky, Eastern church history; Richard M. Gummere, Latin; Edward Y. Hartshorne, sociology; Robert H. Haynes, librarian; Frank W. C. Hersey, English; Werner Jaeger, classics; Sanford A. Lakoff, government; Karl S. Lashley, psychology and neuropsychology; Louis M. Lyons, curator of Nieman Fellowships (journalism); Charles H. McIlwain, history and government; Charles F. Mason, bursar; Francis O. Matthiessen, history and literature; Louis J. Mercier, French and education; Richard S. Meriam, economics and business economics; André Morize, military science and tactics, and French literature; Harris P. Mosher, laryngology, anatomy, and otology; William A. Neilson, English; Arthur S. Pease, Latin and Greek; David T. Pottinger, associate director of Harvard University Press; Fritz Redlich, senior associate, Center for Entrepreneurial History; William T. Reid, Jr., baseball and football coach; John F. C. Richards, Greek and Latin; Arthur Truman Safford, hydraulic engineering; Gaetano Salvemini, history of Italian civilization; George Sarton, history of science; Edgar J. Schoen, Harvard graduate; William E. Sedgwick, English; Walter R. Spalding, music; Alfred North Whitehead, philosophy; Alfred Worcester, hygiene; and John K. Wright, military science and history.

Unpublished finding-aid in the repository.

Access restricted in part.

Information on literary rights available in the repository.

Acquired from various sources by gift, permanent deposit, and other means.

210. *Harvard University Faculty and Other Officers, Living after 1940.*
Papers, especially correspondence, 1954, 1905-70. 12 ft.
In Harvard University Archives (Cambridge, Massachusetts).

Small, separately organized collections, consisting mainly of correspondence, but including notes, manuscripts of writings and speeches, memos and reports, lecture notes and other teaching material, scrapbooks, and biographical and autobiographical papers. Persons, teaching areas, and offices represented include Oakes Ames, botany; Fernand Baldensperger, comparative literature; William Bollay, applied mechanics; John M. Brewer, education; Sergius Ivan Chermayeff, architecture; Walter E. Clark, Sanskrit; Harry E. Clifford, electrical engineering and dean of Engineering School; Reginald A. Daly, geology; Cecil K. Drinker, physiology and dean of Faculty of Public Health; Sidney B. Fay, history; William S. Ferguson, history and dean of Faculty of Arts and Sciences; Ronald M. Ferry, biochemistry; Louis F. Fieser, chemistry; Clifford Frondel, mineralogy; Edwin F. Gay, economics, economic history, dean of Graduate School of Business Administration, and overseer; Alfred C. Hanford, government, dean of Harvard College, and director of Summer School of Arts and Sciences and of Education; William G. Howard, German; Reid Hunt, pharmacology; Edward V. Huntington, mathematics and mechanics; Byron S. Hurlbut, English, and recording secretary and dean of Harvard College; Robert T. Jackson, paleontology; Michael Karpovich, history, and Slavic languages and literature; Charles W.

210. *(Continued)*

Killam, architecture; Kirsopp Lake, history, ecclesiastical history, and early Christian literature; Walter Lichtenstein, curator in the library; David Little, English, assistant dean of Harvard College, secretary to the university, and curator in the library; Alexander G. McAdie, meteorology; Lionel S. Marks, mechanical engineering; George A. Miller, psychology; John Usher Monro, dean of Harvard College; James B. Munn, English; William Bennett Munro, government, history, and overseer; George H. Parker, zoology; George A. R. Reisner, Semitic languages, archeology, and Egyptology; Fred Norris Robinson, English; George W. Robinson, secretary of Graduate School of Arts and Sciences; Frederick A. Saunders, physics; Warren A. Seavey, law; George Sherburn, English; Joseph L. Smith, freehand drawing; Frederic J. Stimson, American and comparative legislation; Charles H. Taylor, history and medieval history; Alfred M. Tozzer, archeology and anthropology; Karl Viëtor, German art and culture; and Henry A. Yeomans, government, and dean of Harvard College.

Unpublished finding-aid in the repository.

Access restricted in part.

Information on literary rights available in the repository.

Acquired from various sources by gift, permanent deposit, and other means of acquisition.

211. *Haverkamp, Harold J., 1912-* .

Papers, 1945-55. 54 items.

In Hope College Archives (Holland, Michigan).

Associate professor of psychology at Hope College, and dean of Central College in Pella, Iowa. Mainly correspondence with J. W. Hollenbach and I. J. Lubbers.

212. *Hawkins, Walace, 1895-1951.*

Papers, 1910-51. ca. 4 ft.

In University of Texas Library, Texas Archives (Austin, Texas).

In part, photocopies.

Lawyer of Texas. Correspondence, journals, telegrams, speeches, lectures, biographical and historical sketches, writings, reviews, scrapbooks, petitions, legal papers, reports, case records, court docker, notebooks, memoranda, obituaries, photos, maps, plates, and other papers. Deals with Hawkins's personal and family life, including genealogy and family history; his academic life as a student at Stanford College and the University of Texas Law School, as principal of Bublin High School, and as a participant in alumni groups; his legal career, including work as Assistant State Attorney General and Attorney General; employment with the Magnolia Petroleum Company, and as a general counsel for that corporation; his political career, including election to the state legislature and participation in events leading to the impeachment of Governor James Ferguson; his military career; his religious interests, including ecclesiastical histories and spiritualism; and his interest in Texas history.

Described in the *University of Texas Archives; A Guide to the Historical Manuscripts Collections in the University Library* (1968), pp. 162-63.

213. *Hazen, George Wintermute, 1852-1909.*

Papers, 1871-1909. 1 vol. and 1 folder.

In Oregon Historical Society Library (Portland, Oregon).

Lawyer. Correspondence, a scrapbook, and other material, relating to the American Patriotic Club of Portland, in which Hazen served as secretary. Includes a phrenological examination (1896).

Information on literary rights available in the library.

214. *Hazzard, Florence (Woolsey), 1903-* .

Papers, 1819-1965. ca. 1 ft. and 2 reels of microfilm.

In Cornell University Library, Department of Manuscripts and University Archives (Ithaca, New York).

In part, transcripts and photocopies.

Author and psychologist. Correspondence, manuscripts of writings, notes, bibliographies, printed matter, photos, and other papers, dealing mainly with Mrs. Hazzard's studies of eminent American women. Includes miscellaneous personal and professional papers of the Hazzard family; and material on the disposition of the Emily Howland papers, the World Center for Women's Archives, the women's rights movement in the United States, and Mrs. Hazzard's work in psychology, especially in odor perception. Women represented include Abigail Adams, Susan B. Anthony, Mary Sheldon Barnes, Elizabeth Blackwell, Katherine Blake, Lillie Devereux Blake, Lydia Maria Child, Prudence Crandall, Margaret Fuller, Rachel Brooks Gleason, Angelina Grimké, Sarah Grimké, Cornelia Hancock, Amanda Sanford Hickey, Julia Ward Howe, Harriet May Mills, Eliza Mosher, Lucretia Mott, Alice Freeman Palmer, May Preston Slosson, Elizabeth Cady Stanton, Lucy Stone, Harriet Tubman, and Emma Willard. Chief correspondents include Mary Ritter Beard, Carrie Chapman Catt, Edward Bradford Titchener, and Marjorie White.

Unpublished guides in the library.

Restricted in part.

Gift of Mrs. Albert S. Hazzard, 1965-67.

215. *Health and Welfare Council, Philadelphia.*

Records, 1922-69. ca. 17 ft. and 35 folders in 4 boxes.

In Temple University Libraries, Urban Archives (Philadelphia, Pennsylvania).

Collection consists of several series of papers, the contents of which overlap. One series is made up of minutes, reports, mimeographed materials, and other records of the executive committees and the five service divisions of the council (aging, family, children, education-recreation, and health) and of its predecessor, the Council of Social Agencies of Philadelphia. A second series includes correspondence, minutes, and other papers of the Family Service Division and Committee on Illegitimacy. Subjects mentioned include adoption, the aged, charities, children, family size, housing, illegitimacy, mental hygiene, Negroes, nursing homes, prisoners, public welfare, social services, and unmarried mothers. People and organizations represented include Marjorie Duckrey, Friends Neighborhood Guild, Lillian Gest, Claudia Grant, Paul Jans, C. F. McNeil, National Federation of Settlements, Philadelphia-Camden Social Ser-

215. *(Continued)*

vice Exchange, William W. Scranton, Henry Serotkin, Wilma Stringfellow, James H. J. Tate, U.S. National Insitute of Mental Health, Wharton Center, and Randolph E. Wise. A third series includes material drawn from the files of Lillian Gest, including mimeographed minutes, reports, correspondence, statements, and executive committee reports from the Conference on Child Care Standards (1952-53), White House Conference on Children and Youth (1950), and West Parkside Area Committee (1944-46). This series also includes much material relating to the Council of Social Agencies, and to the early (from 1922) history of organized welfare and relief in Philadelphia. A fourth series is made up of Lillian Gest's own papers, including executive committee materials, and administrative, budgetary, conference, and Children's Division records.

Unpublished descriptions and finding-aids available at the repository.
Deposited in 1969, 1970, and 1975, by various donors.

216. *Hendricks, James R., 1817-* .

Papers, 1859-1902. ca. 2 ft.
In University of Oklahoma Library (Norman, Oklahoma).

Cherokee judge. Correspondence (family and general), journals, notebooks, speeches, accounts, wills, petitions, statements relating to charges against individuals, and other legal documents; printed matter including advertisements, broadsides, handbills, and a copy of the *Tahlequah Times* (1878); and other papers pertaining to family dates, and Indian customs and remedies. Includes special correspondence and other papers arranged under the subjects of "Blind" and "Insane Asylum". Elections data of the National Party, "Old Settler" affairs, and Tahlequah Lodge of the National Party; and letters from patients for whom Hendricks prescribed medicine and treatment by mail.

217. *Henry, Henrietta (Mitchell),   -1958.*

Papers, 1917-57. 2407 items.
In Mississippi Department of Archives and History (Jackson, Mississippi).

Daughter of T. J. Mitchell, superintendent of the Mississippi State Hospital for the Insane. Collection includes correspondence, recollections, genealogical data, photos, and clippings.

218. *Herrick, Charles Judson, 1868-1960.*

Papers.
In University of Kansas, Kenneth Spencer Research Library, Department of Special Collections (Lawrence, Kansas).

Scholar, teacher, and research scientist whose work focused upon the nervous system and the brain. He and his brother, Clarence L. Herrick, founded the American School of Psychobiology. Major correspondents include various neurologists.

219. *Herrick, Henry Nathan, 1832-1886.*

Papers, 1851-1956. ca. 500 items and 7 vols.
In Minnesota Historical Society Collections (St. Paul, Minnesota).

Baptist minister. Correspondence, diaries (1857-70), sermons, genealogical data, newspaper clippings and Civil War discharge papers. The bulk of the correspondence consists of letters (1864-65) written by Herrick as a chaplain with the Fifth Minnesota Regiment to his wife in Minneapolis. Although the letters place great emphasis on religion in army life, they also contain descriptions of travel on troop ships, war damage, civilian life, Negro troops, army food, and hospitals, battles, and marches. Includes a diary (1864-65) kept by Herrick's wife, Anna Strickler Herrick; a manuscript by their son Charles Judson Herrick, entitled *Chronology of the Herrick Family, 1629-1956;* and genealogical material on the Herrick, Small, Strickler, and Talbot families.

Unpublished descriptions in the library.

Gift of Mrs. Charles Judson Herrick, 1956-57.

220. *Hillcrest Children's Center, Washington, D.C.*
Records, 1815-1966. 25 ft. (ca. 9500 items).
In Library of Congress, Manuscript Divison (Washington, D.C.).

Correspondence, minutes of meetings, committee and staff reports, admittance and application records, journals, ledgers, financial statements, deeds, mortgages, bank checks, budget estimates, index cards; and miscellaneous material, chiefly 1880-1960, reflecting the financial and managerial techniques of the center, which until 1953 provided for the care and protection of homeless youths, and more recently for the treatment of emotionally disturbed children.

Gift of the center, 1968.

221. *Holland, Charlton Gilmore, 1911-* .
Papers, 1936-59. 1300 items.
In University of Virginia Library (Charlottesville, Virginia).

Psychiatrist and archeologist. Correspondence, diary (1944), and other papers. The correspondence is mostly with Holland's wife while he was with the Medical Corps in the Pacific (1942-45), and contains information on psychiatric cases and war medicine. Includes a Tagalog translation, by Eduardo Makabenta, of Poe's "The Raven." Correspondents include J. C. Crawford, Clifford Evans, Lawrence Payton Harris, Betty Jane Meggers, Henry Bearden Mulholland, Julian M. Robinson, the Smithsonian Institution, John Reed Swanton, Charles Frederick Voegelin, and David Cole Wilson. The material is related to the library's Archeological Society of Virginia collection.

Deposit, 1948-60.

222. *Hollingworth, Harry Levi, 1880-1956.*
Papers, 1905-56. 4 ft.
In University of Akron, Archives of the History of American Psychology (Akron, Ohio).

Psychologist and educator. Correspondence, unpublished autobiography, research material in industrial psychology (1912-17), manuscripts of writings, speeches, lectures, notes, awards, and academic records.

222. *(Continued)*
Index guide and unpublished register in the repository.
Open to investigators under restrictions accepted by the repository.
Information on literary rights available in the repository.
Gift of Mr. and Mrs. Benjamin H. Florence, 1966.

223. *Hollingworth, Leta (Stetter), 1886-1939.*
Papers, 1913-39. ca. 4 ft.
In University of Akron, Archives of the History of American Psychology (Akron, Ohio).
Psychologist and professor at Teachers College, Columbia University. Chiefly material relating to the class for gifted children in Speyer School (Public School 500, New York City). Includes records of students with high IQ's, school reports, transcripts of staff meetings and projections for the future of the class. Other papers include early publications, photos, and memorabilia dealing with Dr. Hollingworth's life and career.
Unpublished register in the repository.
Open to investigators under restrictions accepted by the repository.
Information on literary rights available in the repository.
Gift of Mr. and Mrs. Benjamin H. Florence, 1966.

224. *Hollingworth, Leta (Stetter), 1886-1939.*
Papers, 1914-39. ca. 600 items.
In Nebraska State Historical Society Collections (Lincoln, Nebraska).
Psychologist. Chiefly reprints of Dr. Hollingworth's articles, many of them relating to her study of the gifted child; together with biographical material and other papers.
Gift of Mamie Meredith (Lincoln, Nebraska), 1959.

225. *Holmes, Jack Alroy, 1911-1967.*
Papers, 1947-67. 27 cartons.
In University of California at Berkeley, Bancroft Library (Berkeley, California).
Professor of education at the University of California at Berkeley. Personal correspondence, lecture notes, course outlines, notes on visual perception, records of the Berkeley Growth Study, descriptions of reading techniques, particularly regarding remedial reading; notes on educational psychology, and recommendations for the School of Education. Correspondents include the National Reading Association and the *Journal of Experimental Education.*

226. *Holt, Helen Louise Froelich.*
Papers, 1938-59. 9 ft.
In West Virginia University Library (Morgantown, West Virginia).
Legislator, secretary of state, and assistant commissioner of public institutions, of West Virginia. Correspondence, speeches, news releases, lists of Republican officials, and clippings, concerning Mrs. Holt's career as a state official involved

with such subjects as acts of the legislature, aid for the blind and mentally ill, capital punishment, handicapped children, Interstate Highway 77, juvenile delinquency, Korean veterans' bonus bonds, the Meadow River flood control project, positions taken by Mrs. Holt on political issues, prisoner's aid movement, property assessment, reading improvement program in industry, business and occupation tax, salaries of state commission engineers, school appropriations, the Summerville dam project, vocational rehabilitation, workmen's compensation, Weston State Hospital, and West Virginia Training School at St. Mary's. Correspondents include J. G. Bradley, Eugene H. Brown, A. B. Chambers, William Langer, Irvin Stewart, Cecil Underwood, and Robert White.

Unpublished processing notes in the library.

Gift of Mrs. Holt (Washington, D.C.), 1965.

227. *Holt, Homer Adams, 1898-* .

Papers, 1936-41. 350 items.

In West Virginia Department of Archives and History collections (Charleston, West Virginia).

Lawyer, attorney general and governor of West Virginia. Correspondence, reports, and memoranda to heads of state government departments. Much of the correspondence relates to improvements of the state capitol building. Other subjects include coal miners' unions and West Virginia University stadium bonds. Includes reports (1939-41) of fines remitted, punishments commuted, reprieves, and pardons granted; and a compendium of the record of an investigation (1936) of Huntington State Hospital. Correspondents include John Bricker, A. B. Chandler, Howard C. Christy, D. Boone Dawson, Cass Gilbert, Cordell Hull, Philip LaFollette, Herbert H. Lehman, Leverett Saltonstall, and Harold Stassen.

Unpublished guide in the repository.

228. *Hooker, Isabella (Beecher), 1822-1907.*

Papers, 1839-1901. 978 items.

In Stowe-Day Memorial Library and Historical Foundation (Hartford, Connecticut).

Woman suffragist and reformer. Chiefly correspondence between Mrs. Hooker and her husband, John Hooker, a lawyer of Hartford; together with Mrs. Hooker's diary (1901) dealing with her husband's last days and her views on spiritualism. Includes letters to their daughters, Alice (Hooker) Day and Mary (Hooker) Burton; letters written by John Hooker while on travels through Connecticut as recorder for the state supreme court and while on tours to Europe; and letters by Mrs. Hooker from their home at Nook Farm and from the Gleason Water Cure (Elmira, New York) containing reference to her brother, Thomas K. Beecher, Mr. and Mrs. Jervis Langdon, Harriet Beecher Stowe, George H. Warner, and other members of the Warner family.

Card catalog in the library.

Information on literary rights available in the library.

Chiefly the gift of Miss Katherine S. Day, granddaughter of John and Isabella Hooker.

229. *Horner, Matina (Souretis), 1940-* .
Oral history, 1971. 1 tape.
In Radcliffe College, Schlesinger Library on the History of Women in America (Cambridge, Massachusetts).
Recording of an interview. Horner is professor of psychology and president of Radcliffe College (1972-).

230. *Horton, Lydiard Heneage Walter, 1879-1945.*
Papers, 1860-1945. 8 boxes.
In Columbia University Libraries (New York, New York).
In part, transcripts.
Psychologist. Correspondence, diary, typescripts of lectures, research studies, articles, professional case histories, and material gathered by the Cartesian Research Bureau. Includes correspondence and excerpts from the diary (1860) of Samuel Dana Horton. Other correspondents include John Fiske, C. W. Fremantle, Moreton Frewen, James A. Garfield, Frederick W. Holls, Henry James, William James, Robert Todd Lincoln, and William Howard Taft.
Bequest of Marion E. Robinson.

231. *Houstoun, Mary Williamson, 1815-1871.*
Papers, 1802-75. 143 items.
In Georgia Historical Society collections (Savannah, Georgia).
In part, transcripts (handwritten) made from originals by Charles Spaulding Wylly.
Chiefly legal papers concerning Houstoun's estate, kept by executor Dr. Richard Dennis Arnold, of Savannah, Georgia, including family and administrative correspondence, conveyances, surveys, tax lists, slave lists, personal accounts, wills, and records of property; together with family correspondence of Houstoun, her father, James Edmund Houstoun (1777-1829), his wife, Mary Ann (Williamson) Houstoun (who later married Maj. Jonathan Thomas), and their children, John Williamson Houstoun (1817-61), James Edmund Houstoun (1819-52), and Eliza V. (Houstoun) Spaulding (1810-36). Includes material on payment for the care of Mossman Houstoun (1786-ca. 1865) in Pennsylvania Hospital for the Insane; records of Marengo plantation, McIntosh County, Georgia; Woodstock plantation, Chatham County, Georgia, land in Murray County, Georgia, and real estate in Savannah; and 5 letters (1827-28) attributed to Mary Williamson Houstoun, concerning life in the home of Capt. Alexander Campbell Wylly (1759-1833), St. Simons Island, Georgia, and the marriage of his daughter Caroline to James Hamilton Couper.
Unpublished finding-aids in the repository.
Gifts of Caroline L. Meldrim, Savannah, Georgia, from the papers of her father, Judge Peter W. Meldrim, 1952; and Frank B. Screven, a Wylly descendant, 1956.

232. *Howard, James C.,   -1880.*
Papers, 1813-81. 8 boxes.
In State Historical Society of Wisconsin Collections (Madison, Wisconsin).

Early settler. Correspondence from numerous members of the Howard family in several sections of the United States. Includes letters from Howard's brother, Dean S. Howard, a building contractor who invented a new type of dredging machine and who worked on harbors and canals in Upper Canada and the Middle West; from Howard's wife, Sophronia Porter; from his children and their families in Wisconsin, Massachusetts, and California; and from other relatives. The letters touch on the various activities of the correspondents, their health, financial concerns, religious beliefs, and cultural interests; local politics, financial panics, the California gold rush, educational facilities, scientific farming, fruit-growing, wood conservation, spiritualism, and the final settlement of Howard's estate.

233. *Howison, George Holmes, 1834-1916.*
Papers. ca. 1862-1917. 6 boxes, 2 cartons and a portfolio.
In University of California at Berkeley, Bancroft Library (Berkeley, California).
Philosopher and professor of philosophy at the University of California at Berkeley. Correspondence, manuscripts, printed copies of articles and lectures, and notes relating to philosophy and mathematics. Many of the letters from Howison's students reveal the close-knit world of Harvard during the reign of Josiah Royce, William James, Hugo Münsterberg, and George Herbert Palmer; and show the emergence of psychology as a study distinct from philosophy. Major correspondents include George Plimpton Adams, James B. Angell, James R. Angell, Charles Montague Bakewell, James Mark Baldwin, James E. Beard, Nicholas Murray Butler, James Cabot, James McKeen Cattell, William Otis Crosby, John Dewey, Thomas Davidson, Frank Foster, Charles Goddard, William Torrey Harris, Ernest Norton Henderson, William James, Joseph Jastrow, Martin Kellogg, Charles Levermore, Arthur Lovejoy, George Herbert Mead, Sidney Mezes, William Montague, Ernest Moore, George Sylvester Morris, Hugo Münsterberg, George Herbert Palmer, Walter Pillsbury, Charles Rieber, Josiah Royce, Ferdinand Schiller, Thomas Shackleford, George Frederick Stout, George Malcolm Stratton, James Ward, Joseph Worcester, and Harry Manville Wright.
Report and key to arrangement in the library.

234. *Hume, David, 1711-1776.*
Papers, ca. 1738-1817. 4 reels of microfilm.
In American Philosophical Society Library (Philadelphia, Pennsylvania).
Microfilm made from originals owned by the Royal Society of Edinburgh.
Scottish philosopher and historian. Correspondence, manuscripts of poetry and other writings, memoranda, and other papers of Hume and others. Correspondents include Jean le Rond d'Alembert, Marquis de Barbentane, Hugh Blair, Marie Charlotte Hippolyte de Campet de Saujeon, Comtesse de Boufflers, Richard Davenport, George Keith, Earl Marischal, Andrew Millar, William Mure, Sir John Pringle, Adam Smith, and William Strahan.
Calendar published in *Proceedings of the Royal Society of Edinburgh*, vol. 52 (1932), pp. 1-138.
Gift of David Hume, the younger, Hume's nephew.

235. *Humphreys, Lloyd G. 1913-* .
Papers, 1936-69. 5 ft.
In University of Illinois Archives (Urbana, Illinois).
Professor and head of the Department of Psychology, University of Illinois. Correspondence with administrators, colleagues, students, Rand McNally and Company, and with his children, concerning budget, personnel, and staff affairs, preliminary examination questions for doctoral candidates, research projects, publication policies, professional meetings, disagreements between practitioners and scientific investigators in psychology, and personal affairs; committee reports; and a list (1936-64) of publications, reprints, and book reviews. Includes correspondence with committee members of the All-University Committee on Admissions, Board of Scientific Affairs, Clark Committee, Departmental Chairmen of Graduate Training Departments, and the Executive Committee of Liberal Arts and Sciences, of the University of Illinois; and with the Publication Board of the American Psychological Association.
Unpublished finding-aid in the repository.
Information on literary rights available in the repository.
Acquired 1970.

236. *Husserl, Edmund, 1859-1938.*
Archive.
In Raymond Fogelman Library, The New School (New York, New York).
The Husserl Archive at The New School, Established in the Memory of Alfred Schutz, contains transcripts of most of Husserl's stenographic manuscripts. It comprises the texts of the following sets of manuscripts: A, B, C, D, E, F, K, and M. See descriptions of these manuscripts in *Philosophy and Phenomenological Research*, vol. 8, no. 3 (March 1947), pp. 487-91.
Access restricted. Permission to consult this collection must be obtained in advance from the Department of Philosophy of The New School.

237. *Idaho (Territory).*
Records, 1863-90. 20 ft.
In Idaho State Historical Society, State Archives (Boise, Idaho).
Executive, legislative, judicial, and constitutional convention records; correspondence of the governor and the territorial secretary; territorial militia records; reports and records of the Idaho territorial law library, trustees of the capitol, and the Idaho Insane Asylum; county administrative records filed with the territorial secretary; reports and opinions of the territorial attorney general, controller, treasurer, and superintendent of public instruction; proclamations, office inventories, vouchers and accounts, the 1863 and 1864 territorial census and official canvass of the territorial elections.
Transferred to the Idaho State Archives, 1952 and 1954.

238. *Imboden, John Daniel, 1823-1895.*
Papers, 1831-95.
In University of Virginia Library (Charlottesville, Virginia).
Virginia lawyer. Contains one letter from an 1855 inmate at Western State Insane Asylum requesting in-town visiting privileges.

239. *Ingersoll, Robert G., 1833-1899.*

Papers, 1862-1956. 2 boxes.

In University of Wyoming, American Heritage Center (Laramie, Wyoming).

Agnostic and freethinker. Correspondence with his wife, Eva A. Parker Ingersoll, regarding spiritualist contacts she had made with her deceased husband.

240. *Institute of Living.*

Letters and manuscripts.

In The Institute of Living Archives (Hartford, Connecticut).

Historical material relating to the Connecticut Retreat for the Insane, the Hartford Retreat, and the Institute of Living, including annual reports, documents, handbooks, manuscript materials, and the like. Included is the correspondence of Eli Todd, the first superintendent, and fellow physicians and patients' families. Handwritten case reports and stewards' papers, from 1824 to the end of the century, are other archival material relating to the institute.

Much material confidential.

241. *International Society for Clinical and Experimental Hypnosis.*

Records, 1957-67. ca. 2 ft.

In University of Akron, Archives of the History of American Psychology (Akron, Ohio).

Correspondence relating to the founding, meetings, and membership of the society; journal records; and photos of early members. Persons represented include John G. Watkins. Major correspondents include Ernest R. Hilgard, C. Scott Moss, and John G. Watkins.

Unpublished finding-aids in the repository.

In part, access restricted.

Information on literary rights available in the repository.

Gift of H. C. Harding, B. B. Raginsky, and Mr. Watkins, 1967 and 1969.

242. *Iowa State Medical Library.*

Society papers, 1850-1944. 5 vols.

In Iowa State Medical Library (Des Moines, Iowa).

Notes of the secretaries of the Keokuk, Iowa Medical Society (1850-1910); minutes of the Iowa Society for Mental Hygiene (1917); minutes of the Military Surgeons Club of the Iowa State Medical Society (1932-44); and clippings and miscellaneous notes.

Indexed in the library catalog.

Also described in part in *Journal of the Iowa Medical Society*, vol. 11 (April 1921), pp. 127-39.

Gift of Frank M. Fuller, 1931; Julia Ford Hill, 1933; Frederick G. Murray, 1952.

243. *Ives, Margaret, 1903- .*

Papers, 1934-73. 8 ft.

In University of Akron, Archives of the History of American Psychology (Akron, Ohio).

243. *(Continued)*

Psychologist. Correspondence and minutes of meetings of the National Council of Women Psychologists, reflecting Ives's role in international affairs.

Jacksonville State Hospital (cf. Mental Health Care)

244. *James, Ada Lois, 1876-1952.*

Papers, 1816-1952. 39 vols. and 52 boxes.

In State Historical Society of Wisconsin Collections (Madison, Wisconsin).

Suffragist, social worker, and reformer. Correspondence (24 boxes, 1890-1952); diaries (1892-1920, 1930-47); scrapbooks, articles, and financial records; and case histories, minutes, and reports of the Richland County Children's Board (1926-51). Two boxes of family correspondence (1816-1904) contain material on Miss James's parents, David G. James and Laura Briggs James, reflecting her father's interest in employment for women, women suffrage, spiritualism, birth control, and socialism. Among the volumes are diaries (1865, 1882-1904), and proceedings (1885-1903) of the meetings of the Wisconsin Women's Suffrage Association kept by her mother. Ada James's correspondence is chiefly of the period from 1911 to 1918 when she was active in the suffrage movement as president of the Political Equity League (1911-13) and a member of the Wisconsin Women's Suffrage Association and the National Women's Party. Many letters written in 1911 and 1912 concern the suffrage bill introduced into the Wisconsin legislature by her father, a state senator, and the resultant state referendum. Letters written during World War I reflect her developing belief in pacifism and her interest in prohibition. Those of the early 1920s contain material on progressivism, including information on Miss James's service as vice-president of the Wisconsin Progressive Association in 1929, as vice-chairman of the Republican State Central Committee in 1922, and her rift with Robert M. La Follette, Sr., over his support of John J. Blaine in the 1924 campaign. After 1925 her correspondence deals principally with social work, particularly the founding of the Children's Board. Correspondents include Jane Addams, Olympia Brown, Carrie Chapman Catt, Jessie Sylvia Pankhurst, and Theodora Youmans.

Records of the Richland County Children's Board are not available for public use.

245. *James, William, 1842-1910.*

Papers.

In Harvard University, Houghton Library (Cambridge, Massachusetts).

General and family correspondence, many of the letters personally written by James. Major psychological correspondents include James R. Angell, James Mark Baldwin, H. P. Bowditch, W. B. Cannon, J.R.I. Delboeuf, John Dewey, Theodore Flournoy, George S. Fullerton, H. N. Gardiner, Edmund Gurney, G. Stanley Hall, Ernst Mach, H. R. Marshall, Hugo Münsterberg, Theodule Ribot, E. D. Starbuck, George F. Stout, Carl Stumpf, James Sully, E. L. Thorndike, and James Ward.

A general index is available.

246. *James, William, 1842-1910.*
Papers. 34 letters.
In Johns Hopkins University, Milton S. Eisenhower Library (Baltimore, Maryland).
Psychologist and philosopher. Major correspondents include Daniel C. Gilman and Arthur O. Lovejoy.

247. *James Family, William.*
Papers, 1825-1900. ca. 1200 items and 13 vols.
In Colby College Library, Special Collections (Waterville, Maine).
Includes letters of Elizabeth Tillman (James) Seelye (1833-81), daughter of William James who married Julius Seelye, president of Amherst College; and letters of Katherine Barber (James) Prince (1834-90), daughter of William James who married psychiatrist William Prince. Correspondence concerns charitable activities with missions and children's homes.
Unpublished guide available.

248. *Jarrett, Mary C., 1877-1961.*
Papers, 1913-49. 8 boxes.
In Smith College Library, Sophia Smith Collection (Northampton, Massachusetts).
Specialist in gerontology and psychiatric social work, and director of the Smith College School of Social Work. Correspondence includes letters to Lillian (Moller) Gilbreth, a specialist in industrial engineering.
Published guide available.

249. *Jastrow, Joseph, 1863-1944.*
Papers, 1875-1961. 995 items and 14 vols.
In Duke University Library (Durham, North Carolina).
Psychologist and professor at the University of Wisconsin. Correspondence, manuscripts of lectures, speeches, prose, and poetry; and copies of published articles, book reviews, and newspaper clippings. Subjects include the Jastrow family of Philadelphia and the Szold family of Baltimore, the University of Wisconsin at Madison, Judaism in Baltimore and Philadelphia, and the Zionist movement. Correspondents include Marcus Jastrow and Henrietta Szold.
Card index in the library.
Gift, 1959.

250. *Jastrow, Joseph, 1863-1944.*
Papers, 1915-42. 1 box.
In State Historical Society of Wisconsin Collections (Madison, Wisconsin).
Professor, psychologist and author. A small amount of correspondence concerning the Nazi mind; an article by Jastrow entitled "Hitler: Mask or Myth"; a series of radio lectures for laymen on psychology; and notes on the relationship of state and university.

251. *Jennings, Elizabeth, 1926-* .
Papers, 1954-66. 12 boxes.
In Washington University Library (St. Louis, Missouri).
   British poet. Correspondence (chiefly 1956-58), poems, essays, notes for a journal and an essay, a script for the British Broadcast Corporation book reviews; notebooks containing personal items, poetry, essays, reviews, and manuscripts for books; and other papers relating to Miss Jennings's acceptance of the Somerset Maugham Award, her poetry, her mental illness, and personal experiences in Rome. Correspondents include Richard Church, Robert Conquest, Helen Lehmann, William Somerset Maugham, William Stanley Merwin, Edwin Muir, Victoria Mary Sackville-West, Edith Sitwell, Constantine Trypanis, John Wain, and Cecely Veronica Wedgwood.
   Unpublished register available in the library.
   Purchase, 1967.

252. *Jerome, Charles Waldron, 1868-1927.*
Papers, (some undated) 1855-1966. ca. 2 ft.
In Minnesota Historical Society Collections (St. Paul, Minnesota).
   Businessman of South Dakota and Minnesota. In part, photocopies (positive) made in 1968 from 100 original letters loaned by Russell Lewis of St. Paul, Minnesota. Correspondence, reports, poems, articles; genealogical material on the Jerome, Sardeson, and Waldron families; printed matter and other papers of Jerome and his wife, Eva Sardeson Jerome (1875-1966), relating to organizations active in Minnesota politics, mental health programs, and combatting racial discrimination in employment and housing (1909-66). Includes writings by Jerome's father, Charles Theodore Jerome (1840-99), and letters and newsletters to Mrs. Jerome from Perry Oliver Hudson, a Methodist missionary in Japan.
   Unpublished inventory in the repository.
   Deposited by Mr. Jerome, 1924, and gift of Russell Lewis, 1968.

253. *Johnson, Adelaide.*
Papers, ca. 1878-1946. ½ cubic ft.
In Smithsonian Institution, National Museum of History and Technology, Division of Political History (Washington, D.C.).
   Pamphlets, photos, obituaries, clippings, newspapers, and periodicals of Johnson, a sculptor. The material documents her artistic work and her interest in suffrage, temperance, spiritualism, the peace movement, and vegetarianism.
   Open to scholars.

254. *Johnson, Beth McCullough, 1909-1973.*
Papers, 1957-69. 12 cubic ft.
In Florida State Archives (Tallahassee, Florida).
   Papers of Mrs. Johnson, a member of the Florida House of Representatives (1957-62) and first female member of the Florida Senate (1962-68). Includes speeches, material about her campaigns and elections, and information about her work in mental health, traffic safety, and higher education.
   Published guide available.

255. *Johnson, Eleanor Hope, 1871-1969.*
Papers. ca. 6 ft.
In Hartford Seminary Foundation, Case Memorial Library (Hartford, Connecticut).
Social worker and psychology teacher at Hartford Seminary Foundation. Correspondence, articles, pamphlets, and clippings, relating to race relations, 1942 and after. Includes World War I letters from Major John B. Johnson, and Red Cross letters written during World War II.
Unpublished partial index in the repository.

256. *Johnson, Thomas Cary, 1859-1936.*
Papers, 1899-1921. 1 ft.
In Historical Foundation of the Presbyterian and Reformed Churches Collections (Montreat, North Carolina).
Professor at Austin School of Theology (Texas) and Union Theological Seminary (Richmond, Virginia). Chiefly lectures and notes on the medieval church, the German Reformation, the nineteenth century church, Presbyterianism in the United States, church government, missions, and spiritism. Includes research notes for Johnson's books, *A History of the Southern Presbyterian Church* (1894), and *Virginia Presbyterianism and Religious Liberty in Colonial and Revolutionary Times* (1907); and extensive notes for class lectures on Henry C. Sheldon's *History of Christian Doctrine* (1881), and Philip Schaff's *History of the Christian Church.*
Unpublished finding-aid in the repository.
Gift of Miss Anne F. Johnson, 1941.

257. *Johnston, John Black, 1868-1939.*
Papers, 1892-1937. ca. 3 ft.
In University of Minnesota Library, University Archives (Minneapolis, Minnesota).
Professor of anatomy and neurology; and dean of the College of Science, Literature, and the Arts, University of Minnesota. Correspondence; manuscripts of *Education for Democracy* (1934); notes, articles with drawings, and speeches on anatomy of the nervous system and neurology. Chief correspondents include Charles Judson Herrick and Johnston's publishers and editors.
Unpublished description in the library.
Open to investigators under library restrictions.
Information on literary rights available in the library.

258. *Jones, Thomas Thweatt, 1906- .*
Papers, 1757-1976. 6437 items and 61 vols.
In Duke University Library (Durham, North Carolina).
Physician, of Durham, North Carolina. Correspondence (chiefly 1947-74), addresses, writings, memoranda, reports, printed material, clippings, and other papers, relating to Jones' activities with the Durham Council of Alcoholism and Medical Society of the State of North Carolina, and his interest in alcoholism, mental health, and agathanasia (death with dignity); and letters, addresses,

258. *(Continued)*
    writings, legal and financial papers, and other papers relating to family history
    and genealogy.
    Unpublished finding-aid in the repository.
    Gifts, 1974-75.

259. *Journal of Philosophy.*
    Correspondence, 1892-1943. 121 items.
    In Columbia University Libraries (New York, New York).
    Letters addressed to editors of the journal, Wendell T. Bush and Frederick J. E.
    Woodbridge; together with four typewritten manuscripts of John Dewey con-
    taining his holograph corrections. The letters, from numerous philosophers,
    include thirteen from John Dewey, thirty-three letters and thirteen post cards
    from William James, sixteen letters from Josiah Royce, and fifteen from George
    Santayana.
    Gift of the journal, 1965.

260. *Journal of the Experimental Analysis of Behavior.*
    Records, 1958-72. 34 ft.
    In University of Akron, Archives of the History of American Psychology (Akron,
    Ohio).
    Editorial correspondence, evaluations of manuscripts submitted for publica-
    tion, and other records, relating to the founding of the journal and its earliest
    issues.
    Unpublished finding-aids in the repository.
    Access restricted.
    Information on literary rights available in the repository.
    Gift of the Society for the Experimental Analysis of Behavior, 1968 and after.
    Additions to the collection are expected.

261. *Juvenile Protective Association of Chicago.*
    Records, 1904-55. 4 ft.
    In University of Illinois at Chicago Circle Library (Chicago, Illinois).
    Correspondence, annual reports, speeches, reports, financial records, statis-
    tics, published material, bylaws, lists, legislation, notes, criminal codes, photos,
    memoranda, affidavits, minutes, and surveys. Most of the material concerns
    investigations of violations of child labor laws in factories, small shops, industrial
    homework, street trades, and the stage, in Illinois; and commercialized prostitu-
    tion. Includes correspondence relating to the provision of uniform educational
    and protective standards for stage children; and reports on illegitimate births,
    juvenile delinquency, mentally defective children, employment of women and
    girls, immoral life in Kalamazoo, Michigan, news alley, child neglect, baby
    farms, and minors employed in taverns and bowling alleys.
    Unpublished guide and index cards in the library.
    Gift of the association.

262. *Kalamazoo County, Michigan.*
Records, 1833-1963. ca. 1571 items and 213 vols.
In Western Michigan University, Regional History Collections (Kalamazoo, Michigan).

County directories (1931-63); state and federal census; records pertaining to the county treasurer, highway commissioner, board of health, superintendent of the poor, the Asylum for Insane, Kalamazoo, Michigan (1863-79), the cemetery board for Kalamazoo Township (1861-62), physicians, and the appointment of sheriffs; school district minutes and class records; justice of the peace dockets; marriage records, including those kept by Amos D. Allen, justice of the peace (1866-81); registers of electors; election tickets; tax rolls and other tax records; chattel mortgages; land patents; soldiers' discharges (1862-65, 1899-1902); Civil War bounty bonds (1865); Spanish American War relief records; records of the Rural Real Property Identification Survey (WPA); and other records of Kalamazoo County, Michigan, and in particular of Alamo, Charleston, Comstock, Cooper, Kalamazoo, Pavilion, Richland, and Wakeshma Townships.

Described in *Guide to the Regional History Collections*, Western Michigan University, compiled by Phyllis B. Burnham (1964) p. 21 and *Supplement* (1966) pp. 19-20.

Acquired from various sources.

263. *Kalamazoo State Hospital.*
Records, 1855-1964. 2 ft. and 3 items.
In Western Michigan University, Regional History Collections (Kalamazoo, Michigan).

Annual statements (1925-60), regulations and bylaws (1867-1913), reports (1855-1914) of the board of trustees, real estate inventory and financial statement (1837), "History of State Hospital" (1964) by Seth O. Craft, and other papers relating to the hospital at Kalamazoo, Michigan; and other materials on mental hospitals in Michigan.

In part, gift of Mrs. Katherine Habel, 1964.

264. *Kallen, Horace Meyer, 1882-1974.*
Papers, 1924-50. 24 ft.
In Yivo Institute for Jewish Research Library (New York, New York).

Educator and writer. In part, transcripts. Correspondence, clippings, and papers on education and on many liberal and Jewish causes. Correspondents include Henri Bergson, Louis D. Brandeis, John Dewey, Theodore Dreiser, James T. Farrell, Kurt Lewin, Sinclair Lewis, Walter Lippman, H. L. Mencken, and George Santayana.

Information on literary rights available in the repository.

Gift of Dr. Kallen, 1954.

265. *Keller, David Henry, 1880-1963.*
Papers, 1894-1962. 5 ft.
In Syracuse University Library (Syracuse, New York).

Psychiatrist and author. Correspondence, consisting mainly of letters from

265. *(Continued)*

Keller to Col. H. C. Worden (Klamath Falls, Oregon), relating to Col. Worden's purchase of Keller's manuscripts; together with published works and manuscripts of Keller's short stories and novels of science fiction, fantasy, and horror.

Unpublished description in the library.

Information on literary rights available in the library.

Purchase, 1968.

266. *Kelley, Truman Lee, 1884-1961.*

Papers, 1930-54. 1 ft.

In Harvard University Archives (Cambridge, Massachusetts).

Professor of education at Harvard. Correspondence and other papers.

Open to investigators only upon prior application to the repository.

Information on literary rights available in the repository.

267. *Kellogg, John Harvey, 1852-1943.*

Papers, 1873-1942. 15 ft. and 78 vols.

In University of Michigan, Michigan Historical Collections (Ann Arbor, Michigan).

Superintendent and surgeon of Battle Creek Sanitarium. Correspondence; household accounts (1897-1900); lecture notes, transcripts of informal question and answer sessions; manuscripts of speeches, books and articles; notebooks containing brief comments on trips in the United States and abroad; and student notebooks of the University of Michigan, and Bellevue Hospital in New York.

Gift of Gertrude W. Goodwin, 1960-62.

268. *Kellogg Family.*

Diaries, 1805-1946. 159 vols.

In New York Historical Society Collections (New York, New York).

Journal (1805) of Tryphena Ely White (1784-1816), who later married Frederick Kellogg (1766-1832), describing life in a frontier community (later named Belle Isle) in Onondaga County, New York, together with a printed edition (1905); diaries (33 volumes, 1863-96) of her son, Charles White Kellogg (1815-96) of Brooklyn, New York, containing information on the fancy livestock business, a tour of the South on horseback, and his interest in spiritualism; diaries (1863-1902) of his daughter, Gertrude Kellogg (1843-1903), an actress of Brooklyn, relating to her career and professional connections; diaries (83 volumes, 1861-1946) of her sister, Fanny Kellogg (1848-1947), relating mostly to daily life in Brooklyn and her visits to Port Kent, New York; and journal (1870) of Julia Burwell (Snow) Kellogg (1842-92), wife of Peter Comstock Kellogg (son of Charles White Kellogg), concerning life in Brooklyn and relationships with other members of the Kellogg family.

Gift, 1973.

269. *Kempf, Edward John, 1885-1971.*

Papers, 1911-72. 8 ft.

In Yale University Library (New Haven, Connecticut).

Psychiatrist and psychologist. Correspondence, research material, drafts of articles and books, and other papers, relating to Kempf's work in psychiatry, psychology, and psychosomatic medicine, and his criticism of Freud. Correspondents include Albert Einstein, Anna Freud, Walter Lippmann, William C. Menninger, Adolph Meyer, and Gardner Murphy.

Unpublished register in the repository.

Information on literary rights available in the repository.

Gift of Mrs. Kempf, 1974.

270. *Kentucky Eastern State Hospital (Lexington).*
Records, 1828-1940. ca. 4000 sheets.
In University of Louisville, Medical School Library (Louisville, Kentucky).

Photocopies of originals in the hospital, and in the Filson Club (Louisville, Kentucky).

Correspondence, bonds, court hearings, trial writs; and query and answer sheets issued by the medical superintendent and accompanied by brief case histories of several patients of a mental hospital. Persons represented include William Arvin, George W. Barrow, F. M. Dickinson, J. Dudley, G. A. Hull, John W. Hunt, Andrew McCalla, and Vina Marks.

All items except those copied from the Filson Club have also been microfilmed (positive and negative, 5 reels each).

271. *Kilday, Paul Joseph, 1900-1968.*
Papers, 1942-61. ca. 200 ft.
In University of Texas Library, Texas Archives (Austin, Texas).

U.S. representative from Texas. In part, photocopies. Correspondence, writings, press releases, charts, memoranda, maps, photos, reports, pamphlets, broadsides, and clippings, concerning the activities of Kilday as a congressman, on the House Committee on Armed Services, and on the Joint Committee on Atomic Energy. Material also relates to issues of national concern; people and problems of Bexar County, Texas; Wherry Housing Sub-Committee; Atomic Energy Commission; Civil Aeronautics Administration; Federal Communications Commission; General Services Administration; National Labor Relations Board; Securities and Exchange Commission; Selective Service System; Smithsonian Institution; Interstate Commerce Commission; Civil Service Commission; fisheries, mental health, labor, civil rights, Hawaii statehood, federal advertising, aid to education, railroads, merchant marine, income taxes; reciprocal trade, agriculture, firearms, urban renewal, social security, pressure campaign petitions, National Investors Council; foreign commerce, civil defense, Texas State Commission for the Blind; Texas Employment Commission; and the San Antonio Public Housing Project. Persons represented include F. C. Bolles, Frances P. Bolton, Frank W. Boylin, Lyndon B. Johnson, John F. Kennedy, Joe Kilgore, Henry Cabot Lodge, Gus R. Mauermann, Sam Rayburn, Morris Shipley, James T. Wadsworth, and Ralph Yarborough.

272. *Kirk, Samuel Alexander, 1904- .*
Papers, 1933-67. ca. 1 ft.
In University of Illinois Archives (Urbana, Illinois).

272. *(Continued)*

Professor of education and director of the Institute for Research on Exceptional Children at the University of Illinois. Correspondence, manuscripts of articles and speeches, publications, and reports, relating to the organization, policies, financial support, and administration of the institute. Includes papers relating to the education of the mentally handicapped, the Illinois test of psycholinguistic abilities, research in special education, professional meetings, a presidential mission to study Russian techniques and developments in treating mental retardation (1962), a controversy (1949-65) concerning certification of teachers for the deaf, and a controversy (1946-55) over the results of Dr. Bernadine G. Schmidt's treatment of the mentally handicapped.

Unpublished finding-aid in the repository.

Information on literary rights available in the repository.

Acquired, 1967.

273. *Kite, Elizabeth Sarah, 1864-1954.*

Papers, 1889-1955. 23 items and 3 boxes.

In Rutgers University Library (New Brunswick, New Jersey).

Educator, historian, and archivist. Correspondence, writings, clippings, and photos, about Miss Kite and her work; and notes of the Kite family, including James Kite's Quaker stories and poems. Miss Kite's writings include a biography, *Silas Deane, a Neglected Connecticut Patriot,* articles on religious subjects and French aid to America during the Revolution, miscellaneous historical articles; and articles on the feebleminded, published in the *Training School Bulletin* or *The Surveyor,* and chiefly relating to her work at the Vineland Training School (New Jersey) and with the Pineys, occupants of the New Jersey pine barrens. Places represented include Trenton, New Jersey, and Washington, D.C.

Gift of St. Alban Kite.

274. *Klyce, Scudder, 1879-1933.*

Papers, 1911-33. ca. 7 ft. (4800 items).

In Library of Congress, Manuscript Division (Washington, D.C.).

Author and naval officer. Correspondence and drafts of published and unpublished articles, and a typescript of Klyce's book, *Universe.* Relates to his ideas on logic, philosophy, religion, mathematics, and psychology. Correspondents include Robert Daniel Carmichael, James McKeen Cattell, Clarence Day, John Dewey, Dorothy Canfield Fisher, Waldo Frank, David Starr Jordan, Theodore William Richards, William Emerson Ritter, Upton Sinclair, and Robert Andrews Taylor.

Unpublished register in the library.

Gift of Mrs. Klyce, 1933.

275. *Knopf, Sigard Adolphus, 1857-1940.*

Papers, 1895-1941. ca. 5 ft.

In National Library of Medicine (Bethesda, Maryland).

Physician. Correspondence, articles, drafts, press clippings, certificates, documents, and printed matter. The correspondence relates to tuberculosis, controlled diaphragmatic respiration, birth control, cremation and burial, and psychical research. Includes a bibliography of pamphlets and books written by Dr. Knopf. Correspondents include Jane Addams, Maurice A. Bigelow, Frank Billings, John S. Billings, Vincent J. Bowditch, Lawrason Brown, Andrew Carnegie, Alexis Carrel, Grover Cleveland, Calvin Coolidge, Harvey W. Cushing, Allan Roy Dafoe, Walter Damrosch, Frederic S. Dennis, Irving Fisher, Robert Fletcher, Simon Flexner, Harry Emerson Fosdick, Giovanni Galli, Warren G. Harding, Bruno Heymann, Frederick Ludwig Hoffman, John Haynes Holmes, Elbert Hubbard, Cordell Hull, Abraham Jacobi, Henry Barton Jacobs, Harold W. Jones, Herbert Maxon King, Arnold Klebs, Robert Koch, Mrs. Robert Koch, Henry O. March, Charles H. Mayo, William J. Mayo, Charles L. Minor, S. Weir Mitchell, James E. Murray, Sir William Osler, Sir Robert William Philip, Mazyck P. Ravenel, John D. Rockefeller, Theodore Roosevelt, Margaret Sanger, Henry E. Sigerist, George M. Sternberg, Nathan Straus, William Howard Taft, Franz Torek, Edward Livingston Trudeau, Raymond A. Vonderlehr, William H. Welch, C.E.A. Winslow, Leonard Wood, and J. L. Yates.

Unpublished register in the library.

Gift of Mrs. S. A. Knopf, 1942-50.

276. *Köhler, Wolfgang, 1887-1967.*

Papers, 1914-67. ca. 5000 items.

In American Philosophical Society Library (Philadelphia, Pennsylvania).

Psychologist. Correspondence, research notebooks, articles, speeches, lectures, notes, reports, reprints, films, slides, and other papers relating to Köhler's cofounding of Gestalt psychology. Includes material on research with apes; the Gifford, Hitchcock, and Langfeld lectures; and Ford Foundation and National Science Foundation grants.

Table of contents in the library.

Open to investigators under restrictions accepted by the library.

Information on literary rights available in the library.

Gift of Mrs. Köhler, 1967.

277. *Kohs, Samuel Calmin, 1890-   .*

Papers, 1916-60. 4 ft.

In American Jewish Historical Society Collections (Waltham, Massachusetts).

Psychologist and social worker. Correspondence, autobiographical sketch, lecture notes and bibliographies for courses at the New York Graduate School for Jewish Social Work and other academic institutions; psychological tests devised by Kohs, manuscripts and published versions of speeches and articles, memorabilia, and other papers, relating to Kohs's career and his involvement with Jewish communal institutions. Much of the material relates to the National Coordinating Committee for Aid to Refugees and Emigrants coming from Germany, and Kohs's work with Jewish immigrants. Correspondents include Harry Barron, Jacob Billikopf, and William Haber.

Gift of Mr. Kohs, 1969.

278. *Krippner, Stanley.*
Papers.
In Kent State University, Special Collections (Kent, Ohio).
Traces Krippner's paranormal experiences and his pioneering research at Maimonides Hospital's dream laboratory. Major correspondents include Charlotte Bühler, Virginia Glenn, Timothy Leary, Gardner Murphy, J. B. Rhine, and Alan Watts.

279. *Krumboltz, John Dwight, 1928-* .
Papers, 1957-78. 4 boxes and 16 vols.
In Stanford University Archives, Green Library (Stanford, California).
Psychologist and professor of education and psychology at Stanford University. Material on education research and research psychology, class notes, workshop notes, conferences, and professional oganizations accrued by Krumboltz from 1957 to 1978, is included. Topics include consulting (teacher education, behavior modification in children, vocational education), correspondence (competency materials for an M.A. program), case studies, miscellaneous correspondence (students' rights), human relations training, course material (educational psychology and research methods, measurement accountability, work effectiveness skills, career skills assessment), and behavioral systems training.

280. *Lamont, Corliss, 1902-* .
Papers, 1891-1975. 125 items.
In Columbia University Libraries (New York, New York).
Philosopher. Correspondence with George Santayana, letters by Santayana to others; poetry manuscripts of, interviews and notes on, and correspondence about Santayana.
Gift of Mr. Lamont, 1975.

281. *Lansburgh, Therese Weil, 1919-* .
Papers, 1968-75. ca. 2 ft.
In Smith College, Sophia Smith Collection (Northampton, Massachusetts).
Social worker. Correspondence, agenda, minutes, addresses, notes, newsletters, and reports, documenting Lansburgh's leadership in the Day Care and Child Development Council of America, the Maryland Committee for Day Care of Children, the Maryland Association for Mental Health, the Children's Lobby, and the Richmond Fellowship. Includes selected learning toys.
Gift.
Additions to the collection are expected.

282. *Lasker, Mary, 1900-* .
Oral history, 1965-72. 14 tapes and 1525 pages.
In Columbia University Library, Oral History Collection (New York, New York).
Interviews with Lasker recalling her work in the development of national institutes for cancer, heart disease, and blindness. Her medical research discusses an interest in psychoanalysis.

283. *Laura Spelman Rockefeller Memorial.*
Records, 1918-41. 58 ft.
In Rockefeller Archive Center (Pocantico Hills, North Tarrytown, New York).
Correspondence, minutes and dockets; financial, administrative, and individual appropriations papers; reports, information files, clippings, pamphlets, charts, maps, and other papers, chiefly before 1930. Includes material on child study, education, emergency relief, leisure, parent education, public health, race relations, religion, social studies, and social welfare. Organizations represented include American Home Economics Association, American Red Cross, Association for the Study of Negro Life and History, Boy Scouts of America, Child Study Association, National Conference on Outdoor Recreation, National Negro Business League, National Research Council, National Urban League, Neighborhood Teacher Association, Playground and Recreation Association of America, Social Science Research Council, Welfare Council, Young Men's Christian Association, and Young Women's Christian Association. Correspondents include Franz Boas, William Sloane Coffin, William E. Dodd, Lawrence Dunham, Richard T. Ely, Walter L. Fleming, Guy Stanton Ford, Arnold Gesell, Herbert Hoover, Waldo G. Leland, Albert R. Mann, Charles R. Mann, Charles E. Merriam, Wesley C. Mitchell, Robert R. Moton, Howard Odum, Anson Phelps Stokes, F. W. Taussig, Carter G. Woodson, and Monroe N. Work.
Unpublished inventory and partial index in the repository.

284. *Lazarus, Moritz, 1824-1903.*
Papers, 1854-1902. ca. 300 items.
In Leo Baeck Institute Collections (New York, New York).
German professor of psychology and philosopher. In part, transcripts made from original letters in the Lazarus Archives, National and University Library, Jerusalem. Correspondence, manuscript of *Carnaval—Eine Psychologische Studie* (1882); album entitled *Sprueche des Lazarus,* containing a collection of thoughts selected from Lazarus's writings and illustrated with drawings by his wife, Nahida Ruth Remy-Lazarus, on his seventieth birthday (1894); an early manuscript version of Mrs. Lazarus's book *Ich Suchte Dich* (1898); a family tree, photos, and a list of holdings in the Jerusalem Lazarus Archives. Correspondents include Berthold Auerbach, Georg Brandes, Salomon Buber, Ignaz Goldziher, Paul Heyse, David Kaufmann, Paul Lindau, Moses Montefiore, and Heymann Steinthal. In German.
Information on literary rights available in the repository.
Acquired chiefly from the estates of Rabbis Arnold Taenzer and Leo Baerwald.

Lewis Audiovisual Research and Teaching Archive
(cf. Audio Cassette Collection).

285. *Liddell, Howard Scott, 1895-1962.*
Papers, 1937-62. ca. 265 items and 1 vol.
In Cornell University Library, Department of Manuscripts and University Archives (Ithaca, New York).

285. *(Continued)*

Director of Behavior Farm Laboratory and professor of psychology and psychobiology at Cornell University. Correspondence with colleagues concerning psychological experiments, particularly Pavlovian responses; other topics of professional interest, administration of the psychology department at Cornell; and other material.

Access restricted.

286. *Livermore, Mary Ashton (Rice), 1820-1905.*

Papers, 1863-1903. 45 items.

In Boston Public Library (Boston, Massachusetts).

Temperance and suffrage leader. Correspondence includes letters to Lilian Whiting containing discussions of Livermore's interest in spiritualism.

287. *Loeb, Jacques, 1859-1924.*

Papers, 1889-1924. ca. 11,000 items.

In Library of Congress, Manuscript Division (Washington, D.C.).

Physiologist and educator. General professional correspondence (ca. 8000 items), family correspondence (ca. 1500 items), biographical data, speeches, awards, photos, and other material. Loeb's scientific writings include drafts of his books *Forced Movements, Tropisms, and Animal Conduct* (1918), *Proteins and the Theory of Colloidal Behavior* (1922), and *Regeneration From a Physicochemical Viewpoint* (1924); laboratory notebooks relating principally to his research on bryophytes, gelatin, and frogs, which led to his development of the tropism theory; and scientific articles (in English and German) on such topics as colloid chemistry, genetics, osmosis, and proteins. Correspondents include Svante Arrhenius, Bernard Berenson, James B. Conant, Paul De Kruif, Paul Ehrlich, Albert Einstein, Sigmund Freud, Julian Huxley, Ivan Pavlov, and Harlow Shapley.

Finding-aid in the library.

Information on literary rights available in the library.

Gift of Dr. Loeb's children, Leonard B. and Robert F. Loeb and Mrs. Anne L. Osborne, 1960-63.

288. *Loeb, Jacques, 1859-1924.*

Papers, 1906-24. ca. 2 ft.

In Rockefeller University Archives, Rockefeller Archive Center (Pocantico Hills, North Tarrytown, New York).

Physiologist and educator at Rockefeller Institute for Medical Research (New York, New York). In part, transcript (typewritten) of a letter from Albert Einstein to Leonard Loeb. Administrative and other correspondence, bibliography, collected reprints (7 vols.), and photos. Includes letters to Simon Flexner about coming to the institute; a letter from Albert Einstein to Leonard Loeb asking for support to pay an assistant mathematician; and condolence letters from Einstein, Curt Herbst, Hans Meyer, Otto Myerhoff, and Ivan Pavlov.

Unpublished inventory in the repository.

Information on literary rights available in the repository.

Gift of the Rockefeller University administration.

289. *Logan-Fisher-Fox Collection.*
Papers, 1700-1930. ca. 6000 items.
In Historical Society of Pennsylvania Collections (Philadelphia, Pennsylvania).

Papers of three prominent Philadelphia Quaker families, relating chiefly to family and commercial affairs, the medical profession, attitudes toward Indians, the American Revolution, and the role of women in the Quaker family. Includes 1700 pieces of correspondence (1810-40) of William Logan Fisher (1781-1862) of New England, relating to family affairs, economics, politics, slavery, abolition, and Fisher's interest in spiritualism and his expulsion from the Quaker community of New Bedford, Massachusetts; diary (1849-61) of Mary Fisher Fox; and papers of Elizabeth R. Fisher and Sarah Lindley Fisher (William Logan Fisher's second wife), all depicting the life of a nineteenth century Quaker wife and mother; correspondence (1777-1810) of Thomas Fisher (1741-1810), relating to his imprisonment in 1777 for treason to Winchester, Virginia; his activities as a brewer and merchant in Philadelphia, and his philanthropic interests; correspondence (1763-76) of William Logan (1718-76) reflecting British and American Quaker views on the conflict between Britain and the colonies and its effects on trading and social relationships; papers of his son, William Logan (1747-72), relating to his activities as a medical student and apothecary apprentice; Ann Mifflin's account (1802) of missionary work among the Indians; papers of James Logan (1674-1754), secretary to William Penn, relating to Logan's business concerns and dispute with the Pennsylvania Assembly, and his essay (1703) on Flanders; and letters of Samuel Fox (1800-49) and George Fox (1806-82) to their brother Joseph M. Fox, describing the medical profession in Philadelphia and the family countinghouse in New York.

Unpublished finding-aid in the repository.
Information on literary rights available in the repository.

290. *Lord, Herbert Gardiner, 1849-1930.*
Correspondence, 1892-1905. 50 items.
In Columbia University Libraries (New York, New York).

Professor of philosophy. Letters to Lord from George Washington Cable, John Dewey, Josiah Royce, Carl Schurz, and others.
Gift of Mrs. R. J. Goerke, Jr., 1970.

291. *Louttit, Chauncey McKinley, 1901-1956.*
Papers, 1917-56. ca. 25,000 items.
In Yale University Library (New Haven, Connecticut).

Psychologist, educator, and author. Includes correspondence concerning Louttit's teaching and administrative duties, his tour in the Navy during World War II, the controversy with president Asa Smallidge Knowles while Louttit was dean of faculty at Sampson College, his deanship at the Galesburg Undergraduate Division of the University of Illinois, and his chairmanship of the Department of Psychology at Wayne University.

Unpublished register in the library.
Information on literary rights available in the library.
Gift of Richard T. Louttit, 1960.

292. *Lovejoy, Arthur Oncken, 1873-1962.*
Papers, 1910-63. ca. 5000 items.
In Johns Hopkins University Library (Baltimore, Maryland).
Professor of philosophy at Johns Hopkins University. Family and academic correspondence, lecture notes, criticism, and other papers.
Information on literary rights available in the library.
Gift.

293. *Lunatic Asylum West of the Alleghany Mountains.*
Records, 1860-67.
In West Virginia University Library (Morgantown, West Virginia).
Lists employees of the institution, occupations, wages, number of patients treated, expenses of the institution, list of those under treatment during these years (no names), date of admission, sex, form of insanity, cause, age at first "attack," recommendations of the director, table of comparison with other asylums, and a copy of the Act of Legislature changing the name of the Lunatic Asylum at Weston.

294. *McCulloch, Warren Sturgis, 1898-   .*
Papers, ca. 1935-68. 31 ft.
In American Philosophical Society Library (Philadelphia, Pennsylvania).
Neurologist and psychologist. Correspondence, notes, lectures, and studies, relating to computers, neurology, space biology, biological psychiatry, and chemical warfare. Includes biological computer studies and studies conducted for the U.S. Army. Correspondents include Andre John Angyan, Herman J. C. Berenden, Warren M. Brodey, Thomas Edward Burke, Frank Fremont-Smith, John F. Fulton, Hugh W. Garol, Francis P. Gerty, John R. Green, William McConnachie Harrowes, Charles E. Henry, Harold E. Himwich, Hudson Hoagland, Arthur S. Iberall, Kenneth W. Jarwin, Herbert H. Jasper, Stuart A. Kauffman, William L. Kilmer, Yale David Koskoff, Don de Koven, John Kremer, Jerome Y. Lettvin, William K. Livingston, Donald M. McKay, Turner McLardy, Filmer S. C. Northrop, A. Gordon Pask, Jean Piaget, Juan de Dios Pozo-Olano, Antoine Remond, Arnold B. Scheibel, Stephen L. Sherwood, Lloyd E. Slater, John M. Stroud, Theodore Tausig, Charles C. Thomas, Alettus Albertinus Verveen, Arthur A. Ward, Jerome J. Wolken, Carter Zeleznik, and American Society for Cybernetics.
Unpublished finding-aid in the repository.
Information on literary rights available in the repository.
Gift of Mrs. Rook Metzger McCulloch, 1970.

295. *McDonald, John Cooper, 1936-   .*
Papers, 1963-72. ca. 19 ft.
In Ohio Historical Society Collections (Columbus, Ohio).
Lawyer and state legislator, of Heath and Columbus, Ohio. Correspondence, speeches, memoranda, reports from state agencies, legislative case files; and administrative files on budget, finances, legislation, state commissions, and taxes.

Includes material on education, housing, mental health, prison reform, and welfare.

Information on literary rights available in the repository.

Gift of Mr. McDonald, 1973-74.

296. *McDougall, William, 1871-1938.*

Papers, 1915-71. 1 box.

In Duke University Archives (Durham, North Carolina).

Professor of psychology at Duke University (1927-38). Correspondence, newspaper clippings, photos, writings, and other papers (mainly in the period 1920-44) relating to McDougall's work in psychology and appreciations of his career, to the McDougall family, and to friends of the McDougall family. Includes a few items of McDougall's professional correspondence with colleagues; but the bulk of the collection consists of letters to McDougall during his illness in 1938, obituaries of McDougall from newspapers in the United States and Europe; letters to McDougall's wife, Anne Hickmore McDougall (1879-1964), on the occasion of his death; and correspondence of other members of the McDougall family.

Gift of Mrs. Lesley McDougall Brown, 1978.

Gift of Professor Harold McCurdy, 1980.

297. *MacKay-Scott, Ruth (Jarvis).*

Papers, 1928-41. 2 vols., 2 boxes, and 1 folder.

In Radcliffe College, Schlesinger Library on the History of Women in America (Cambridge, Massachusetts).

Civic leader of Evanston, Illinois. Personal and official correspondence, newspaper clippings, and printed material, chiefly relating to MacKay-Scott's duties as an officer of the Woman's Club of Evanston. Includes material relating to the American Social Hygiene Association, Chicago Venereal Disease Prevention Program, Evanston Council of Social Agencies, League of Women Voters of Evanston, birth control clinics, and mental hygiene. Family members represented include her husband, Andrew MacKay-Scott; her son, Andrew MacKay-Scott, Jr.; her daughter, Jean Margaret (MacKay-Scott) Sample; and her mother; Emily Little Jarvis.

Unpublished finding-aid in the repository.

Deposited by Mrs. MacKay-Scott's daughter-in-law, Dr. Anne Firor MacKay-Scott, 1966.

298. *Malone, John,   -1906.*

Malone Theatre Collection, 1872-1910, 1928. 3 boxes.

In New York Public Library (New York, New York).

Actor and Shakespearean student. Letters of theatrical people, mostly American, collected by Malone, together with some of Malone's personal correspondence and that of his family; Marcus Moriarty's autobiography of his theatrical career, his correspondence, and a few contracts; a few letters on nontheatrical material on spiritualism and temperance; correspondence (1928) of the Union Square Book Shop; and a genealogy of the Shelley family.

Acquired, 1943.

299. Mannheim, Eunice (Lundbeck), 1907-1960.

Papers, 1926-61. 3 boxes and 1 folder.

In Radcliffe College, Schlesinger Library on the History of Women in America (Cambridge, Massachusetts).

Civic leader, of Amherst, Massachusetts. Correspondence (1954-60) and minutes (1958-60) of the Amherst Board of Selectmen to which Mannheim was the first woman elected; correspondence and other papers relating to her Republican political campaigns for state offices; correspondence and printed material pertaining to Amherst Council of Social Agencies, League of Women Voters of Amherst, Massachusetts Area Mental Health Centers, and other organizations in which she was active; and general correspondence, speeches, notes, appointment calendars, school yearbook, newspaper clippings, and photos. Persons represented include Leverett Saltonstall.

Unpublished finding-aid in the repository.

Gift of Mrs. Mannheim's husband, L. Robert Mannheim, 1975.

300. Marsh, James, 1794-1842.

Papers, 1821-74. 80 items.

In University of Vermont Archives (Burlington, Vermont).

Philosopher and educator. In part, transcripts and photocopies (positive). Correspondence (mostly 1821-42); an undated manuscript, "A Sermon on Conscience," by Marsh; questions on fine arts, metaphysics, and psychology, probably used for class examinations; and notes of lectures kept by some of Marsh's students. The correspondence concerns Samuel Taylor Coleridge, religion, American education, and other topics; and includes letters from Marsh to Coleridge; letters (1845) from Samuel Cox censuring Marsh and the philosophy of Coleridge; and a letter (1874) from A. G. Pease covering one of the Cox letters. Other correspondents include William Chamberlain, Rufus Choate, Richard H. Dana, Edward Everett, Josiah Quincy, George Ripley (1802-80), Jared Sparks, George Ticknor, and Noah Webster.

Incomplete card index in the library.

301. Mead, George Herbert, 1863-1931.

Papers, 1920-30. ca. 6000 items.

In University of Chicago Library (Chicago, Illinois).

Philosopher and professor at the University of Chicago. Classroom notes taken by students of Mead, which formed the basis of the three volumes published after his death, entitled *Mind, Self, and Society* (1934), *Movements of Thought in the Nineteenth Century* (1936); and *The Philosophy of the Act* (1938).

Gift, 1949.

302. Meduna, Ladislas Joseph, 1896-1965.

Papers, 1942-59. ca. 3 ft.

In University of Illinois Archives (Urbana, Illinois).

Professor of psychiatry at the University of Illinois. Correspondence, notes, notebooks, electroencephalograph tracings, copies of articles; manuscripts and illustrations for the first and second editions of Meduna's book *Carbon Dioxide*

Therapy; manuscripts of *Oneirophrenia* (1950), reviews, photos, and other papers relating to carbon dioxide inhalation therapy, metrazol convulsive therapy, research, the presence of an anti-insulinic factor in the blood of schizophrenics, and the nature of psychoses and psychoneuroses.

Unpublished finding-aid in the repository.

Received 1965.

Menninger Foundation (cf. Clippings)

303. Mental Health Care.

Oral histories. 10 items.

In Sangamon State University, Brookens Library, Oral History Office (Springfield, Illinois).

Transcripts of tape-recorded interviews, conducted by Roger Streitmatter, with administrators and staff of Jacksonville State Hospital (Illinois), relating to the hospital's retardation unit, changes in the use of patient labor and dietary services, patient treatment and care, and various therapies and recreation from the 1900s to the present. Persons interviewed include Russell Barnes, Harold Bushnell, Dale Charles, Mamie Cole, Eleanor DeLong, Oscar Gronseth, Flo Lasley, Albert McCarthy, Allen Rupel, and Roy Wright.

Unpublished finding-aids in the repository.

Information on literary rights available in the repository.

Permanent deposit 1971-76.

Original tape recordings have been retained.

Illinois State Historical Library, Springfield, also has copies of the tapes and of seven transcripts.

Microfiche copies of the transcripts have been made by the Microfilm Corporation of America.

304. Metcalf, George R., 1914-   .

Papers, 1950-65. ca. 25 ft.

In Syracuse University Library (Syracuse, New York).

New York state senator. Correspondence, speeches, printed material, legislation, reports, and other papers, relating to New York state legislative hearings, discrimination, housing, education, Blue Cross, health insurance, hospital problems, and mental health.

Unpublished list in the library.

Information on literary rights available in the library.

Gift of Mr. Metcalf, 1966.

305. Meyer, Adolf, 1866-1950.

Papers, ca. 1885-1948. ca. 300 ft.

In Johns Hopkins University, Alan Mason Chesney Medical Archives (Baltimore, Maryland).

Professor of psychiatry at Johns Hopkins University, and leading figure in psychology and mental health. Correspondence, diaries, notebooks, manuscripts

305. *(Continued)*

of writings; lecture notes, documents, and pictures; largely relating to psychiatry but also covering Meyer's personal life.

There is both an inventory and name index for this vast collection of over 7100 correspondents.

Access permitted to accredited scholars.

Gift of the estate of Dr. Meyer, 1963.

306. *Michigan State Agencies.*

Records of state agencies, 1805-1957. 1 ft. (4 items), 17 vols., and 1 reel of microfilm.

In University of Michigan, Michigan Historical Collections (Ann Arbor, Michigan).

Michigan territorial records consisting of an extract of proceedings of the governor and judges of the territory about land for the Detroit jail and courthouse (1812), and a list of import taxes (1805); minutes, reports, extracts, and financial records (1911-13) of the Public Domain Commission; minutes (1883-1932) of the State Board of Dentistry, and a register of licensed dentists (1907-57); daily weather records (1880-93) for the Ann Arbor area, kept for the State Board of Health; records (1934-38) of the State Emergency Welfare Relief Commission, composed of directives of the state relief administrator, William Haber, and containing information on the operation of all New Deal agencies in Michigan; Newaygo and Northport Road survey (1859) made by the State Land Office; records (1903-07) of the State Prison of Southern Michigan at Jackson; reports (1900) of the comprehensive Michigan Railroad Appraisal, directed by Mortimer E. Cooley for the State Tax Commission, together with appraisals of plank roads and canals built in Michigan; and an account book (1878-81) of the Eastern Michigan Asylum (later Ypsilanti State Hospital).

There is a composite collection consisting of groups of papers or single items listed and described in *Guide to Manuscripts in the Michigan Historical Collections of the University of Michigan,* by R. M. Warner and I. C. Brown (1963), entry nos. 2727, 2752, 2755-57, 2759, 2761, 2762, and 2765.

Acquired from various sources.

307. *Michigan, University of. Michigan Historical Collections.*

Records of organizations, 1832-1955. ca. 245 items and 42 vols.

In University of Michigan, Michigan Historical Collections (Ann Arbor, Michigan).

Minutes, financial records, correspondence, membership lists, constitutions, historical and biographical material, addresses, poetry, program notes, and other records of social clubs, literary and dramatic societies, charitable organizations, political parties and organizations, consumers' cooperatives, labor organizations, historical societies, medical associations, and other professional groups. Also includes societies interested in such matters as temperance, child study, protection, and civic improvement. Places represented include Albion, Ann Arbor, Brooklyn, Flushing, Grand Rapids, Greenville, Hillsdale, Kalamazoo, Lansing, Milford, Monroe, Redford, and Ypsilanti; and the counties Eaton, Jackson, Oakland, St. Joseph, and Washtenaw.

There is a composite collection consisting of groups of papers or single items listed and described in *Guide to Manuscripts in the Michigan Historical Collections of the University of Michigan,* by R. M. Warner and I. C. Brown (1963), pp. 212-24.

Acquired from various sources, 1938-63.

308. *Michigan State Home and Training School, Coldwater Parents' Council.*

Records, 1949-62. 300 items.

In University of Michigan, Michigan Historical Collections (Ann Arbor, Michigan).

Correspondence, constitution, history, reports, and minutes, relating to an institution created for the treatment of mentally deficient children.

Gift of the council.

309. *Michigan State Home and Training School, Lapeer.*

Records, 1893-1904. 300 items.

In University of Michigan, Michigan Historical Collections (Ann Arbor, Michigan).

Correspondence relating to the location and construction of the Lapeer State Home and Training School (formerly the Michigan Home for the Feeble-Minded and Epileptic); and correspondence of Dr. William A. Polglase, first superintendent of the school, relating to the erection of the building, supplies, staff, purchasing, and admissions. Correspondents include John Havener, Julian Hess, Cyrus G. Luce, John T. Rich, James Schermerhorn, John C. Sharp, and Loren A. Sherman.

Gift of Beryl Bishop, 1959.

310. *Mill, John Stuart, 1806-1873.*

Papers, 1812-88. ca. 500 items.

In Yale University Library (New Haven, Connecticut).

Philosopher. Correspondence, fragmentary notes, printed material, and other papers, relating to Mill, Harriet (Hardy) Taylor Mill, Helen Taylor, British politics, and logic. Includes 232 letters by Mill.

Unpublished register in the library.

Information on literary rights available in the library.

Purchase, 1930.

311. *Miller, Arnold W.*

Papers, 1847-1928. 10 vols. and 8 folders.

In Michigan State University, Historical Collections and Archives (East Lansing, Michigan).

Farmer. Correspondence, chiefly from friends and relatives in Kansas and Vermont, including information on agricultural business conditions and spiritualism; four Civil War diaries (1862-65) written by Miller while serving with the third Michigan Cavalry; legal documents, account books, and receipts.

Gift of Mrs. L. J. Marshall.

312. *Mills, Charles Karsner, 1845-1931.*
Papers, 1864-1931. ca. 4000 items.
In Historical Society of Pennsylvania Collections (Philadelphia, Pennsylvania).
Neurologist. Scrapbooks containing Mills's correspondence, lectures, pamphlets, programs, and invitations to professional and social affairs. Includes information on the progress of medical science, treatment of insanity and other diseases, institutional work, and men in the medical profession.
Presented by Mrs. Andrew Weisenburg.

313. *Minnesota Society of Neurology and Psychiatry.*
Records, 1909-41. 1 vol.
In Minnesota Historical Society Collections (St. Paul, Minnesota).
Minutes, constitution, bylaws, accounts, and obituaries of deceased members of the Minnesota Society of Neurology and Psychiatry (1932-41) and of its predecessor organization, the Minnesota Neurological Society (1909-32).
Descriptive inventory in the repository.
Gift of the society, 1961.

314. *Mohn, Fredrik Voss, 1856-1942.*
Papers, 1838-1942. 83 items.
In St. Olaf College, Norwegian-American Historical Association Archives (Northfield, Minnesota).
Physician and professor of mental and nervous diseases at California Eclectic Medical College, Los Angeles. Correspondence, articles on medical, political, and religous topics, including socialized medicine; legal papers (1838-71) in Norwegian, and clippings.
Information on literary rights available in the repository.
Gift of Dr. Mohn.

315. *Monroe, Walter Scott, 1882-1961.*
Papers, 1912-56. ca. 1 ft.
In University of Illinois Archives (Urbana, Illinois).
Professor of education, director of educational research, and acting dean of the College of Education, University of Illinois. Correspondence, class notes and records, working papers, reprints and other papers, relating to arithmetic and reading tests, development and validity of standardized tests, educational research, tests and measurements, learning theory, teacher training, literature, the *Encyclopedia of Educational Research,* and classroom lectures.
Received 1966.

316. *Moore, Merrill, 1903-1957.*
Papers, 1903-58. 211 ft.
In Library of Congress, Manuscript Division (Washington, D.C.).
Psychiatrist and poet. Diaries, notebooks, biographical material, genealogical records, correspondence, literary papers, scrapbooks, and other manuscript and printed material. Collection reflects not only Moore's interest in the treatment of alcoholism, drug addiction, and various psychological disorders, but his literary

pursuits as well. A few of the papers relate to his hobby, shell collecting. Prominent names in a large file of correspondence and other major correspondents include Alexandra Adler, Conrad Aiken, George E. Armstrong, Olga Barsis, Donald G. Davidson, Babette Deutsch, Dudley Fitts, Rockwell Kent, Charlotte Lowell, Winifred Overholzer, John Crowe Ransom, Allen Tate, Louis and Jean Untermeyer, Albert C. Wedemeyer, and William Carlos Williams. The collection also includes the correspondence of Moore's wife, Ann Leslie (Nichol) Moore.

Published guide to the collection available from the repository.
Partially closed.
Information on literary rights available in the repository.
Gift of Mrs. Moore, 1958.

317. *Moore, Merrill, 1903-1957.*
Papers, 1929-58. ca. 1 ft. (570 items).
In Vanderbilt University Library (Nashville, Tennessee).

Correspondence, chiefly with Hill Turner, Vanderbilt alumni secretary; 173 sonnets, including 63 entitled "Homage to New Zealand"; manuscripts of articles on alcoholism, neurotic soldiers, shell collecting, and on Moore; reprints and clippings of scientific articles by Moore; newspaper and magazine clippings about Moore; photos, and recordings. Includes material on the Fugitives, a group of poets at Vanderbilt University, and on the U.S. Army Medical Corps during World War II.

Unpublished register in the library.

318. *Morgan, Laura (Puffer), 1874-1962.*
Morgan-Howes family papers, 1892-1962. 7 file boxes.
In Radcliffe College, Schlesinger Library on the History of Women in America (Cambridge, Massachusetts).

Primarily correspondence, reports, press releases, articles, and minutes of meetings, documenting Mrs. Morgan's career as a lecturer, writer, teacher, world traveler, suffragist, press correspondent, and worker for disarmament and world organization. Includes the smaller collection of Mrs. Morgan's sister, Ethel (Puffer) Howes (1872-1950), psychologist and first director of the Institute for the Coordination of Women's Interests at Smith College. Persons represented include Carrie Chapman Catt, Dame Kathleen Courtney, Mary Agnes Dingman, Arthur Henderson, Herbert Hoover, Julia Ward Howe, Raymond Beveridge Morgan, Annie Russell, Ellery Sedgwick, M. Carey Thomas, Woodrow Wilson, and Mary E. Woolley.

Inventory in the library.

319. *Morris, George Sylvester, 1840-1889.*
Papers, 1852-1935. 1 ft.
In University of Michigan, Michigan Historical Collections (Ann Arbor, Michigan).

Professor of philosophy at Johns Hopkins University and the University of Michigan. Correspondence; a diary kept by Morris during his student days, and

319. *(Continued)*
three diaries of European trips; memorials after Morris's death; papers relating to his son, Roger S. Morris; notebooks of class lectures and other notes; and one volume of notes on Professor F. A. Trendelenburg's lectures on psychology in Berlin, 1867-68. Correspondents include Charles K. Adams, James B. Angell, John Dewey, Daniel C. Gilman, Moses C. Tyler, Frederick Ueberweg, and Robert M. Wenley.
Gift of the estate of Mrs. G. S. Morris, 1936.

320. *Morrison, Henry Clinton, 1871-1945.*
Papers, 1925-37. ca. 400 items.
In University of Chicago Library (Chicago, Illinois).
Professor of education and superintendent of the laboratory schools at the University of Chicago. Correspondence with Charles Hubbard Judd regarding Morrison's work, manuscripts of writings, and biographical material.
Unpublished guide in the library.
Deposited by the Department of Education, University of Chicago, 1966.

321. *Münsterberg, Hugo, 1863-1916.*
Papers. 300 letters, 700 items.
In Boston Public Library, Rare Book Department (Boston, Massachusetts),
Psychologist. Letters to Münsterberg from over 1000 persons and some correspondence from Münsterberg. Seventy items classified under such categories as: applied psychology, addresses, articles, reports, souvenirs, the Amerika-Institut, and the Saint Louis Congress. The letters date from 1890 to 1916. Major correspondents include James R. Angell, R. P. Angier, James Mark Baldwin, Henri Bergson, W. V. Bingham, Franz Boas, H. E. Burtt, Nicholas Murray Butler, M. W. Calkins, Andrew Carnegie, James McKeen Cattell, Edmund B. Delabarre, Knight Dunlap, C. W. Eliot, R. M. Elliott, R. W. Emerson, Benno Erdmann, Kuno Francke, G. Stanley Hall, E. B. Holt, William James, Pierre Janet, Joseph Jastrow, C. H. Judd, Oswald Külpe, George T. Ladd, H. S. Langfeld, A. L. Lowell, William McDougall, Max Meyer, C. S. Meyers, G. H. Palmer, R. B. Perry, A. H. Pierce, Morton Prince, D. C. Rogers, Josiah Royce, Carl Stumpf, James Sully, Edward B. Titchener, L. T. Troland, H. C. Warren, John B. Watson, R. S. Woodworth, and Robert M. Yerkes.

[This entry is reprinted, with permission, from: Edwin G. Boring, "Psychologists' Letters and Papers," *Isis* 58 (1967): 103-107.]

322. *Murphy, Lois Barclay, 1902- .*
Papers, 1935-71. 25 containers.
In National Library of Medicine (Washington, D.C.).
Family and personal correspondence, plans and evaluations of parent-child centers (1966-71), talks on mental retardation, and reports of a task force on the mental health of children (1968). Case studies (1959-71) and a typescript of *Development, Vulnerability and Resilience* (1970) are included along with correspondence written during her work with children in Nigeria and India (1941-63).

323. *Murphy, Patrick Livingston, 1848-1907.*
Papers, 1848-1944. 243 items.
In University of North Carolina Library, Southern Historical Collection (Chapel Hill, North Carolina).

Physician and superintendent of the North Carolina Hospital for the Insane at Morganton. Correspondence, chiefly 1880-1907, pertaining to Murphy's career; early family letters, a physician's fee book (1875-76), two scrapbooks of clippings about the state hospital at Morganton (1897), and other papers.

Unpublished description in the library.

Gift of Dr. James B. Murphy, Dr. W. A. Murphy, and May Murphy, before 1940.

324. *Murray, Elsie, 1878-1965.*
Papers, ca. 1896-1965. 43 ft.
In Cornell University Library, Department of Manuscripts and University Archives (Ithaca, New York).

Psychologist, professor of psychology at Sweet Briar, Vassar, Wells, and Wilson Colleges; research associate at Cornell University, and director of French Azilum (incl.), and the Tioga Point Museum in Bradford County, Pennsylvania. Correspondence (personal and professional), diaries, accounts; a journal (1926-27) kept as secretary of the Cornell University music department; test forms and materials, drafts of scientific writings, research and testing notes, class notes as student and professor, manuscripts of Miss Murray's unpublished fiction; material relating to her interest in music, poetry, and social psychology; photos, newspaper clippings, and printed and mimeographed matter. Includes material relating to color blindness and various aspects of color vision, color studies for the Office of Naval Research, color perception tests and apparatus, the aesthetics of color, intelligence and other mental tests, the activities of the Inter-Society Color Council, the New York and American Psychologist Associations, and other professional organizations. The correspondence with Karl M. Dallenbach and Joseph Peterson mainly concerns publication of the *American Journal of Psychology*. Other correspondents include Frank Allen, Madison Bentley, Edwin G. Boring, Forrest Lee Dimmick, Knight Dunlap, Dean Farnsworth, James J. Gibson, Walter F. Grether, J. P. Guilford, Samuel P. Hayes, Dorothea and Leo Hurvich, Deane B. Judd, Sidney M. Newhall, Dorothy Nickerson, R. W. Pickford, Lars-Gunnar Romell, Christian A. Ruckmick, Howard C. Warren, Harry P. Weld, and manufacturers of psychological testing apparatus.

Gifts of Miss Murray, 1965, Miss Helen J. Cady, 1966, and Mrs. Toby Clarey, 1967.

325. *National Association of Social Workers.*
Records, 1917-63. ca. 53 ft.
In University of Minnesota Social Welfare History Archives (Minneapolis, Minnesota).

Chiefly records of the association and its predecessor organizations: American Association of Group Workers (1936-55), American Association of Medical Social Workers (1917-56), American Association of Psychiatric Social Workers (1921-58),

325. *(Continued)*

American Association of Social Workers (1918-55), Association for the Study of Community Organization (1944-55), National Association of School Social Workers (1922-55), Social Work Research Group (1949-56), and the Temporary Inter-Association Council of Social Work Membership Organizations (1946-55); together with records of the National Committee on Social Work in Defense Mobilization (1950-55), pertaining explicitly to social work involvement in the national defense effort. Subjects covered include the U.S. armed forces, the recruitment, education, placement, and practice of social workers; group, medical, psychiatric and school social work; play and recreation, and World War II. Other organizations represented include the Academy of Certified Social Workers, American Hospital Association, American National Red Cross, American Public Health Association, American Public Welfare Association, Council on Social Work Education, International Conference of Social Work, National Foundation of Infantile Paralysis, National Social Welfare Assembly, United Community Defense Services, U.S. Public Health Service, U.S. Selective Service System, and U.S. Veterans Administration. Correspondents include Jane Addams, Joseph P. Anderson, Harriet M. Bartlett, Bertram M. Beck, Margaret Blenkner, Elizabeth and Karl De Schweinitz, Arthur Dunham, Ethel Ginsburg, Melvin Glasser, Dora Goldstine, Ernest B. Harper, Mary Hemmy, Fred K. Hochler, Joe R. Hoffer, Donald S. Howard, Dorothy C. Kahn, Gisela Konopka, Janet Korpela, Florence Ray, Elizabeth Healy Ross, Harold Silver, Sanford Solender, Addie Thomas, and Walter M. West.

Unpublished description in the library.

Open to investigators under library restrictions.

Information on literary rights available in the library.

Deposited by the association, 1964.

326. *National Association of Social Workers. Chicago Area Chapter.*
Records, 1921-55. 10 ft.

In Chicago Historical Society Library (Chicago, Illinois).

Correspondence, annual reports, minutes of the Chicago area chapter and its predecessors, including minutes (1924-55) of the executive committee, of the membership committee (1924-51), and of the personnel practices committee; and other material. Provides data on the formation of the chapter in 1924, and its relationship to the national organization, standards and ethics of social workers, codes of conduct for welfare agencies, employment practices and personnel regulations, welfare legislation, public aid matters, improved service to the general public, and other items concerning the Great Depression and changing welfare needs during and after World War II. Includes material relating to the American Association of Group Workers, the American Association of Medical Social Workers, and the Chicago Round Table of Psychiatric Social Work.

Unpublished guide in the library.

Information on literary rights available in the library.

Gift of the chapter, 1966 and 1970.

327. *National Council on Family Relations.*
Records, 1939-75. 13 ft.
In University of Minnesota, Social Welfare History Archives. (Minneapolis, Minnesota).
The records document the council's efforts to promote consultation and cooperation among professional family-life workers, including clergymen, counselors, educators, home economists, nurses, physicians, lawyers, social workers, and psychologists. Included in the collection are files on annual meetings, correspondence with state and regional family relations councils, financial records, and membership cards.

328. *Nesbitt, Charles Torrence.*
Papers, 1899-1947. 437 items and 3 vols.
In Duke University Library (Durham, North Carolina).
Physician and public health official of Wilmington, North Carolina. Correspondence, scrapbooks, and other papers, relating to Nesbitt's career, especially his service as superintendent of health (1911-17) and public health and sanitation in Wilmington. Includes an autobiographical account of Nesbitt's medical education at the University of Pennsylvania, Bellevue Medical College, and Baltimore Medical College, and his experiences as a young physician, with references to early psychiatric practices, and political and social affairs and homosexuality in New York City during the 1880s. Physicians discussed in the memoirs include Austin Flint, Jr., Edward Gamaliel Janeway, Frederick Peterson, George Reuling, and John Allen Wyeth. Correspondents include Rupert Blue, Albert Pike Bourland, Edward Hatch, Jr., Jacob Lott Ludlow, Angus Wilton McLean, Arthur Wilson Page, Walter Hines Page, Watson Smith Rankin, Leo L. Redding, Charles Wardell Stiles, Frank Porter Stockbridge, Henry Walters, and George Chandler Whipple.
Card index in the library.
Purchase, 1958.

329. *Newman, Emma E.*
Papers, 1845-1921. ca. 200 items.
In Henry E. Huntington Library (San Marino, California).
Mental healer and "Christian metaphysician." Diaries, commonplace books, lectures, and sermons.
Acquired from Martha Caroline Pritchard, 1948.

330. *Newman, Philip Charles, 1914-   .*
Papers, ca. 1949-64. ca. 1000 items.
In Columbia University Libraries (New York, New York).
Labor economist and consultant. Correspondence, notes, reports, and miscellaneous papers, relating to Newman's work and to that of his wife, Ruth Newman, a clinical psychologist.
Gift of Mrs. Newman, 1969.

331. *New York Psychoanalytic Institute.*
Business and financial records, 1880- . 20 ft.
In New York Psychoanalytic Institute, Abraham A. Brill Library (New York, New York).

Includes records of the New York Psychoanalytic Society (founded in 1911) and the New York Psychoanalytic Institute (founded in 1913), the first such society and institute to be founded in the United States. The history of the institute is intertwined with the psychoanalytic movement both in the United States and Europe, since European psychoanalysts found an intellectual outlet in the work of the institute upon their immigration to the United States. The collection includes scientific papers presented at society meetings twice monthly during the academic year; the annual Freud Anniversary and Brill Memorial Lectures; more than thirty Freud holographs; additional Freudiana. Books, manuscripts, and papers of members of the society and other psychoanalysts include Berta Bornstin, Anna Freud, Smith Ely Jelliffe, Theodor Reik, and Fritz Wittels. Photographs of psychoanalysts and psychoanalytic events, motion pictures of Ernest Jones and Anna Freud, oral history tapes and transcripts, and biographical data on society members and other psychoanalysts are included in the archives.

332. *North Carolina Mental Health Association.*
Records, 1913-61. 3 boxes.
In North Carolina Division of Archives and History (Raleigh, North Carolina).

Minutes, correspondence, committee material, and a history of the association, including information on Dorothea Dix, mental health, the National Association for Mental Health, and other records of the association.

Published guide available.

333. *Ogden, Robert Morris, 1877-1959.*
Papers, 1889-1959. ca. 21 ft.
In Cornell University Library, Department of Manuscripts and University Archives (Ithaca, New York).

Professor of psychology and dean of the College of Arts and Sciences, Cornell University. Correspondence (1889-1949) pertaining to Ogden's work as psychologist, author, and educator, and to his membership in various scientific societies, especially the Southern Society for Philosophy and Psychology; personal and family correspondence; notes, essays and other manuscripts of writings; personal accounts, Cornelliana, reprints and other printed matter; clippings, photos, and accounts of the estate of Mrs. John Dorsey.

Gifts of Mrs. Ogden and Frank S. Freeman, 1959-61.

334. *O'Hare, Kate Richards, 1877-1948.*
Papers, 1919-20. 1 vol.
In Radcliffe College, Schlesinger Library on the History of Women in America (Cambridge, Massachusetts).

Socialist. Correspondence to members of her family concerns the psychology of women and developments in psychoanalysis.

Unpublished guide available.

335. *O'Neill, C. William, 1916-1978.*
Papers, 1939-59. ca. 77 ft.
In Ohio Historical Society Collections (Columbus, Ohio).
State legislator, governor of Ohio, and chief justice of the Ohio Supreme Court. Private and public papers from O'Neill's career in the Ohio General Assembly (1939-50), as attorney general of Ohio (1951-57), his 1956 and 1958 gubernatorial campaigns, and from his term as governor (1957-59), including correspondence and records relating to interstate highways, the Ohio Department of Mental Health and Correction, and the right-to-work amendment.
Inventory in the repository.
Gift of Judge O'Neill, 1959.

336. *Oral History Collection, 1926, 1951-68.*
32 items.
In National Library of Medicine (Bethesda, Maryland).
Transcripts or tape recordings of interviews with physicians and other persons connected with medical matters; addresses; and a tape recording of the "William Stewart Halsted Centenary" program, (Baltimore, Maryland, 1952). Three of the oral histories were conducted by the American Gastroenterological Association. Topics covered include medical education, military medicine, public health, social medicine, costs of medical care, blood banks, drugs, quackery, cancer treatment, medical research, biochemistry, gastroenterology, immunology, psychiatry, and surgery. Persons interviewed include J. Arnold Bargen, Stanhope Bayne-Jones, Daniel L. Borden, Arthur Carlisle Christie, Burrill B. Crohn, Ward Darley, Raymond Osborne Dart, Michael Marks Davis, John Miller Train Finney, Warfield Monroe Firor, Robert Philipp Fischelis, Morris Fishbein, Gilbert S. Goldhammer, Albert Baird Hastings, Michael Heidelberger, Lister Hill, Andrew Conway Ivy, Boisfeuillet Jones, George P. Larrick, Zigmond Meyer Lebensohn, Warren Egbert Magee, Rudolph Matas, William Shainline Middleton, Wilder Graves Penfield, Herbert Percy Ramsey, Harvey Brinton Stone, Albert Szent-Györgyi, Vivien Thomas, Rexford Guy Tugwell, Donald Dexter Van Slyke, and Lawrence Richardson Wharton. Other persons and organizations mentioned include Alfred Blalock, Simon Flexner, William Stewart Halsted, Sir William Osler, Franklin D. Roosevelt, the American College of Surgeons, American Medical Association, Committee on the Costs of Medical Care, Johns Hopkins University School of Medicine, Rockefeller Institute for Medical Research (New York), U.S. Food and Drug Administration, and U.S. National Institutes of Health.
Catalogued and indexed individually in the library, where most of the original tapes are retained.
In part, restricted.

337. *Orbison, Hannah D. (Jones), 1820-1878.*
Papers, 1829-78. 3 ft.
In Troy-Miami County Local History Room (Troy, Ohio).
Teacher. Contains pamphlets (1844-46) written by O. S. Fowler concerning the use of phrenology and physiology in choosing a marriage partner.

338. Overholser, Winfred, 1892-1964.

Papers, 1917-64. 10 ft. (ca. 5000 items).

In Library of Congress, Manuscript Division (Washington, D.C.).

Psychiatrist, educator, and superintendent of St. Elizabeth's Hospital in Washington, D.C. A few letters, scrapbooks, notes for book reviews, addresses, and special projects; printed matter, and other papers, relating to Overholser's career in psychiatry and his research in forensic psychiatry.

Unpublished finding-aid in the library.

Open to investigators under restrictions accepted by the library.

Gift of Winfred Overholser, Jr., and the American Security and Trust Company, 1965.

339. Owen, Robert Dale 1801-1877.

Papers, 1831-73. 71 items.

In University of Illinois, Illinois Historical Survey Collections (Urbana, Illinois).

Microfilmed in 1952 from originals owned by Aline Owen Neal.

Social and educational reformer, U.S. representative, diplomat, and spiritualist. Correspondence, memoranda, and legal papers, including Owen's certificate of naturalization (1831). Most of the papers are from the 1870s and many of them concern spiritualism. Includes a memorandum (1863) to Abraham Lincoln on the pardoning power as an element of reconstruction. Correspondents include James Freeman Clarke, Charles W. Elliott, and Henry James.

Unpublished catalog microfilmed with the collection.

340. Owens, John W.

Papers, 1880-1926. 1 folder.

In Oregon Historical Society (Portland, Oregon).

Lecturer in phrenology. Includes correspondence, clippings, and a notebook.

341. Pace, Edward Aloysius, 1861-1938.

Papers, ca. 1890-1963. 4 ft.

In The Catholic University of America Archives (Washington, D.C.).

Priest, professor, and dean of the School of Philosophy and Vice Rector, The Catholic University of America. Personal and professional correspondence, lecture notes, articles, pamphlets, and clippings, relating to his career as student, teacher, and scholar, and to his participation in professional associations.

342. Pacific State Hospital, Pomona, California.

Archival Records and Clippings, 1921- .

In Lanterman State Hospital and Developmental Center (Pomona, California).

Institution for the mentally retarded and developmentally disabled. Collection includes 3 drawers of "selected archival materials," clippings dating from the founding of the hospital, and a large unpublished history, completed in 1959, by Anna Shotwell. See also Hugh Kohler, "Pacific State Hospital, 1921-1965," *Pomona Valley Historian*, vol. 8, no. 1, January 1972.

343. *Pappenheim, Bertha, 1859-1936*
Papers, 1903-68. ca. 100 items.
In Leo Baeck Institute Collections (New York, New York).

German Jewish social worker and feminist leader. Correspondence (1904-36), reports (1914-41) relating to a home for unmarried mothers and homeless children, which Mrs. Pappenheim founded at Isenburg, Germany; poems and prayers written for the home, photos of the home, summary of a lecture (1959) by Dr. Richard Karpe relating to the treatment of Anna O. (Bertha Pappenheim) by the psychoanalyst Joseph Breuer; facsimile edition (1936) of "Gebete" (handwritten prayers in German) with an epilogue by Margarete Susman; *Prayers—Gebete* (1946), print of German text with English translations by E. Forchheimer; and newspaper and magazine articles by and about Miss Pappenheim. In German.

Gifts and loans from Dr. Dora Edinger (New York City) and other sources, since 1963.

344. *Partlow, William Dempsey, 1877-1954.*
Papers, 1907-50. ca. 2490 items.
In University of Alabama Library (Tuscaloosa, Alabama).

Psychiatrist, teacher, and superintendent of Bryce Hospital in Alabama. Correspondence, autobiography, short biography, addresses, publications by Dr. Partlow, and newspaper clippings. Correspondents include Frank W. Boykin and George H. Denny.

Unpublished finding-aid in the library.

Open to investigators under library restrictions.

Gift of Dr. Partlow's daughter, Mrs. Harry Pritchett, 1962.

345. *Paterson, Donald Gildersleeve, 1892-1961.*
Papers, 1915-61. 7½ ft.
In University of Minnesota Archives, Walter Library (Minneapolis, Minnesota).

Psychologist. Professor of psychology, University of Minnesota, 1921-60. Secretary of the American Psychological Association, 1931-37.

346. *Patten, Everett Frank, 1895-1966.*
Papers, 1924-50. ca. 140 items.
In University of Akron, Archives of the History of American Psychology (Akron, Ohio).

Psychologist. Chiefly correspondence between Patten and Clark L. Hull, relating to research design and implementation, personnel, and other professional matters.

Unpublished finding-aids in the repository.

Information on literary rights available in the repository.

Gift of Mrs. Patten, 1967-70.

347. *Paul, George H.*
Papers, 1834-89. 16 boxes.
In State Historical Society of Wisconsin Collections (Madison, Wisconsin).

Newspaperman, politician, and businessman. Correspondence and business

347. (Continued)

records concerning the Democratic Party in Wisconsin, the University of Wisconsin (especially the building program and the resignation of President John Bascom); the Milwaukee post office, the Kenosha post office, the early history of Kenosha, the *Burlington Sentinel*, the work of a preceptress at a girls' school at Little Falls, New York. (1849); California in 1849; a trip to Kenosha via the Great Lakes in 1851; Madison, the legislature, and political figures during the session of 1853; the arrest of a Democrat at Fond du Lac during the Civil War, the Milwaukee Cement Company, the Barstow-Bashford controversy, state and local political campaigns, especially those of 1852 and 1872; reimbursement of the builders of the state capitol after the disaster of 1882; the Potter Law and injunction suits of the 1870s; the National Civil Service Law in the 1880s; and investigation of the Milwaukee County Insane Asylum in the 1880s. Includes a list of voters in Kenosha in 1855, several letters of Paul while employed as an editorial assistant to Fernando Wood for a few months in 1861; business papers concerning the *Milwaukee Daily News*, letters of Congressman Charles A. Eldredge on relations between President Johnson and Congress in 1866; and one of the earliest letters written on a typewriter (1874). Records of the Milwaukee post office (1885-89) consist almost exclusively of duplicate form reports submitted to the Post Office Department at Washington.

348. Pease, Rufus D.

Papers, 1838-90. 1 box.

In Dickinson College Library (Carlisle, Pennsylvania).

Papers relating to Pease's career as lecturer on physiology, spiritualism, etc. Includes testimonials from audiences.

Described in *Archives and Manuscript Collections of Dickinson College* (1972), p. 48.

Gift of Samuel and Anna D. Moyerman and their son, Barry Moyerman, 1962-66.

349. Peaslee, Charles Hazen, 1804-1866.

Correspondence, 1831-52. 51 items.

In New Hampshire Historical Society Collections (Concord, New Hampshire).

Lawyer and U.S. representative of Concord, New Hampshire. One-quarter of the correspondence concerns the organization of the New Hampshire Asylum for the Insane and the controversy over its location, 1838-39. Scattered letters mention the election campaign of 1832, candidates for senator in 1839, pension claims, and appointment of postmasters.

350. Pennsylvania Association for Retarded Children, Allegheny County Chapter.

Records, 1950-62. 22 ft.

In University of Pittsburgh Libraries, Archives of Industrial Society (Pittsburgh, Pennsylvania).

Correspondence, constitution and bylaws, financial reports, budgets, allotments, receipts, bills, payroll, membership lists, printed matter, publicity, and other records, relating to the chapter's activities and projects. Includes material on the Health and Welfare Association, National Association for Retarded Children, and the Pennsylvania Association for Retarded Children.

Gift of the Allegheny County Chapter, 1966.

351. *Pillsbury, Walter Bowers, 1872-1960.*
Papers, 1898-1960. 3 ft.
In University of Michigan, Michigan Historical Collections (Ann Arbor, Michigan).

Professor of psychology and chairman of the psychology department at the University of Michigan. Correspondence, lecture notes, manuscripts of writings, and examination questions. Includes the working papers of the psychological laboratory and the psychology department after its organization in 1929. Correspondents include Henry C. Adams, Fayette W. Allport, James R. Angell, George F. Arps, Henry M. Bates, Edwin G. Boring, Norman A. Cameron, Moses Gomberg, Clark L. Hull, Clarence T. Johnston, Charles H. Judd, Kurt Lewin, Norman R. F. Maier, Carl Murchison, Carl E. Seashore, Edward B. Titchener, Edward C. Tolman, Robert M. Wenley, Lloyd S. Woodburne, Robert M. Yerkes, and Clarence S. Yoakum.

Gift of Walter M. Pillsbury, 1960.

352. *Pitman Family.*
Papers, ca. 1850-1954.
In Cincinnati Historical Society Collections (Cincinnati, Ohio).

Correspondence; biographical and genealogical material; spiritual and religious notes and material of Melrose Pitman (1889-   ) on the Anthroposophical Society in America; designs and wood carvings, home decorations, and a sketchbook of Benn Pitman (1822-1910), shorthand expert and master wood carver of Cincinnati; photos, art work, and sketches by Agnes Pitman; articles on the Pitman shorthand system; scrapbooks of newspaper clippings; pamphlets, and other printed matter.

Unpublished index in the repository.

Gift of Miss Melrose Pitman, 1963 and 1970.

353. *Popper, Hermine (Isaacs) 1915-1968.*
Papers, 1941-68. 4 boxes.
In Radcliffe College, Schlesinger Library on the History of Women in America (Cambridge, Massachusetts).

Author and editor. Correspondence, writings by Popper and by authors edited by her, and collaborations, drafts, notes, and research material. Bulk of the collection concerns writings by Martin Luther King and manuscript of *Up From Poverty* (1968) by Popper and Frank Riessman. Includes material on psychoanalysis, poverty, and civil rights. Persons represented include Helene Deutsch, Peter F. Drucker, Gregory Rochlin, Victoria Sackville-West, Bertram Schaffner, Isabel Wilder, and Thornton Wilder.

Unpublished finding aid in the repository.

Gift of Mrs. Popper's husband, Robert Lyman Popper, 1969.

354. *Pruette, Lorine Livingston, 1896-1977.*
Papers, 1915-74. 4 file boxes, 1 folder, and 6 folders of photographs.
In Radcliffe College, Schlesinger Library on the History of Women in America (Cambridge, Massachusetts).

The papers of Pruette, psychologist, writer, and lecturer, consisting primarily of writings and correspondence, with some biographical and personal material.

355. *Psycho-Acoustic/Psychophysics Laboratory, Harvard University.*
Papers and records, 1940-72. 14 ft.
In Harvard University Archives (Cambridge, Massachusetts).

Correspondence and related records of the director, S. S. Stevens, with outside persons and groups, and with Harvard University administration. Includes processed documents, memos, notes, photographs, building specifications, budget papers, reports, computer programs (1965, 1969), equipment inventories, and personnel records. Much of the material relates to research contract work, especially during World War II, and includes items relating both to administrative and scientific/technical matters.

Prior permission necessary for access. (Contact repository for information on access.)

356. *Psychoanalytic Movement.*
Oral history, 1963-66. 1802 pages.
In Columbia University Library, Oral History Collection (New York, New York).

Transcripts of tape-recorded interviews with analysts and persons active in the psychoanalytic movement, discussing the early history of psychoanalysis and its subsequent ramifications, varying theories and predictions, research development into the nature of the thought process, and cross-cultural studies. Persons interviewed for this project include Michael Balint, Raymond de Saussure, Edward Glover, Willi Hoffer, and Rene A. Spitz. Autobiographical interviews relating to this collection which are in the library's biographical oral history collection include Dr. Heinz Hartmann, Dr. Abraham Kardiner, Dr. Rudolph Loewenstein, Margaret Mahler, Dr. Sandor Rado, and Theodore Reik.

Described in the *Oral History Collection of Columbia University* (1964), p. 154; *Supplement* (1966), p. 28; and *Supplement* (1968), p. 27; the autobiographical interviews are described in the biographical section of these catalogs.

Partially restricted.

357. *Psychologists' Oral History Interviews, 1965-68.*
ca. 12 items.
In University of Akron, Archives of the History of American Psychology (Akron, Ohio).

Transcripts of tape-recorded interviews with Samuel Beck, psychologist at Michael Reese Hospital and American pioneer in the Rorschach technique of personality assessment; Evelyn Fitzsimmons Douglas, secretary to G. Stanley Hall; Pauline H. Havre (in which she reviews a course by Sigmund Freud to which the wives of American physicians studying in Vienna, 1926-27, were admitted); Elaine F. Kinder, psychologist active in comparative and clinical specialities, and originator of rotating internship in clinical psychology; Norman R. F. Maier, professor at the University of Michigan and industrial psychologist; Frederick C. Thorne, editor of *Journal of Clinical Psychology;* Harold Burt and Sidney Pressey, emeriti faculty at Ohio State University (relating to their graduate student days at Harvard and their careers at Ohio State); and Valentin Wertheimer and Mrs. John Hornbostel, son and widow of Max Wertheimer.

Open to investigators under restrictions accepted by the repository.

Information on literary rights available in the repository.

Additions to the collection are anticipated.

358. *Putnam, James Jackson, 1846-1918.*

Papers, 1907. 1 item.

In Radcliffe College, Schlesinger Library on the History of Women in America (Cambridge, Massachusetts).

Neurologist. Major correspondent is Elizabeth Glendower Evans and concerns the views of Josiah Royce and William James.

Published and unpublished guides available in the repository.

359. *Quetelet, Lambert Adolphe Jacques, 1796-1874.*

Selected correspondence. 2 reels of microfilm.

In American Philosophical Society Library (Philadelphia, Pennsylvania).

Microfilm made from originals in the possession of the Bibliothèque Royal de Belgique, Brussels.

Astronomer, meteorologist, and statistician. Correspondents include Charles Babbage, Samuel Brown, Thomas G. Clemson, Robley Dunglison, James P. Espy, Michael Faraday, William Farr, James D. Forbes, James A. Garfield, Charles Frederic Gauss, James Melville Gilliss, Arnold Guyot, William R. Hamilton, Joseph Henry, Edward C. Herrick, Sir John F. W. Herschel, George W. Hough, Alexander von Humboldt, Joseph C. G. Kennedy, Auguste A. de la Rive, Urbain J. J. Le Verrier, Humphrey Lloyd, Hubert A. Newton, Sir Edward Sabine, E. A. Sanford, Lemuel Shattuck, Charles Wheatstone, William Whewell, and Edward L. Youmans.

Information on literary rights available in the library.

360. *Quimby, Phineas Parkhurst, 1802-1866.*

Papers, 1859-66. ca. 100 items.

In Library of Congress, Manuscript Division (Washington, D.C.).

Mental healer. Drafts of letters, handwritten copies of essays, and notes for essays or lectures by Quimby on such subjects as wisdom, happiness, health and disease, spiritualism, science, Christ, religion, life and death, and mind and matter; as well as accounts of his experiences in healing. Includes letter (1862-65) from Mary M. Patterson (Mary Baker Eddy) to Quimby.

Gift, 1953.

361. *Rand, Benjamin, 1856-1934.*
Papers, 1897-1933. 3 boxes.
In Harvard University Archives (Cambridge, Massachusetts).
Philosopher and librarian at Harvard University. Professional correspondence and scholarly papers.
Permission to quote from the collection will be required until 1984.
Information on literary rights available in the repository.

362. *Rank, Otto, 1884-1939.*
Papers, ca. 1903-30. ca. 25 boxes.
In Columbia University Libraries (New York, New York).
Psychiatrist. Correspondence, manuscripts of Rank's writings daybooks, notebook of dreams, poems, and other papers by and about Rank. Includes the manuscript of *Der Künstler*, and Rank's own listing and comments on his writings and publications. The correspondence includes letters (1906-24) between Sigmund Freud and Rank, some on the controversy over Rank's book *The Trauma of Birth;* a few letters to and from Sandor Ferenczi; and copies *or* originals of the circular letters (1920-24) by members of the inner circle, Abraham Eitingon, Sandor Ferenczi, Sigmund Freud, Ernest Jones, and Rank.
Gift of Jessie Taft and Mrs. Pierre Simon, 1957.

363. *Rapaport, David, 1911-1960.*
Papers, 1948-60. 18 ft. (14,000 items).
In Library of Congress, Manuscript Division (Washington, D.C.).
Psychologist. Correspondence, drafts of articles and lectures, notes and memoranda, dated during the time Rapaport was research associate at the Austen Riggs Center in Stockbridge, Massachusetts. Some subjects of Rapaport's research while at the center were memory theory and the organization and pathology of thought. Much of the correspondence is concerned with research in the behavioral sciences, especially psychology and sociology, and many papers relate to the effects of this work on other disciplines.
Unpublished register in the library.
Open to investigators under restrictions accepted by the library.
Information on literary rights available in the library.
Deposited by Mrs. Rapaport, 1962.

364. *Reitman, Ben Louis, 1879-1942.*
Papers, 1905-51. 2 ft.
In University of Illinois at Chicago Circle Library (Chicago, Illinois).
Physician. Correspondence, statements, articles, reports, speeches, poems, notes, cartoons, lists, clippings, photos, reprints, and other papers, relating to Reitman's life as a hobo, field manager for Emma Goldman, the anarchist, and physician specializing in the prevention of venereal diseases. Topics covered include birth control, the pimp, venereal diseases, war, free speech, socialism, communism, capitalism, sex censorship and education, juvenile delinquency, illegitimate births in Chicago, female transients; economic conditions (1924-32) in the United States, France, Great Britain, and Germany; Illinois county jails, the

eugenic marriage laws of Wisconsin, Michigan, and Indiana; women's employment, flophouses, immorality, and the employment of children in street trades in Chicago. Includes the incomplete manuscript of "Box-car Bertha" Thompson's autobiography, *Sister of the Road*, and the unpublished manuscript of Reitman's *Following the Monkey*.

Unpublished guide and subject entry cards in the library.

Acquired in 1969.

365. *Reitman, Ben Louis, 1879-1942*.

Papers, 1905-51.

Addition, 1910-51. 5 ft.

In University of Illinois at Chicago Circle Library (Chicago, Illinois).

Physician. Correspondence, legal documents, poems, and clippings, pertaining to Reitman's family and his professional activities. Includes material relating to anarchy, communism and socialism, Jewish charities, mental institutions, tramps, unemployment, and venereal diseases. Persons represented include Alexander Berkman, Emma Goldman, and Lucy Parsons.

Unpublished guide and subject entry cards in the library.

Gift of Dr. Reitman's daughters, 1971.

366. *Rethlingshafer, Dorothy, 1900-1969*.

Papers, 1926-66. ca. 4 ft.

In University of Akron, Archives of the History of American Psychology (Akron, Ohio).

Psychologist. Chiefly material relating to the publication of Miss Rethlingshafer's books, *Motivation as Related to Personality* (1963) and *Principles of Comparative Psychology* (1973); together with professional and personal correspondence, class and reading notes, and research reports. The bulk of the papers' dates are in the 1950s and 1960s. Major correspondents include Joseph V. Brady, Willard Caldwell, James A. Dinsmoor, John L. Fuller, Sherman Ross, William R. Thompson, and Rolland H. Watters.

Unpublished finding-aids in the repository.

Information on literary rights available in the repository.

Gift of S. T. Margulis and H. S. Pennypacker (University of Florida) 1969.

367. *Reymert, August, 1851-1932*.

Papers, 1832-1927. 236 items.

In St. Olaf College, Norwegian-American Historical Association Archives (Northfield, Minnesota).

Lawyer of New York City. Correspondence, biographical sketches and genealogical chart of the Reymert family; articles, reports, clippings, and photos, relating largely to family affairs in America, Norway, and Scotland. Includes letters by Reymert's uncle, James Denoon Reymert, concerning opportunities for law practice on the American frontier, and monographs on psychology by Martin L. Reymert, director of Mooseheart Laboratory in Mooseheart, Illinois.

Information on literary rights available in the repository.

Gift of Martin L. Reymert.

368. *Rice, Elizabeth Prince, 1900-* .
Papers. 3 cartons and 1 box.
In Radcliffe College, Schlesinger Library on the History of Women in America (Cambridge, Massachusetts).
Associate professor of public health and social work at the Harvard School of Public Health. Correspondence concerns her work in mental health and social welfare.

369. *Ridenour, Nina, 1904-* .
Papers. 7 boxes.
In Menninger Foundation Archives (Topeka, Kansas).
Director of the education division of the National Association for Mental Health. Correspondence and manuscripts relate to her work in New York City regarding mental health.
Unpublished guide available.

370. *Rinsland, Henry D., 1918-1950.*
Papers, 1918-50. 2 ft.
In University of Oklahoma Library, Western History Collections (Norman, Oklahoma).
Professor of education and national leader in testing and measurements. Papers include original manuscripts, published and unpublished on vocabulary and spelling tests, and research notes on testing. Samples of tests devised for the U.S. armed forces, various civilian groups, and educators are included.

371. *Roethke, Theodore, 1908-1963.*
Papers, 1935-48.
In University of Virginia Library (Charlottesville, Virginia).
Comments and reflections on Roethke's mental illness. Correspondents include Peter H. and Katinka L. DeVries.

372. *Rosenblith, Walter, 1913-* .
Papers, 1958-76. ca. 43 ft.
In Institute Archives and Special Collections, Massachusetts Institute of Technology (Cambridge, Massachusetts).
Neuroscientist, electrical engineer, and academic administrator. Most of the collection relates to Rosenblith's service as MIT Provost, but several files include material relating to his work on experimental neurology, brain models, and biophysics, and with the International Brain Research Organization and the American and Eastern Psychological Associations.
Access restricted.
Container list available in Archives.

373. *Ross, Josephine, 1906-1972.*
Papers, 1953-62. 5 in.
In University of Akron, Archives of the History of American Psychology (Akron, Ohio).

Psychologist who participated actively in the International Council of Psychologists. Correspondence, manuscripts, and recordings of therapy sessions reflect her work in psychoanalysis.
Unpublished guide available.

374. Royce, Josiah, 1855-1916.

Correspondence, 1875-1917.
In Johns Hopkins University Library (Baltimore, Maryland).
Personal and professional correspondence. Major correspondents include George B. Coale, Davis R. Dewey, Daniel C. Gilman, and Arthur O. Lovejoy.

375. Royce, Josiah, 1855-1916.

Papers, 1882-1916. 25 ft.
In Harvard University Archives (Cambridge, Massachusetts).
Professor of philosophy at Harvard University. Personal and professional correspondence, manuscripts of lectures and articles, and notes.
Information on literary rights available in the repository.

376. Royce, Josiah, 1855-1916.

Papers, 1882-1916. 25 ft.
In University of California at Los Angeles Library (Los Angeles, California).
Professor of psychology at Harvard University. A collection of writings by and about Royce, copies of his correspondence, clippings, photographs, a typescript copy of a journal written by his mother, Sarah Eleanor Royce, entitled "Across the Plain" (1849); and other Royce memorabilia collected by the Department of Philosophy, University of California at Los Angeles, in memory of Josiah Royce.

377. Royster, Hubert Ashley, 1871-1959.

Correspondence, 1927-49. 50 items.
In University of North Carolina Library, Southern Historical Collection (Chapel Hill, North Carolina).
Physician and surgeon of Raleigh, North Carolina. Correspondence, relating to personal and professional topics, from Dr. Benjamin K. Hays of Oxford, North Carolina, and James King Hall (1875-1948), a psychiatrist of Richmond, Virginia.
Unpublished description in the library.
Gift of Dr. Royster, 1951.

378. Rubin, Theodore Isaac, 1923-   .

Papers, 1960-66. 50 items.
In Boston University Libraries (Boston, Massachusetts).
Author and psychiatrist. Correspondence, holograph and typewritten copies of Rubin's works in variant drafts, notes, galleys, and other papers.
Inventory in the library.
Information on literary rights available in the library.
Gift of Mr. Rubin, 1965-66.
Additions to this collection are anticipated.

379. *Ruml, Beardsley, 1894-1960.*
Correspondence and papers, 1917-59. 7 ft.
In University of Chicago Library (Chicago, Illinois).
Applied psychologist, educator, businessman, and government advisor on finance and fiscal policy. Biographical material and sketches; correspondence, speeches and articles concerned with national economic conditions and policy; miscellaneous correspondence of a mixed personal and professional nature; clippings and reprints of articles on Ruml, including interviews and autobiographical material. The speech files contain drafts of numerous articles and correspondence related to the Laura Spelman Rockefeller Memorial. Major correspondents include Mortimer J. Adler, William Benton, T. E. Blackwell, and J. D. Zellerbach.
Unpublished guide in the library.
Information on literary rights available in the library.
Gift of Mrs. Ruml, 1960.

380. *Rush, Benjamin, 1745-1813.*
Papers, 1762-1813. 17 ft. (ca. 6500 items).
In Library Company of Philadelphia Collections (Philadelphia, Pennsylvania).
Physician. Correspondence, medical writings, three small notebooks containing Rush's diary for 1777-78 covering debates in the Continental Congress; journals, and daybooks. Correspondence relates to Rush's medical career, land speculation, Dickinson College, controversies with Shippen and Cobbett, and family affairs. Includes letters from Dr. David Ramsay.
Some of the letters appear in *Letters of Benjamin Rush*, edited by L. H. Butterfield (1951).
Bequest of Dr. James Rush, 1869.

381. *Rush, Benjamin, 1745-1813.*
Papers, 1768-1813. ca. 100 items.
In American Philosophical Society Library (Philadelphia, Pennsylvania).
In part, microfilm.
Physician. Correspondence, diaries, biography, commonplace book, and memorandum book. Correspondents include Thomas Bradford, William Cullen, Benjamin Franklin, Thomas Jefferson, Robert Patterson, Richard Price, and Benjamin Vaughan. Includes one reel of microfilm made from papers in the College of Physicians of Philadelphia. Some of the papers are filed in other collections of the library.
Catalogued individually in the manuscripts catalogue of the library.
Purchases and deposits.

382. *Rush, Benjamin, 1745-1813.*
Papers, 1775-1814. 60 items.
In New York Public Library (New York, New York).
Handwritten transcripts (1840?).
Physician. Chiefly letters to Rush relating to public affairs during the Revolu-

tion, and extracts from Rush's diary (1792-1806). Correspondents include John Dickinson, Charles Lee, and Anthony Wayne.

Formerly part of the library's Bancroft Collection.

383. *Rush, James, 1786-1869.*
Papers, 1802-69. 12 ft. (2700 items).

In Library Company of Philadelphia Collections (Philadelphia, Pennsylvania).

Physician, psychologist, and author. Correspondence, an incomplete manuscript of Rush's *Philosophy of the Human Voice;* invitations and visiting cards, and other papers. Includes correspondence of his student days at Edinburgh and London.

Bequest of Dr. Rush, 1869.

384. *Rutland Corner House, Boston, Massachusetts.*
Records, 1877-1966. ca. 7 ft.

In Radcliffe College, Schlesinger Library on the History of Women in America (Cambridge, Massachusetts).

Superintendent's correspondence, annual reports, minutes of board meetings, evaluation records, vital statistics, and visitors books, of a home for working women, which later became a lodging for women awaiting placement by community agencies, and finally a home for female psychiatric patients.

Unpublished inventory in the library.

Information on literary rights available in the library.

Gift of Mrs. Herbert P. Gleason on behalf of Rutland Corner House, 1970.

385. *St. Louis State Hospital.*
Records, 1869-1935. 35 books.

In University of Missouri-Columbia School of Medicine Library and Missouri Institute of Psychiatry (St. Louis, Missouri).

Patients historical registers (1869-1911), including admission dates and patient population statistics. Miscellaneous records (1869-1935) include employee population statistics, clinical records, day and night restraint records, admissions and discharges, staff wages, goods received, and correspondence.

Use of records is restricted.

386. *St. Paul Phrenological Society.*
Records, 1890-99. 3 vols. and 1 box.

In Minnesota Historical Society Collections (St. Paul, Minnesota).

Correspondence, essays on phrenology written by members of the organization; minutes of meetings, financial records, constitution, and bylaws, of a society formed to study phrenology and to build a collection of phrenological publications, pictures, and objects. Includes information about lectures given at meetings of the society and elsewhere, and about the purchase of items for its collection; includes a report of an interview of Professor George Morris with Coleman and James Younger in the state prison at Stillwater, Minnesota; and character studies by Morris of various inmates of the prison.

387. *St. Peter State Hospital, St. Peter, Minnesota*
Records, 1862-1972. 21 ft.
In Minnesota Historical Society, Southern Minnesota Historical Center, Mankato State College (Mankato, Minnesota).
Correspondence, research notes, building plans, ledgers and photos, relating to a state mental hospital

388. *Salisbury, Helen.*
Papers, ca. 1890-1927. 1¼ in.
In Iowa State Historical Society Library (Iowa City, Iowa).
Letters and documents collected by Salisbury, including photos and programs of the Hospital for the Insane in Independence, Iowa.

389. *Sanborn, Herbert Charles, 1873-1967.*
Papers, 1900-66. ca. 16 ft. (ca. 10,715 items).
In Vanderbilt University Library (Nashville, Tennessee).
Author, educator, and professor of philosophy and psychology at Vanderbilt University in Nashville, Tennessee. Correspondence, research notes, student notebooks, business papers, manuscripts of writings; essays, articles, book reviews written by Sanborn, newspaper and magazine clippings on political and racial themes, phonodiscs of bird calls; photos, and miscellaneous papers, relating to Sanborn's teaching career. Includes material on dogs, goats, philosophy, politics, psychology, racial and ethnic themes, and social problems.
Unpublished register in the library.
Information on literary rights available in the library.
Gift of Mrs. Sanborn.

390. *Santayana, George, 1863-1952.*
Papers, ca. 1880-1946. 8 boxes.
In Columbia University Libraries (New York, New York).
Philosopher and author. Correspondence and literary manuscripts. Includes the manuscripts of *Realm of Spirit; Persons and Places* (vols. 1 and 3); *Idea of Christ in the Gospels,* and *Apologia Pro Mente Sua.*
Gift of Corliss Lamont, 1954 and 1958.

391. *Saperstein, Esther.*
Papers, 1949-67. 6 ft.
In University of Illinois at Chicago Circle Library (Chicago, Illinois).
Member of the Illinois legislature. Correspondence, biographical sketches, schedules of activities, legislative bills, minutes, memoranda, agendas, reports, studies, press releases, bylaws, and other papers. The material relates to Mrs. Saperstein's campaigns and legislative career, the improvement of mental health facilities in the state, raising the age of compulsory education in the public school system, redressing grievances over pensions of retired schoolteachers, legislative scholarships allotted to Mrs. Saperstein, discrimination against women in industry, projected highway needs of the state, and high school equivalency testing program for inmates of penal institutions and other irregular students. Corporate

bodies represented include the Cook County Department for Public Aid, Governor's Task Force on Education, Illinois Cities and Villages Municipal Problems Commission, Illinois Commission on Children, Illinois Mental Health Planning Board, Illinois State Toll Highway Commission, Juvenile Protective Association, Mental Health Association of Chicago, National Association for Retarded Children, Organization for Rehabilitation through Training, and Public School Teachers' Pension and Retirement Fund of Chicago. Correspondents include Richard J. Daley, Arthur J. Goldberg, and Otto Kerner.

Unpublished guide and index cards in the library.

Gift of Mrs. Saperstein, 1967.

392. *Sargent, Helen Durham, 1904-* .
Papers, 1910- .

In Menninger Foundation Archives (Topeka, Kansas).

Psychologist. Speeches, research data, and notes, regarding child development and the rehabilitation of the blind.

393. *Savage, Alexander Duncan, 1848-1935.*
Papers, 1860-1974. 3 ft. (ca. 1500 items).

In University of Virginia Library (Charlottesville, Virginia).

Museum curator, educator, and classicist. Chiefly personal correspondence, together with financial papers, translations and articles; a children's story entitled "The Stone in the Road"; biographical data, sketches, post cards, clippings, and photos. Includes Savage's descriptions of classes taught by Basil Lanneau Gildersleeve and Maximilian Schele De Vere at the University of Virginia, and the Universities of Bonn and Leipzig in Germany, where Savage also studied; descriptions of vacations on Staten Island and Virginia beaches; and material on the scandal at the New York Metropolitan Museum of Art, where Savage was assistant director in charge of classical antiquities, involving director Luigi Palma di Cesnola's supervision of reconstruction of antique statues. Includes letters from Savage's parents, Thomas Staughton Savage and Elizabeth (Rutherford) Savage, relating to life in Pass Christian, Mississippi, and Rhinecliff, New York, where his father held Episcopal pastorates; and letters from his brother, Dr. Thomas Rutherford Savage, describing medical practice at the Michigan State Insane Asylum in Kalamazoo. Correspondents include Luigi Palma di Cesnola, Gaston Feuardent, Richard Watson Gilder, Basil Lanneau Gildersleeve, and James Albert Harrison.

Unpublished guide in the repository.

394. *Scheerer, Martin, 1900-1961.*
Papers, 1939-61. ca. 12 ft.

In University of Akron, Archives of the History of American Psychology (Akron, Ohio).

Psychologist and professor at the University of Kansas. Lecture and class notes, student papers and examinations, reading notes, annotated reprints, experimental data, a large cartoon collection, and very little correspondence.

Index guide and unpublished register in the repository.

394. *(Continued)*
Open to investigators under restrictions accepted by the repository.
Information on literary rights available in the repository.
Gift of Mrs. Scheerer, 1968.

395. *Schilling, Robert, 1843-1922.*
Papers, 1852-1922. 1 box.
In State Historical Society of Wisconsin Collections (Madison, Wisconsin).
Forms part of the Society's Labor Collection.
Labor leader, reformer and politician. Correspondence, articles, speeches, a diary (1863-65), an autograph book from a Greenback Party in Wisconsin, and two volumes of names of workers for a Populist Party in Wisconsin and other states. Articles and speeches concern spiritualism, bimetallism, prohibition, and America's support of England in World War I.

396. *Scholer, Gustav, 1851-* .
Papers, 1874-1929. 6 boxes.
In New York Public Library (New York, New York).
Physician of New York City. Correspondence (1887-1929), minutes, notes of lectures on nursing in mental and nervous diseases, records (1920-22) of prescriptions, manuscripts of writings, German songs, printed matter, and other papers and records, relating to Scholer's career and interests, including his service as examining surgeon for the U.S. Bureau of Pensions, coroner of the city and county of New York, manager of Manhattan State Hospital (Ward's Island, New York), contract surgeon in the U.S. Army during World War I; his presidency of the Arion Society of New York, New York Turnverein, and West Side Tax Payers' Association; and his participation in German singing societies, the Hudson-Fulton Celebration (1909), the National Liberal Immigration League, war relief work, and German-American and Republican organizations. Includes writings by Joseph B. Mauch, and account books, minutes, and other records (1874-1911) of the Verein der Deutschen Patrioten von 1848-1849.
Described in *Dictionary Catalog of the Manuscript Division, New York Public Library* (1967), vol. 2, pp. 294-95.
Gift of Richard Helbig, 1930 and 1935.

397. *Scholle, Howard, 1885-1966.*
Scholle collection, 1861-1963. 70 items.
In Scoville Memorial Library (Salisbury, Connecticut).
Forms part of the library's Scoville Memorial Library Historical Collection.
In part, transcripts (typewritten) of originals in the possession of Francis Robinson (Lakeville, Connecticut).
Manuscripts of writings and other papers relating to Salisbury, Connecticut. Includes a history of Montgomery Lodge (Lakeville, Connecticut, 1933-63) by Harry Bellini; "Ore Hill Mine" (1960), by John Maloney; "Veterans' Graves in Salisbury," by Scholle; "Men of Worth of Salisbury Birth," by Malcolm Day Rudd; two volumes of typewritten and printed copies of manuscript articles prepared for future publication in book form by Scholle; and a record book

(1861-1913) and other papers of the School for Imbeciles in Lakeville, Connecticut.

Malcolm Day Rudd's articles were published in the *Lakeville Journal* from 1933 and 1946 on.

Gift of Mr. Scholle.

398. *Schools' and Students' Papers, 1819-1950.*
Addition, 1790-1923. 21 vols.
In Maryland Historical Society Library (Baltimore, Maryland).
  In part, transcripts.
  Copybooks, notebooks, and exercise books of students: F. W. Alexander (1855-56), Elizabeth Ann (Mattingly) Edwards (ca. 1845), Lot Robbins (1839), A. M. Rogers (ca. 1850-65), M. Stall (ca. 1810), William Watson (1790-91), and an unidentified member of the Ogle family (ca. 1795-1820); in the fields of arithmetic, chemistry, English, geometry, Latin, literature, mathematics, natural philosophy, and religion. Includes lectures on ethics (1792) and related papers of Rev. Charles Nesbit; lectures on psychology and fine arts, translations of "Prometheus Bound," and "Questions on Political Economy and Government" (1853, 1858) of Prof. J. Torrey, D.D.; a minute book (1919-23) of the Pi Delta Pi fraternity, composed of young men in Baltimore schools, including membership list; constitution, bylaws, membership list, and minutes (1820-22) of the Juvenile Polemical Society (location unknown); and an autograph album (1874) of Mary Ella Clendenin for the Lutherville Female Academy (Maryland).
  The Nesbit lectures and Torrey notebook contain indexes.
  A composite collection consisting of small groups of papers or single items listed and described separately in the repository.
  Acquired from various sources.

399. *Schroeder, Theodore Albert, 1864-1953.*
Papers, ca. 1842-1957. 54 ft.
In Southern Illinois University Archives (Carbondale, Illinois).
  Lawyer, author, and psychologist. Correspondence, legal case files, and bibliographies, relating to Schroeder's work as an evolutionary psychologist (1918-53) seeking to apply a psychological approach to writings on religion, law, sociology, and other topics; as an advocate of free speech (1900-ca. 1918) in New York City, where he was involved in the cases of Moses Harman, Jay Fox, Emma Goldman, Alexander Berkman, and Michael Mockus and led a movement to incorporate the Free Speech League (predecessor of the American Civil Liberties Union); and in Albany, New York (1911); and as a lawyer in Salt Lake City, Utah (1889-91), where he helped found the Democratic Party and the First Unitarian Society. Correspondents include Leonard D. Abbott, Alexander Berkman, Ilsley Boone, William Montgomery Brown, Anthony Comstock, Aleister Crowley, Clarence Darrow, Oscar DePriest, J. Carlisle DeVries, John Dewey, Havelock Ellis, Emma Goldman, Samuel Gompers, Benjamin L. Reitman, Upton Sinclair, and Lincoln Steffens.
  Inventory and name index in the repository.
  Information on literary rights available in the repository.
  Purchase, 1969.

400. Schroeder, Theodore Albert, 1864-1953.
Papers, 1846-ca. 1940. 3 boxes.
In New York Public Library (New York, New York).

Lawyer, author, and psychologist. Miscellaneous correspondence, manuscripts and reprints of Schroeder's articles and essays, notes, and printed ephemera, reflecting his interest in esoterica; together with material collected by Schroeder on Mormonism, including letters (1846-52) to Brigham Young from his wives, and letters to James T. Cobb of Salt Lake City, regarding the origin of the Book of Mormon.

Purchased from John E. Edwards, 1966.

401. Schroeder, Theodore Albert, 1864-1953.
Papers, ca. 1950-52. 60 items.
In Columbia University Libraries (New York, New York).

Lawyer. Correspondence, documents, books, pamphlets, and clippings relating to the development and dissemination of Schroeder's theory of evolutionary psychology. Most of the letters are from Schroeder to Mrs. Ethel Clyde, his friend and patron, and to Lesley Kuhn of Psychological Library, his publisher.

Gift of Ethel Clyde and Lesley Kuhn, 1962.

402. Schurman, Jacob Gould, 1854-1942
Papers, 1878-1942. ca. 26 ft.
In Cornell University Library, Department of Manuscripts and University Archives (Ithaca, New York).

President of Cornell University and diplomat. Correspondence, printed and manuscript copies of Schurman's speeches and writings, and newspaper clippings. The correspondence consists of letters written to Schurman during his tenure as president of Cornell (1892-1920) and letters relating to foreign affairs and national politics. Includes material relating to Schurman's position as a member of the Philippine Commission, to Republican Party politics, to peace problems after World War I, and to his service as U.S. minister to China (1921-25). Correspondents include George Frederick Behringer, William Edgar Borah, William Jennings Bryan, James Bryce, Albert Dinwiddie, Edward Eggleston, Charles William Eliot, Hamilton Fish, Joseph Benson Foraker, Gilbert Hovey Grosvenor, Othon Guerlac, Warren G. Harding, John Hay, Edward Mandell House, Charles Evans Hughes, Jean Jules Jusserand, Frank Kellogg, William McKinley, Hugo Münsterberg, Benjamin Barker Odell, William Lyon Phelps, Theodore Roosevelt, Jacob Henry Schiff, William Sowden Sims, Charles Proteus Steinmetz, Oswald Garrison Villard, John Wanamaker, Henry Lane Wilson, and Erving Winslow.

Unpublished guide in the library.

Also described in *Annual Reports of the Curator and Archivist: Collection of Regional History and University Archives, Cornell University* (1948-50), pp. 60-63; (1958-62), pp. 104-5.

403. The Scott Company.
Records, 1919-23. 3 boxes.
In Northwestern University Archives (Evanston, Illinois).

Records of the consulting firm established by Walter Dill Scott, a Ph.D. in psychology and educational administration (Leipzig, 1900), and professor of psychology and pedagogy at Northwestern University. The collection has been divided into five categories: general administrative records, business contracts, the testing and rating of materials, personnel materials for companies, and publications. Much of the material is promotional literature and guides to management of the corporation.

No restrictions.

Gift of Leonard W. Ferguson (Ohio University).

404. *Sears, Robert R., 1908-* .
Papers, 1944-65. 4½ ft.
In Stanford University Archives, Green Library (Stanford, California).

Professor of psychology at Stanford University. The collection is made up of several sections. One set of material pertains to American Psychological Association and includes agenda, minutes, constitutional information, and correspondence. Another set contains folders with correspondence, agenda, and minutes from several other miscellaneous committees and societies. A third set includes manuscripts, drafts, data, and correspondence, relating to two of Sears's books, *Patterns of Child Rearing* and *Identification in Child Rearing*. A final set includes data and other material from various psychological research projects, including the Kansas City Thumb Sucking Study.

Written permission of Dr. Sears required for access.

Gift of Dr. Robert R. Sears.

Additions to the collection are expected.

405. *Segal, Arthur, 1875-1944.*
Papers, 1919-68. ca. 2 ft.
In Leo Baeck Institute Collections (New York, New York).

European artist. Correspondence, manuscripts of writings (1919-44) on art, painting, architecture, the principles of optics, the therapeutic value of art, and related topics; autobiographical writings, lectures and broadcasts, newspaper clippings, and photos. Includes letters from S. Friedländer, psychiatrist and publicist, and from various psychoanalysts in support of Segal's application for a stay in England and the founding of his painting school for professionals and nonprofessionals, intended for psychotherapeutic rehabilitation for neuropsychological cases. In German and English.

Information on literary rights available in the repository.

Gift of Mr. Segal's daughter, Marianne Segal (London), 1968.

406. *Senn, Milton J. E.*
Papers, 1944-65. 10 containers.
In National Library of Medicine (Washington, D.C.).

The collection consists of miscellaneous writings and correspondence regarding the Gesell Clinic, Institute of Child Development, Cornell-New York Hospital, and the development of the Yale University Child Study Center. Copies of

406. *(Continued)*

lectures, seminar notes, and unpublished manuscripts regarding child study and development are included. Major correspondents include Louise Ames, Arnold Gesell, and Frances L. Ilg.

407. *Shaw, Ruth Faison, 1887-1969.*

Papers, 1913-68. 1 ft. plus 2 vols.
In University of North Carolina Library, Southern Historical Collection (Chapel Hill, North Carolina).

Personal correspondence and papers of Miss Shaw of New York, artist, educator, innovator in fingerpainting techniques; and consultant for the use of fingerpainting in psychiatric therapy at North Carolina Memorial Hospital in Chapel Hill (1959-69). Included are social and personal letters and two scrapbooks of clippings and photographs.

408. *Shelton Family.*

Papers, 1864-66, 1908. 10 items and 4 vols.
In University of Iowa Libraries (Iowa City, Iowa).

Diaries of Mary E. Shelton and Rhoda Amanda Shelton describing their nursing experience with Annie (Turner) Wittenmayer during the Civil War, and at the Hospital for the Insane (later the Iowa State Hospital) in Mount Pleasant, Iowa; and the Civil War diary of Orteus Carnefix Shelton, lieutenant in the forty-fifth Regiment of Iowa Infantry.

Gift of Helen Stewart Classen and Lucy S. Stewart, 1957.

409. *Sheppard, Moses.*

Papers, 1794-1927. 2 ft.
In Friends Historical Library of Swarthmore College (Swarthmore, Pennsylvania).

In part, transcripts.

Quaker humanitarian and businessman of Baltimore. Correspondence on the subjects of antislavery, colonization in Liberia, plans for a mental hospital, and on personal affairs; documents relating to the Sheppard Asylum, the American Colonization Society, spiritualism, and a variety of other topics; material relating to the libel trial of William Lloyd Garrison; lists of applicants for Liberia; business papers, deeds, wills, and financial records. Correspondents include Henry Ward Beecher, Matthew Carey, and Robert S. Finley.

Checklist in the library.

Gift of the Sheppard Asylum (Baltimore, Maryland), 1958.

410. *Sherwin, Martha May (Reynolds).*

Papers, 1919. 1 box.
In Vassar College Library (Poughkeepsie, New York).

Professor of psychology and child study at Vassar College (1917-18). Collection of papers and correspondence from when she was doing Y.W.C.A. work in France during 1919. Includes snapshots, guidebooks, postcards, and miscellaneous pieces, including Y.W.C.A. information publications.

411. *Shipley, Walter Cleveland, 1903-1966.*
Papers, 1941-66. ca. 2 ft.
In University of Akron, Archives of the History of American Psychology (Akron, Ohio).
Psychologist and professor at Wheaton College. Primarily lecture notes, course outlines, and examinations, together with reading lists and other course-related material, including student research projects. Includes material relating to the Shipley Institute of Living Scale and ephemera relating to Shipley's career. Major correspondents include R. G. Holroyd, Charles F. Mason, and Joseph Zubin.
Index guide and unpublished register in the repository.
Information on literary rights available in the repository.
Gift of Esther U. Sharp (formerly Mrs. Walter Shipley), 1968.

412. *Sizer, Nelson, 1812-1897.*
Papers, 1883. 6 items.
In University of Iowa Libraries (Iowa City, Iowa).
Phrenologist. Correspondence, catalog, pamphlet, and leaflet, pertaining to a description of a phrenological character which he presented to the Fowler and Wells Phrenological Cabinet in New York City.
Unpublished guide available.
Open to scholars.

413. *Smith, Bunnie Othaniel, 1903-   .*
Papers, 1949-69. ca. 7 ft.
In University of Illinois Archives (Urbana, Illinois).
Professor of education and department head, University of Illinois. Correspondence with college and university administrators, students, officers of the American Educational Research Association, Educational Testing Service, National Education Association, Philosophy of Education Society, and other professional organizations and governmental officials; and manuscripts by Smith and others and other material concerning curriculum development, teacher training, the M.A. degree program, critical thinking and courses. Correspondents include Myron Lieberman, R. Bruce Raup, Harold Rugg, and Willard Spaulding.
Unpublished finding-aid in the repository.
Information on literary rights available in the repository.
Acquired, 1970.

414. *Smith, Henry Arthur.*
Papers, 1820-1929. 3 boxes.
In Minnesota Historical Society Collections (St. Paul, Minnesota).
Farmer and journalist. Correspondence and diaries, account books, books of poetry, clippings, and miscellaneous papers, relating to Smith's career as publisher of the *Mantorville Express* and the *Kasson Express,* and to pioneer life in Dodge County, Minnesota. Contains information on a trip made in 1820 by wagon from St. Louis through Indiana and Ohio; on weaving, knitting and other household crafts in Massachusetts; Baptist revivals in London, Michigan; and

414. *(Continued)*

spiritualist meetings attended by Smith. Includes papers of Smith's family in Massachusetts.

Described in *Minnesota History*, vol. 24 (1943), pp. 354-55.

Gift of Smith's daughter, Mrs. Ralph H. Brinks.

415. *Solomon, Barbara (Miller), 1891- .*

Papers, 1925-74. 7 cartons and 4 boxes.

In Radcliffe College, Schlesinger Library on the History of Women in America (Cambridge, Massachusetts).

Psychiatric social worker and vice president of the Massachusetts Society for Social Hygiene (1928-56). Correspondence, minutes, reports, and other materials, concerning Solomon's work with the American Association of Psychiatric Social Workers, the American National Red Cross, Boston State Hospital, Boston Psychopathic Hospital, and various hospital administrations, regarding psychiatric social work.

Access restricted.

416. *Sontag, Lester W.*

Correspondence, 1937-42; reprints to 1969. 1 container.

In National Library of Medicine (Washington, D.C.).

417. *Southard, Elmer Ernest, 1876-1920.*

Papers, ca. 1900-1919. 5 ft.

In Harvard University, Countway Library of Medicine (Boston, Massachusetts).

Physician. Professional papers; cases for the study of the anatomy of mental disease; drafts of articles; lectures in psychiatry (1916); criminology notes and letters; and autopsy reports.

Gift.

418. *South Carolina Psychological Association.*

Records, 1955, 1970-79. ca. 150 items.

In Winthrop College Library (Rock Hill, South Carolina).

Correspondence, charter of incorporation, bylaws and constitutions, membership directories, treasurer's reports, and newsletters, of an organization for professional psychologists.

Unpublished finding aid in the repository.

Permanent deposit by the organization through S. K. Mathews, past president.

419. *South Carolina Women Doctors.*

Collection, 1890-1940. 5 folders.

In Medical University of South Carolina Library (Charleston, South Carolina).

Biographical material about the state's women doctors, including Sarah C. Allen, a pioneer in psychiatry who graduated from the Women's Medical College of New York Infirmary in 1894.

420. *Southern Society for Philosophy and Psychology, 1932-76.*
In University of Virginia Library (Charlottesville, Virginia).
Minutes, correspondence, membership lists, programs, newsletters, accounts, yearbooks, and other papers.

421. *Spelman Fund of New York.*
Records, 1928-49. 42 ft.
In Rockefeller Archive Center (Pocantico Hills, North Tarrytown, New York).
Correspondence, reports, minutes, dockets, financial ledgers and journals, audits, administrative records, publications, bulletins, newsletters, and other papers, chiefly from the 1930s. Includes material on state leagues of municipalities, city and state planning organizations, state governmental departments, American Legislators' Association, American Municipal Association, American Public Welfare Association, American Public Works Association, American Society of Planning Officials, Civil Service Assembly, Council of State Governments, Federation of Tax Administrators, International City Managers' Association, National Association of Housing Officials, Public Administration Clearing House, and Public Administration Service. Correspondents include Winthrop W. Aldrich, Louis Brownlow, Cleveland E. Dodge, Robert M. Hutchins, Fiorello LaGuardia, Charles E. Merriam, Frances Perkins, John D. Rockefeller, III; Beardsley Ruml, Harold Stassen, Charles P. Taft, II; Joseph Willits, and Arthur Woods.
Unpublished inventory and partial index in the repository.

422. *Spender, Herbert, 1820-1903.*
Papers, 1849-1903. 148 items.
In Knox College Library (Galesburg, Illinois).
English philosopher. Professional and personal correspondence. Correspondents include W. R. Alger, Lady Amberley, J. E. Boehm, Sir Andrew Clark, Moncure D. Conway, Mary Cross, Sir John Evans, John Fiske, Sir Robert Giffen, Thomas Hodgskin, Lady Hooker, Edward Lott, Mrs. Lyn Lynton, W. C. McBain, Charlotte Shickle, Sidney Williams, and Edward Youmans.
Open to investigators under library restrictions.
Information on literary rights available in the library.
Gift of the Bookfellow Foundation.

423. *Starch, Daniel, 1883-1979.*
Papers.
In Morningside College (Sioux City, Iowa).
Early industrial psychologist, educated at Morningside College, State University of Iowa, and Harvard University. Taught psychology at Wellesley College, Harvard University, and the Universities of Iowa and Wisconsin. From 1924, Starch was consulting psychologist and director of research for the American Association of Advertising Agencies.

424. *Starr, Frederick, 1858-1933.*
Papers, 1876-1930. ca. 5 ft. (ca. 700 items).
In University of Chicago Library (Chicago, Illinois).

424. *(Continued)*

In part, photocopies (negative).

Professor of anthropology at the University of Chicago. Business and personal correspondence; diaries (1876-1926), stories, word lists and other notes on the Onondaga; Pampangan glossary; field notes from Mexico (1894-1928), the Belgian Congo (1905-06), New Mexico (1899), Indian territory (Kansas), and the Northwest; notes on observations of captive chimpanzees; notes on Cuba (1916), the State Asylum for the Feeble Minded in Lincoln, Illinois, the Pan American Exposition in Buffalo, New York (1901), and the Chicago World's Fair, 1893; 23 scrapbooks containing newspaper clippings of articles by and about Starr, book reviews, lecture notices, and personal interviews; student and class notes; and ca. 500 photos, mostly taken in Japan.

Unpublished guide in the library.

Information on literary rights available in the library.

Gift of the Library of the College of William and Mary, 1963; scrapbooks given by Lucy Starr, 1942.

425. *Steefel, Genevieve Fallon, 1899-* .

Papers, ca. 1923-62. ca. 17 ft. (ca. 17,500 items).

In Minnesota Historical Society Collections (St. Paul, Minnesota).

Correspondence, notes, records, reports of organizations, newspaper clippings, published material and other papers, relating to organizations in which Mrs. Steefel, wife of Prof. Lawrence D. Steefel of the University of Minnesota, was active. Represented are the American Association for the United Nations; American Association of University Women; American Council on Race Relations; Citizens' League of Minneapolis; Committee for the Resettlement of Japanese-Americans; Council House for Senior Citizens of Minneapolis; Fair Employment Practices Commission; First Unitarian Society of Minneapolis; Governor's Mental Health Commission; Highlander Folk School (Monteagle, Tennessee); Independent Voters of Minnesota; League of Women Voters; Mayor's Council on Human Relations; Minneapolis Family and Children's Service; Minneapolis Institute of Arts; Minnesota Conference on Children and Youth; Minnesota Independent Citizens' Committee of the Arts, Sciences, and Professions; Minnesota Mental Hygiene Society; National Council Against Conscription; Radcliffe College Development Fund; Unitarian Service Committee; Walker Art Center; Women's International League for Peace and Freedom; and the Zonta Club of Minneapolis. Correspondents include Joseph Hurst Ball, John Anton Blatnik, the Rev. Arthur Foote, Hubert H. Humphrey, Walter Henry Judd, William Bogard Pearson, Robert Clifton Weaver, Luther William Youngdahl, and the Rev. Reuben Kenneth Youngdahl.

Unpublished inventory in the repository.

Gift of Mrs. Steefel (Minneapolis), 1963.

426. *Stetson, Raymond H., 1872-1950.*

Correspondence.

In Oberlin College Archives (Oberlin, Ohio).

Professor of psychology. Major correspondents include Frederick B. Artz,

Arthur L. Benton, Alfred W. Hubbard, Clarence V. Hudgins, J. M. Pickett, Robert K. Richardson, A. T. Slater-Hammel, and James M. Snodgrass. Restricted in part.

427. *Stevens, Stanley Smith, 1906-1973.*
Papers, 1931-73. 11 ft.
In Harvard University Archives (Cambridge, Massachusetts).

Professor of psychology and psychophysics, and director of Laboratory of Psycho-Acoustics and of Laboratory of Psychophysics. General correspondence and related papers, professional and personal, including correspondence with individuals, professional societies and other organizations and journals; correspondence and other papers relating to Harvard University along with notes, manuscripts of speeches, and data; reprints by Stevens are included, and some relate directly to his work.

Information on literary rights available in the repository.

428. *Stigall, B. M.*
Correspondence, 1920-30. 5 folders.
In University of Missouri Library, Western Historical Manuscripts Collection (Columbia, Missouri).

Educator. Correspondence written while Stigall was assistant superintendent of schools in Kansas City, Missouri. Material relates to educational matters such as techniques of recitation, segregation of pupils on a basis of IQ tests, social and educational significance of mental surveys, value of tests given to soldiers of World War I, and one letter dealing with formal discipline. Correspondents include Allan Abbott, Wilford M. Aikins, W. N. Bagley, J. Carleton Bell, Thomas H. Briggs, Otis Caldwell, Flora J. Cooke, C. O. Davis, H. W. Dutch, Eleanore A. Field, P. C. Harris, Charles C. Hughes, Alexander Inglis, Charles H. Judd, L. V. Koos, J. Richard Lunt, F. M. McMurry, H. C. Morrison, S. Chester Parker, John Rush Powell, L. W. Rader, H. H. Ryan, E. B. de Sauze, Raleigh Schloring, L. W. Smith, David Snedden, Edward L. Thorndike, and Joseph K. Van Denburg.

Gift of Mr. Stigall.

429. *Stogdill, Emily, 1893-1976.*
Papers, 1923-66. 1¼ ft.
In University of Akron, Archives of the History of American Psychology (Akron, Ohio).

Psychologist. Lecture notes, reading notes, and early publications, including notes taken from lectures by Edgar A. Doll, A. Toops, and H. H. Goddard.

Unpublished guide available.

Psychologist and professor of psychology at the University of California at

430. *Stratton, George Malcolm, 1865-1957.*
Papers, ca. 1888-1957. 2 boxes and 9 cartons.
In University of California at Berkeley, Bancroft Library (Berkeley, California).

430. *(Continued)*

Psychologist and professor of psychology at the University of California at Berkeley, and at Johns Hopkins University in Baltimore, Maryland. Correspondence, clippings, notes, manuscripts of books and articles, relating primarily to his career as a psychologist. Major correspondents include Michael Amrine, Charles M. Bakewell, James M. Baldwin, James McKeen Cattell, Robert H. Gault, George Holmes Howison, Stanley A. Hunter, William James, James A. Joyce, E. B. McGilvary, John C. Merriam, Ira Remsen, Edward C. Tolman, H. B. Torrey, D. Warnotte, Howard C. Warren, John B. Watson, and Robert M. Yerkes.

Report and key to arrangement in library.

431. *Stripling, Francis T.*
Correspondence, 1864-69.
In University of Virginia Library (Charlottesville, Virginia).
Superintendent and physician at the Western State Insane Asylum.

432. *Student Notebooks, 1871-1931.*
ca. 3 ft. and 111 vols.
In Cornell University Library, Department of Manuscripts and University Archives (Ithaca, New York).

Lecture and field notebooks, laboratory notebooks and reports, model account books, syllabi, and other class work from courses in: ancient (European, English, American) and modern history; mechanical and electrical engineering; agriculture, animal husbandry, astronomy, botany, chemistry, classics, economics, education, elocution, English, entomology; French, geology, German, history, history of architecture, historical geography, industrial organization, international law, law, mechanics, meteorology, ornithology, philosophy, history of philosophy; physics, physiology, political science, psychology, rhetoric, sociology, waterpower, and zoology. These courses were taught at Cornell University by professors Felix Adler, Hjalmar H. Boyesen, George Lincoln Burr, Hiram Corson, Willard Fiske, A. Gudeman, Jeremiah W. Jenks, Ziba H. Potter, William C. Russel, Charles C. Shackford, H. Morse Stephens, Andrew D. White, Burt G. Wilder, and William D. Wilson. The notebooks were kept by Cornell students Carl William Badenhausen, E. Eugene Barker, Maurice C. Burritt, Nelson W. Cady, Gilbert Holmes Crawford, Thomas Curran, Harriett Mathilda Davidson, Herbert D. A. Donovan, William Gurley, Francis W. Halsey, Harry Hayward, Albert Huntington Hooker, Ida C. Kerr, Daniel Chauncey Knowlton, John Turrill Carr Lowe, Robert M. Ogden, Roger Williams Parkhurst, Henry W. Sackett, Abby E. Thayer, John Graham Thompson, Hector Tyndale, Mynderse Van Cleef, and Mary Willcox.

Described in *Reports of the Curator and Archivist: Collection of Regional History and University Archives, Cornell University* (1948-50), p. 68; (1950-54), pp. 29-30; (1954-58), p. 111; (1958-62), p. 107; (1962-66), p. 177.

433. *Sutherland, Robert L., 1903-1976.*
Papers, 1937-73.
In University of Texas Archives (Austin, Texas).

Personal and business papers of Sutherland, president/director of the Hogg Foundation. Records relate to his extension of principles of mental health to the University of Texas student counseling; terms as sociology professor; major role in planning and implementing legislation leading to community health programs in Texas; involvement in restructuring of foundations resulting from tax legislation; juvenile delinquency studies and research on Negro youth; dental, medical, and legal school programs of behavioral studies; bonds of cooperation forged between philanthropies in Texas and the southwest; investigation of the Charles Whitman Case; and co-authoring of a widely used sociology text. Correspondents include McGeorge Bundy, H. E. Butt, Merrimon Cuninggim, Norman Hackerman, F. George Farrar, Ima Hogg, Jack Holland, Wayne Holtzman, Ira Iscoe, J. Lee Johnson, Robert F. Kennedy, Charles A. LeMaistre, Ernest Neal, Manning M. Pattillo, Alan Pifer, Harry Ransom, Mrs. Bert Kruger Smith, Homer C. Wadsworth, and Nils Wessell.
No restrictions.
Donated by Robert L. Sutherland.

434. *Swain, David Lowry.*
Papers, 1763-1895. ca. 1200 items.
In North Carolina Division of Archives and History (Raleigh, North Carolina).
Includes a letter to Swain from Dorothea Dix concerning an institution for mental health care.
Published guide available.

435. *Swift, George Lucien.*
Papers, 1723-1900. 198 items and 1 vol.
In Cornell University Library, Department of Manuscripts and University Archives (Ithaca, New York).
Correspondence, notebooks, accounts, handbills, clippings, and lithographs, relating to Swift's tours as lecturer on telegraphy, electromagnetism, galvanism, popular science, and spiritualism. Other family members represented include E. B. Swift, Lewis Swift, and W. A. Swift. Correspondents include Herman Swift, Hiram Swift, Job Pierce, and Sabina Underwood.

436. *Szasz, Thomas, 1920- .*
Papers, 1949-78. 26 ft.
In Syracuse University Library (Syracuse, New York).
Professor of psychiatry at the State University of New York, Upstate Medical Center (Syracuse, New York). The collection is divided into six series: writings; legal files; correspondence; general files; writings—others; and miscellaneous printed material. The bulk of the correspondence (1956-70) is between Dr. Szasz and several publishers concerning matters involved in the publication of his writings. Also of interest are letters (1964) to the editor *Harper's Magazine*, and a small amount of correspondence with Charles A. Aring, Roy M. Grinker, Joost A. M. Meerloo, and E. Fuller Torrey. The legal papers (1959-62) concern a decision in a case before the U. S. Court of Appeals, in which Dr. Szasz gave testimony.

GUIDE TO MANUSCRIPT COLLECTIONS

436. *(Continued)*
The writings (1949-69) consist of miscellaneous writings, articles, book reviews, interviews, introductions, and speeches.
Restricted access to legal files and case studies.
Gift of Dr. Szasz, 1969 and later.

437. *Tallant, Robert, 1909-1957.*
Papers, 1936-57. ca. 470 items.
In New Orleans Public Library, Louisiana Department (New Orleans, Louisiana).
Author. Correspondence, literary manuscripts, notes, radio scripts, plot outlines, research material, scrapbooks, photos, notebooks, pamphlets, and other papers, relating to voodoo, spiritualism, and Negro folklore.
Finding-list in the library.
Open to investigators under restrictions of the repository.
Information on literary rights available in the library.
Gift of the Tallant family, 1957.

438. *Tallmadge, Nathaniel Pitcher, 1795-1864.*
Papers, 1812-60. 2 boxes and 4 reels of microfilm.
In State Historical Society of Wisconsin Collections (Madison, Wisconsin).
U.S. senator from New York and territorial governor of Wisconsin. Correspondence; memoranda and drafts of Tallmadge's speeches; and clippings from Washington and New York State newspapers. Correspondence relates mainly to political matters, including Tallmadge's support of the United States Bank; enforcement of claims against France (1834-35); and political appointments. Two letters concern Tallmadge's New York business interests; and two, written at Washington, D.C., relate to politics and to Tallmadge's experiments in spiritualism. Letters of James D. Doty, from 1841 to Tallmadge's appointment as governor of Wisconsin Territory in 1844, concern land speculation, patronage, and politics. Additional correspondents include members of Tallmadge's family, as well as George Bancroft, Nicholas Biddle, James Buchanan, Rufus Choate, Henry Clay, Edward Everett, William Floyd, Horace Greeley, Duff Green, William H. Harrison, Andrew Jackson, William Marcy, William C. Rives, William H. Seward, John Tyler, Martin Van Buren, and Thurlow Weed.

439. *Teal, Frederick F., 1875-1968.*
Scrapbook, 1862-1901. 1 vol.
In Nebraska State Historical Society Collections (Lincoln, Nebraska).
Physician, of Norfolk and Omaha, Nebraska. Correspondence and newspaper clippings relating to Teal's career, his service as superintendent of the Nebraska Hospital for the Insane (Norfolk, Nebraska), and destruction of the hospital by fire.
Gift of Dr. Teal, 1955.

440. *Tennessee Central State Hospital (Nashville).*
Records, 1891-1934. ca. 3 ft. (500 items and 50 vols.).
In Tennessee State Library and Archives (Nashville, Tennessee).
Correspondence (1926-27) of Superintendent W. S. Farmer; receipts (1891-1923) for patients' belongings and money; accounts (1898-1909) of W. D. Cartwright, steward; steward's cashbook (1904-11); history (1904-13) concerning individual patients; weekly reports (1916-32) of removals, discharges, and deaths; records of packages received by patients; and other records.
Unpublished register in the repository.
Information on literary rights available in the repository.
Deposit of Dr. William Tragle, Mrs. Martha Penn Davis, and Mrs. Hermione Embry.

441. *Terman, Lewis Madison, 1877-1956.*
Papers, 1910-59. 33 ft.
In Stanford University Archives, Green Library (Stanford, California).
Professor of psychology at Stanford University (1916-42); emeritus (1942-56). Correspondence, tables, calculations, charts, notebooks, news clippings, reprints, and other papers, relating to Terman's marriage study of gifted subjects, his investigations of the gifted and child prodigies, and tests and testing. Includes examples and keys of the Army Alpha and Beta Tests, the Stanford Revision of the Binet-Simon Intelligence Scale, the Stanford Achievement Test, the Terman-McNemar Test of Mental Ability, the Terman Group Study Test, the Attitude-Interest Analysis Tests, and the Male-Female Tests; and first and second drafts of Terman's mental and physical traits of gifted children (*Genetic Studies of Genius*, vol. 1, 1925), *Children's Reading* (1926), and biographical data for early mental traits of 300 geniuses (*Genetic Studies of Genius*, vol. 2, 1926). Major correspondents include Frank Angell, Elizabeth Bonbright, Edwin G. Boring, Herbert S. Conrad, Fred Duncan, Norman Fenton, Morris Fishbein, Arnold L. Gesell, Florence Goodenough, Leta Hollingworth, Emile Holman, Lowell Kelly, Truman Kelley, Heinrich Klüver, Harvey Lehman, Robert L. Thorndike, Ruth Tolman, and Robert M. Yerkes.
Partially restricted.
Gift of Terman Study Group, 1967, 1972; and Frederick Terman, 1976.

442. *Teuber, Hans-Lukas, 1916-1977.*
Papers, 1946-77. ca. 37 ft.
In Institute Archives and Special Collections, Massachusetts Institute of Technology (Cambridge, Massachusetts).
Sensory psychologist and physiologist. Collection includes correspondence, manuscripts of publications, reprints, conference files, research notes, tapes and transcripts of course lectures, appointment calendars for 1951 and for 1959 through 1976, some administrative papers concerning the MIT Department of Psychology, and material concerning the *Handbook of Sensory Physiology*. Also included are 9 linear feet of videotapes of Teuber's psychology courses dated 1968 to 1970.

443. *Thilly, Frank, 1865-1934.*
Papers, 1889-1935. ca. 3 ft.
In Cornell University Library, Department of Manuscripts and University Archives (Ithaca, New York).

Professor of philosophy. Correspondence and lecture notes relating to Thilly's career at the University of Missouri, Princeton University, and Cornell University; notes in German (ca. 1889-90) taken by Thilly while studying at the Universities of Berlin and Heidelberg under Kuno Fischer, Friedrich Paulsen, and others; newspaper clippings; and other papers. Correspondence (1904-21) with Woodrow Wilson concerns Thilly's call to Princeton, administrative matters during Thilly's years there, and his recommendations of several men for national and local office during Wilson's terms as president. Other correspondents include Felix Adler, Ernest Albee, Benjamin Cardozo, Lord Charnwood, Morris R. Cohen, James E. Creighton, Charles W. Dabney, John Dewey, Livingston Farrand, James Morgan Hart, John Grier Hibben, William James, Hugo Münsterberg, Friedrich Paulsen, Cuthbert W. Pound, Josiah Royce, Nathaniel Schmidt, Jacob Gould Schurman, T. V. Smith, William Ritchie Sorley, William Strunk, Jr., William Howard Taft, Joseph P. Tumulty, Andrew Dickson White, and Stephen S. Wise.

Unpublished guide in the library.
Gift of Gertrude Thilly, 1962.

444. *Thompson, Helen, 1897-   .*
Correspondence, 1926-36. 1 container.
In National Library of Medicine (Washington, D.C.).

445. *Thorndike, Edward Lee, 1874-1949.*
Papers, 1900-38 and undated. ca. 100 items.
In Library of Congress, Manuscript Division (Washington, D.C.).

Educator. Articles, lectures, speeches, and research notes associated with Thorndike's pioneer studies in educational psychology. Includes three items of correspondence.

Unpublished finding-aid in the library.
Gift of Mrs. Thomas W. Cope, 1966, 1968.

446. *Thurber, Henry Thomas, 1854-1904.*
Papers, ca. 1871-ca. 1900. 8 vols. and 1 wallet.
In Detroit Public Library, Burton Historical Collection (Detroit, Michigan).

Lawyer of Detroit, and private secretary to President Grover Cleveland. Personal and legal correspondence, including correspondence (1894-96) kept by Thurber while secretary to President Cleveland; and correspondence (1872-1900) pertaining to the Connecticut General Life Insurance Company of Hartford; a notebook on psychology which Thurber kept while a student at the University of Michigan; two address books; and minutes (1871-72) of meetings of the Ladies Home Missionary Society of the First Presbyterian Church of Detroit.

447. *Titchener, Edward Bradford, 1867-1927.*
Papers, 1888-1929. 5 ft.
In Cornell University Library, Department of Manuscripts and University Archives (Ithaca, New York).
Professor of psychology at Cornell University. Largely correspondence presenting a picture of the professional status and varied interests of Titchener, a scholar of international reputation; and containing much information on fellow psychologists, psychology departments at other universities, and the struggle of a relatively young discipline to establish itself in the academic world. Correspondents include Frank Angell, James R. Angell, J. W. Baird, J. Mark Baldwin, E. G. Boring, J. McKeen Cattell, Karl M. Dallenbach, John Dewey, Raymond Dodge, Samuel W. Fernberger, G. Stanley Hall, William James, Joseph Jastrow, Charles Judd, A. Kirschmann, Oswald Külpe, Christine Ladd Franklin, Herbert Langfeld, Hugo Münsterberg, A. H. Pierce, Walter B. Pillsbury, Josiah Royce, Edmund Clark Sanford, Carl E. Seashore, E. L. Thorndike, R. A. Tsanoff, Howard C. Warren, John B. Watson, Louis N. Wilson, Howland Wood, and Robert Yerkes.
Unpublished guide available in the library.
Gifts from various persons, 1960.

448. *Titchener, Edward Bradford, 1867-1927.*
Papers, 1888-1929.
Addition, 1887-1940. ca. 275 items and 1 vol.
In Cornell University Library, Department of Manuscripts and University Archives (Ithaca, New York).
Professor of psychology at Cornell University. Correspondence with colleagues and students, mainly concerned with Titchener's and his fellow psychologists' research and writings, and with the *American Journal of Psychology;* photos, and other papers. Includes two letters from Walter Pater and one from Sigmund Freud. Other correspondents include Frank Angell, Edwin G. Boring, J. McKeen Cattell, Raymond Dodge, G. Stanley Hall, Edwin B. Holt, William James, Joseph Jastrow, Oswald Külpe, Herbert S. Langfeld, Walter B. Pillsbury, Edmund C. Sanford, Harry P. Weld, and Paul T. Young.

449. *Tolman, Edward Chace, 1886-1959.*
Papers, 1915-57. 4 ft.
In University of Akron, Archives of the History of American Psychology (Akron, Ohio).
Psychologist and professor at the University of California at Berkeley. Correspondence, manuscripts of writings with annotations, notes and outlines of designs and proposals for future research, charts, calculation sheets; and classroom material, including lecture outlines, notebooks, and chapter drafts for proposed textbooks. Major correspondents include Floyd Allport, Leonard

449. *(Continued)*
Doob, Otto Klineberg, Sigmund Koch, I. Krechevsky, Zing Yang Kuo, Edwin B. Newman, T. C. Schneirla, Helen Service, and Lewis M. Terman.
Index guide and unpublished register in the repository.
Open to investigators under restrictions accepted by the repository.
Information on literary rights available in the repository.
Gift of David Krech, 1967.

450. *Tolman, Edward Chace, 1886-1959.*
Papers, 1949-56. 3 boxes.
In University of California at Berkeley, Bancroft Library (Berkeley, California).
    Professor of psychology at the University of California at Berkeley. Correspondence, statements, legal documents in *Tolman* v. *Underhill* and *Kelley* v. *Regents,* and related cases; printed material, and clippings, relating to the loyalty oath controversy at the University of California.
    Key to arrangement in the library.

451. *Trocchi, Alexander, 1925-* .
Papers, 1947-68. ca. 205 items and 21 boxes.
In Washington University Library (St. Louis, Missouri).
    British author. Correspondence, short stories, poems, essays, articles, autobiographical sketches, unfinished novels, other writings, notes, notebooks, journals, photos, printed material, and other papers, relating to personal and business affairs, the Cardiff Commonwealth Arts Festival (1965), Project Sigma (an international cultural project, Sigma Netherlands), drug experiences, the problem of dangerous drugs, actions by the Dutch authorities against drug users, treatment of schizophrenics, psychiatry, and various art and theater projects. Includes contributions to and papers relating to the business affairs of *Merlin,* a review edited by Trocchi and copublished by Alice Jane Lougee; *Collection Merlin,* an Olympian Press series; and the periodical *Nimbus.* Persons represented include Donald Allen, Richard Alpert, George Andrews, A. J. Ayer, Martin Bax, Samuel Beckett, Oliver Boelen, Patrick Bowles, Stan Brakhage, Basil Bunting, William Burford, William Burroughs, Alfred Chester, Tom Clark, Ira Cohen, Robert Creeley, Edward Dorn, Bernard Frechtman, Maurice Girodias, William Harpe, Henry Chales Hatcher, Michael Hollingshead, Eric Graham Howe, Ted Hughes, Tristam Hull, Stanley Kunitz, Ronald Laing, Beba Lavring, Timothy Leary, Lawrence Lipton, Joan Littlewood, Christopher Logue, George MacBeth, Hugh McDiarmid, Tom McGrath, Norman Mailer, Peter Mathiesen, Daniel Mauroc, Ralph Metzner, Gil Orlovitz, Eric Price, Ann Quin, Herbert Read, Alan Riddell, William Sansom, Richard Seaver, Clancy Signal, Florence Margaret (Stevie) Smith, Stephen Spender, Peter Stansill, Edith Austyn Wainhouse, Arnold Wesker, and Colin Wilson.
    Unpublished finding-aid in the library.
    Purchase, 1967-68.

452. *Tufts, James Hayden, 1862-1942.*
Papers, 1785-1942. ca. 2 ft.
In Amherst College Library (Amherst, Massachusetts).
Professor of philosophy at the University of Chicago. Chiefly genealogical material, together with correspondence and other family papers. Includes letters of Rev. James Tufts, Sr. (1764-1841) and Rev. James Tufts, Jr. (1812-1901). Correspondents include Jane Addams, Mary Whiton Calkins, John Dewey, and Josiah Royce.
Unpublished guide in the library.

453. *Tufts, James Hyden, 1862-1942.*
Papers, 1871-1943. 1 ft.
In Southern Illinois University Library (Carbondale, Illinois).
Professor of philosophy at the University of Chicago. Chiefly correspondence between Tufts and his grown children, Irene and James Warren Tufts; a diary (1871); genealogies of Tufts's father, Rev. James Tufts, and his mother, Mary E. (Warren) Tufts; a memorial volume to Tufts; and other papers. Includes eight letters from John Dewey and one from Alfred North Whitehead.
Unpublished inventory in the repository.
Information on literary rights available in the repository.
Gift of James W. Tufts, 1968-69.

454. *Umstead, John Wesley, 1889-1968.*
Papers, 1939-65. 2 ft.
In University of North Carolina at Chapel Hill Library, Southern Historical Collection (Chapel Hill, North Carolina).
In part, copies.
State legislator from Orange County, North Carolina; and trustee of the University of North Carolina at Chapel Hill. Correspondence (chiefly 1957-60) relating to Umstead's activities on behalf of the university, the North Carolina General Assembly, and the North Carolina Hospitals Board of Control, which supervised mental hospitals throughout the state.
Access restricted in part until the year 2002.

455. *United Charities of Chicago.*
Records, 1867-1971. 30 ft.
In Chicago Historical Society Library (Chicago, Illinois).
Correspondence, minutes, bylaws, financial records, radio scripts, casework, statistical and intake reports, case histories, manuals, handbooks, pamphlets, bulletins, newsletters, other printed material, scrapbooks, filmstrips, and photos, relating to the aged, economic conditions, foreign population, camping programs, divorce, employees' organizations, legal aid, mental hygiene, Negroes, public welfare, children, and unwed mothers in Chicago. Includes correspondence, minutes, and other records of two predecessor organizations, Chicago Bureau of Charities (1894-1909) and Chicago Relief and Aid Society (1867-1909); a

455. *(Continued)*

history (1857-1957) of the organizations by Gudrun Rom; material relating to the Chicago Relief and Aid Society's service to victims of the Chicago fire (1871); correspondence (1919-47) of Joel Hunter (1882-1970), general superintendent of the organization; correspondence (1919-30) of Amelia Sears (1872-1946), assistant general superintendent; and scattered items pertaining to the Social Service Employees' Union.

Unpublished guide in the library.

Access restricted in part.

Information on literary rights available in the library.

Gift of the organization, 1967-73.

456. *United Neighborhood Houses of New York.*

Records, 1898-1961. 45 ft.

In University of Minnesota Library, Social Welfare History Archives (Minneapolis, Minnesota).

Correspondence, committee minutes, reports, and newspaper clippings of a federation of New York City settlement houses, describing its drive for child labor legislation, housing reforms, relief, unemployment programs, education of immigrants, protection of consumer interests, guarantees of civil liberties, interracial harmony, elimination of juvenile delinquency, treatment of physical and mental health of the urban poor, recognition of minority groups' interests, solving domestic problems during World Wars I and II, and urban development. Includes papers (1900-1919) of the Association of Neighborhood Workers, New York, predecessor of United Neighborhood Houses. Organizations represented include the American Association of Social Workers; Association for Improving the Condition of the Poor, New York; Association of Brooklyn Settlements, Brooklyn; Brooklyn Neighborhood Houses Fund; Charity Organization Society, New York; Federal Housing Administration; International Conference of Social Work; League of Mother's Clubs, New York; National Association of Social Workers, National Conference of Social Work; National Federation of Settlements and Neighborhood Houses; National Urban League; United Nations; Welfare Council of New York City; and the Works Progress Administration. Persons represented include Jane Addams, John Lovejoy Elliott, Mark K. Simkhovitch, and Lillian D. Wald.

Unpublished description in the library.

Open to investigators under library restrictions.

Information on literary rights available in the library.

Deposited by the United Neighborhood Houses, 1969.

457. *Upson, Bennett, 1809-1856.*

Papers, 1836-58. ca. 80 items.

In Yale University Library (New Haven, Connecticut).

Collection agent for Atkins, Allen & Company in Bristol, Connecticut. Correspondence between Upson and his wife, Ursula (Hotchkiss) Upson (1815-1863), a spiritualist, of Wolcott, Connecticut, largely concerned with his work collecting debts and selling cotton gins in Alabama, Louisiana, Mississippi, and Texas; together with other family and business correspondence and papers.

Catalogued in the library.

Information on literary rights available in the library.

458. *Vander Lugt, William, 1902- .*

Papers, 1953-71. 500 items.

In Hope College Archives (Holland, Michigan).

Professor of psychology and philosophy, dean, and chancellor of Hope College. Correspondence, a manuscript of a speech to a mock United Nations assembly, office files (1959-66), and clippings.

Inventory of office files in the repository.

459. *Van Waters, Miriam, 1887-1974.*

Papers, 1924-31. 11 ft.

In Harvard Law School Library (Cambridge, Massachusetts).

Psychologist, penologist, penal administrator, and author. Correspondence, case histories, reports, and statistical summaries, concerning Van Waters's work with criminal justice in greater Boston, specifically in the handling of juvenile delinquents in courts, schools, and social agencies.

Unpublished guide available.

460. *Vaux Family.*

Papers, 1686-1893. ca. 4500 items.

In Historical Society of Pennsylvania Collections (Philadelphia, Pennsylvania).

Correspondence, including about 2000 letters to Roberts Vaux, a leader in the movement for free public schools in Philadelphia; papers of his father, Richard Vaux, including diaries (1779-82) and an account book (1789); poetry and prose (1762-1814); papers of Richard Vaux, who was major of Philadelphia (1856-57), including a docket book (1856), expense account, and checkbook (1848-52); notes on the Insane Hospital; ordinances, resolutions, receipts and accounts, minutes of stockholders of the Bank of Northern Liberties; scrapbooks (1831-80), visiting cards, invitations, and printed notices of social and cultural events. Correspondence pertains to social and political reform, penology, regulation of hospitals, and problems of general welfare, as well as to personal affairs and local and national political events. Includes fifty autograph letters from officers in the French army (1686-1789).

Presented by Mrs. Mary Vaux Buckley.

461. *Vermont State Hospital (Waterbury).*

Records.

In Vermont State Hospital Archives (Waterbury, Vermont).

Material documenting the history of the hospital, material generated by research done by the hospital staff, and publications of the hospital staff.

Viewed by appointment only.

462. *Virginia Glenn Memorial Collection of Readings In Human Potential.*
Papers. 150 articles.
In Kent State University, Special Collections (Kent, Ohio).
The collection includes works in the field of parapsychology, psychedelic drugs, dreams, and the occult. Correspondence and a personal collection of offprints are contained in the collection; original contributors include Bernard Aaronson, Stanley Krippner, Gardner Murphy, Ira Progoff, J. B. Rhine, and Ida P. Rolf.

463. *Virginia Southwestern State Hospital (Marion).*
Records, 1887-1948. 57 vols.
In Virginia State Library, Archives Division (Richmond, Virginia).
Letter books, minutes of the board of directors, journals, ledgers, casebooks, lists of patients, supply records, and other administrative records.
Accession analyses in the library.
Transferred from the Southwestern State Hospital, 1952-58.

464. *Voltaire, François Marie Arouet de, 1694-1778.*
Letters, 1715-78. 8 boxes.
In American Philosophical Society Library (Philadelphia, Pennsylvania).
French philosopher. Chiefly letters written by Voltaire and collected from various places.
Described and listed in *American Philosophical Society Transactions*, vol. 48, no. 4 (1958).
Information on literary rights available in the library.

465. *Wakeman, Letha Evangeline (Ward), 1898-1974.*
Papers, 1908-74. 3 ft.
In University of Oregon Library (Eugene, Oregon).
Baptist missionary. Diaries; personal correspondence, including letters from Gilbert Gordon, a missionary teacher at Cameroons Protestant College in Bali; F. Richard Schneider of Eola Village, Oregon; the Winnebago Children's Home in Neillsville, Wisconsin; and the Bureau of Indian Affairs in Bethel, Alaska; missionary letters and publications from the Congo; family letters from Wakeman's children, her mother, and her husband, Andrew Vergil Wakeman, who contracted filariasis in the Congo and whose letters from Oregon State Hospital (Salem) are of clinical interest; memoirs by her mother, Effie Ward, a missionary to Lagos; records of the Oregon Migrant Ministry, including Eola Village, Gleaners Chapel, and Yamhill County Migrant Committee; and a manuscript biography of Wakeman, by Colena M. Anderson.

466. *Wallin, J(ohn) E(dward) Wallace, 1876-1969.*
Papers.
In University of Delaware, Morris Library, Special Collections (Newark, Delaware).

Clinical psychologist, educated at Augustana College and Yale University. Held positions in clinical psychology from 1906 at state training schools, psycho-education clinics, state departments of education, and the like.

467. *Washburn, Alfred Hamlin, 1895-1972.*
Reprints, 1925-52. 1 container.
In National Library of Medicine (Washington, D.C.).

468. *Watson, Elizabeth Lowe, 1843- .*
Papers, 1899-1921. ½ box.
In California Historical Society Library (San Francisco, California).
Suffragist and spiritualist. The collection consists of letters regarding spiritualism and also includes poems by Watson.

469. *Watson, John Broadus, 1878-1958.*
Correspondence.
In Johns Hopkins University Library (Baltimore, Maryland).
Personal correspondence with Jacob Hollander, Arthur O. Lovejoy, and C.W.E. Miller.

470. *Watson, John Broadus, 1878-1958.*
Papers, 1910-58. ca. 100 items.
In Library of Congress, Manuscript Division (Washington, D.C.).
Psychologist and advertising executive. Chiefly printed speeches and articles by Watson, relating to his work in behavioral psychology. Includes biographical information, correspondence (seven items), and two articles by Watson's wife, Rosalie Alberta (Rayner) Watson.
Gift of Ruth Lieb, 1971.

471. *Weaver, Rufus Washington, 1870-1947.*
Papers, 1903-46. 6 ft. (1730 items).
In Southern Baptist Convention, Dargan-Carver Library (Nashville, Tennessee).
Southern Baptist clergyman, college president, and author. Correspondence, sermons, bibliography, biography, manuscripts of unpublished books, scrapbooks, clippings, pictures, and other papers, concerning American Christianity, Baptist history, Christian education, religious liberty; and the relationship of philosophy, psychology, science, and politics to religion. Represented in the collection are Albert Henry Newman (1852-1933), Luther Rice (1783-1836), the Columbia Association of Baptist Churches (Washington, D.C.), the Education Board of the Southern Baptist Convention, the Joint Committee on Public Relations, Mercer University (Macon, Georgia), and the World League of Truth Seekers. Correspondents include Clarence A. Barbour, W. W. Barnes, Edward A. Bechtel, M. L. Brittain, S. P. Brooks, W. O. Carver, W. T. Conner, W. L. Cross, J. M. Dawson, Gov. Hugh Dorsey, Spright Dowell, John D. Freeman, Francis P. Gaines, L. L. Gwaitney, Gov. Thomas Hardwick, J. H. Kirkland, Ryland Knight, W. H. McDaniel, W. J. McGlothlin, E. Y. Mullins, Gov. Clifford Walker, Ray Lyman, Ray O. Wyland, and Bert Young.
Unpublished register in the library.

471. *(Continued)*

Open to investigators under restrictions of the library and the Southern Baptist Historical Commission.

Information on literary rights available in the library.

Gift of the Weaver family, 1954.

472. *Wenley, Robert Mark, 1861-1929.*

Papers, 1879-1929. 7 ft. and 39 vols.

In University of Michigan, Michigan Historical Collections (Ann Arbor, Michigan).

Professor of philosophy at Glasgow University and the University of Michigan. Correspondence, mainly dealing with Wenley's scholarly interests in philosophy and the University of Michigan; three diaries (1896-1927) of Wenley's travels in Europe and activities at the University of Michigan; twenty-one volumes of notebooks on philosophical subjects; and five notebooks of Kate Gibson Wenley. Correspondents include George P. Adams, James B. Angell, James R. Angell, James M. Baldwin, Frederic H. Britton, Marion L. Burton, Nicholas M. Butler, Edward Caird, W. S. Chang, John Dewey, James Donaldson, Robert A. Duff, Robert Flint, Alexander C. Fraser, Robert L. Frost, Michael J. Gallagher, Emma Goldman, Harry B. Hutchins, George T. Ladd, Oscar Levi, Alfred H. Lloyd, David Masson, Henry L. Mencken, J. Clark Murray, Chase S. Osborn, George J. Romanes, Bertrand Russell, Marten Ten Hoor, and Charles B. Vibbert.

473. *Wertheimer, Max, 1880-1943.*

Papers, 1885-1943. 9 cartons.

In New York Public Library (New York, New York).

Psychologist. Letters (1902-43) to Wertheimer from European colleagues relating to his work in Gestalt psychology; manuscripts of his lectures and writings, including *Productive Thinking* (1945); notes, notebooks, and miscellaneous papers. Includes papers of Wilhelm Wertheimer and of E. M. von Hornbostel relating to music and to ethnology. Many of the letters and papers are in German. Correspondents include Max Born, Albert Einstein, Carl Gustav Jung, Wolfgang Köhler, and Karl Mannheim.

Inventory in the library.

Gift of Ann Hornbostel, 1960.

474. *Wertheimer, Max, 1880-1943.*

Scientific and family papers. 10 cartons (ca. 30 cubic ft).

At University of Colorado, held by Michael Wertheimer (Boulder, Colorado).

Extensive correspondence including personal letters from family and friends, and hundreds of letters from scientific colleagues in many areas, including reprints of published articles. Many letters are from European scholars seeking help in leaving Europe in the 1930s, and these are often accompanied by biographical data. Correspondents include his major collaborators, his students, and his assistants, as well as Christian von Ehrenfels and Albert Einstein. There are also many course notes, folders of early drafts of chapters, and other material relevant to his *Productive Thinking;* various old family papers, and hundreds of photographs.

Open only on personal application to Michael Wertheimer.
See Mitchell G. Ash. "Documents of the History of Gestalt Psychology,"
Historiography of Modern Psychology, ed. Josef Brozek (Toronto: Hogrefe,
1980), pp. 187-200.

475. *West Family.*
Papers, 1837-96. 761 items.
In Virginia Historical Society Collections (Richmond, Virginia).
Chiefly correspondence, inventories, and accounts of John Shaddock West
(1815-1878), relating to his general store, John S. West & Company, in Buck-
ingham County, Virginia; and phrenological charts, and business and estate
papers. Other persons represented include William C. Agee.
Collection has been analyzed for the repository.
Gift of Mr. and Mrs. Thomas Branch Scott (Richmond, Virginia), 1973-74.

476. *Weston State Hospital.*
Records, 1860-93. 5 ft. and 1 reel of microfilm.
In West Virginia University Library (Morgantown, West Virginia).
Business records relating to the purchase of supplies, listing of employees, and
statistics on the operation of a hospital for the mentally ill, formerly known as the
Lunatic Asylum at Weston, West Virginia.
Gifts of Charles Williams, 1970, and Richard H. Ralston, 1971.

477. *West Virginia State Board of Control.*
Correspondence, 1909-49. 102 ft.
In West Virginia University Library (Morgantown, West Virginia).
Correspondence of an agency responsible for all state correctional institutions,
educational institutions, and hospitals. Persons serving on the board include J. W.
Barnes, J. A. Chambers, J. S. Darst, James S. Lakin, F. W. McCullough, Edgar B.
Stewart, J. Z. Terrell, W. R. Thurmond, and John B. White. Institutions repre-
sented include Berkeley Springs Park, Berkeley Springs Sanitarium, Bluefield
State College, Colored Old Folks Home (Huntington), Colored Orphans Home
(Huntington), Concord State College (Athens), Demonstration Packing Plant at
Inwood, Demnar Sanitarium, Droop Mountain Battlefield, Fairmount Emergen-
cy Hospital, Fairmount State College, Glenville State College, Gore Hospital,
Hopemont Sanitarium, Huntington State Hospital, Indian Mound Cemetery,
Industrial Home for Colored Boys (Lakin), Industrial Home for Colored Girls
(Huntington), Industrial Home for Girls, Industrial School for Boys (Grafton),
Jackson's Mill 4-H Camp, Lakin State Hospital, McKendree Hospital, Marshall
College (Huntington), Medium Security Prison (Huttonsville), Miner's Hospitals
No. 1 (Welch), No. 2 (McKendree) and No. 3 (Fairmont), New River State
School, Pinecrest Sanitarium, Potomac State College (Keyser), Rutherford Sani-
tarium (Beckley), School for the Deaf and Blind and School for the Colored Deaf
and Blind (Romney), Shepherd College (Shepherdstown), Spencer State Hospi-
tal, Storer College (Harper's Ferry), Welch Emergency Hospital, West Liberty
State College, West Virginia State College (Institute), West Virginia Tech
(Montgomery), West Virginia Training School (St. Mary's), West Virginia Uni-

477. *(Continued)*

versity (Morgantown), and Weston State Hospital. Correspondents include Charles H. Ambler, R. A. Armstrong, Thurman Arnold, Cleveland M. Bailey, Charles Baker, J. J. Cornwell, Brooks Cottle, John W. Davis, William M. O. Dawson, Denzil L. Gainer, W. E. Glasscock, Howard M. Gore, C. Howard Hardesty, Henry D. Hatfield, Thomas E. Hodges, Homer A. Holt, Rush D. Holt, B. M. Laidley, J. F. Marsh, C. W. Meadows, Robert H. Mollohan, E. F. Morgan, Matthew M. Neely, D. B. Purinton, Jennings Randolph, A. M. Reese, John D. Rockefeller II, W. R. Thurmond, Frank B. Trotter, J. R. Turner, and I. C. White. Transferred from State Records Center, 1967.

478. *West Virginia University.*

Archives, 1872-1948. 55 vols., 170 boxes, 8 bundles, and 9 ft of card files.
In West Virginia University Library (Morgantown, West Virginia).

Correspondence and records from the President's Office, 1872-1924; Office of the Registrar, 1897-1924; College of Education, 1896-1945; Department of Philosophy and Psychology, 1921-48; Office of the Treasurer, 1873-1926; College of Engineering, 1895-1929; and Agricultural Experiment Station, 1896-1944. Includes minute books of various faculty committees, ca. 1900.
Transfers, 1954-57.

479. *Wheeler, Benjamin Ide, 1854-1927.*

Papers, ca. 1870-1923. 1 vol., 11 boxes, 2 cartons, and 2 portfolios.
In University of California at Berkeley, Bancroft Library (Berkeley, California).

President of the University of California. Personal correspondence, writings, speeches, genealogical material on the Ide and Wheeler families, clippings relating to the university, and a few personal papers of Wheeler's father, Benjamin Wheeler.
Report and key to arrangement in the library.

480. *White, Andrew Dickson, 1832-1918.*

Papers, 1845-1918. 102 ft.
In Cornell University Library, Department of Manuscripts and University Archives (Ithaca, New York).

Educator and diplomat. Correspondence; manuscripts of speeches, articles and books; lecture notes and outlines; scrapbooks kept while White was a United States ambassador; travel photos, and other papers. The correspondence relates to family affairs and finances, White's college days at Hobart College and Yale University, his professorship at the University of Michigan, his service in the New York State Legislature, the founding and administration of Cornell University, educational ideas, civil service reform, the policies and activities of the Republican Party, the proposed annexation of Santo Domingo, activities and observations in Europe as attaché and later as minister to Germany, ambassador to Germany, and ambassador to Russia; the study and writing of history, and the study of art and architecture. Correspondents include Lyman Abbott, Charles Francis Adams, Charles Kendall Adams, Henry Carter Adams, Herbert Baxter Adams, Felix Adler, Louis Agassiz, Henry T. Allen, James B. Angell, Charles

Babcock, Theodore Bacon, Liberty Hyde Bailey, Ray Stannard Baker, Frederick A. P. Barnard, Henry Barnard, George S. Batcheller, Catherine Beecher, Henry Ward Beecher, Alexander Graham Bell, Douglass Boardman, William E. Borah, Vicenzo Botta, Clifton R. Breckinridge, David J. Brewer, Erastus Brooks, Lord James Bryce, George Lincoln Burr, Nicholas Murray Butler, George C. Caldwell, Andrew Carnegie, Joseph H. Choate, George F. Comfort, Roscoe Conkling, Thomas M. Cooley, Alonzo B. Cornell, Ezra Cornell, Hiram Corson, Augustus W. Cowles, Thomas Frederick Crane, Charles A. Culberson, Melvil Dewey, Timothy Dwight, Richard T. Ely, Edwin Emerson, Jr., Edward P. Evans, Elizabeth Evans, Moses Ezekiel, Francis M. Finch, Willard Fiske, Charles J. Folger, Joseph B. Foraker, Estevan A. Fuertes, Simon Henry Gage, James A. Garfield, William J. Gaynor, Daniel Coit Gilman, Edwin L. Godkin, Horace Greeley, Arthur T. Hadley, Benjamin Hale, Edward Everett Hale, Marcus Alonzo Hanna, George W. Harris, Benjamin Harrison, Albert Bushnell Hart, John Hay, Rutherford B. Hayes, Waterman T. Hewett, Frank Higgins, Frank Hiscock, Frederick Holls, John Wesley Hoyt, Elbert Hubbard, Gardiner Greene Hubbard, Ernest W. Huffcutt, Charles Henry Hull, Robert G. Ingersoll, John Brinckerhoff Jackson, Morris K. Jessup, Jenkin Lloyd Jones, David Starr Jordan, George Kennan, Joseph Kirkland, Philander Chase Knox, Robert Lansing, Pierre Emile Lavasseur, William H. Lecky, Francis Lieber, Henry Cabot Lodge, Seth Low, William G. McAdoo, Samuel Sidney McClure, William McKinley, Isaac Wayne MacVeagh, Edward Hicks Magill, Alfred Thayer Mahan, Samuel J. May, William Henry Miller, Edwin B. Morgan, Edwin D. Morgan, Justin S. Morrill, Theodore T. Munger, Charles Needham, Stanford Newell, Walter Hines Page, Herbet H. D. Peirce, Gifford Pinchot, Thomas Collier Platt, E. S. Plumb, Constantine Pobedonostzeff, Albert N. Prentiss, Harrington Putnam, Henry S. Randall, Whitelaw Reid, James Ford Rhodes, John D. Rockefeller, Sr., John D. Rockefeller, Jr., Theodore Roosevelt, Elihu Root, William C. Russel, Henry Woodhouse Sackett, Henry W. Sage, William H. Sage, Franklin B. Sanborn, Ernest Sarolea, Jacob H. Schiff, Jacob Gould Schurman, Carl Schurz, George Washington Schuyler, Hiram Sibley, James A. Skilton, George Washburn Smalley, Gerrit Smith, Goldwin Smith, Homer B. Sprague, Leland Stanford, Elizabeth Cady Stanton, Theodore Stanton, Robert Stein, Henry Morse Stephens, Anson Phelps Stokes, Jr., Oscar Straus, William Howard Taft, Ida M. Tarbell, William Roscoe Thayer, Baron Thielmann, Robert H. Thurston, Samuel J. Tilden, Robert H. Treman, Clarence Tucker, Joseph P. Tumulty, Moses Coit Tyler, Hendrik Willem Van Loon, Henry Villard, Lester Frank Ward, Charles Dudley Warner, Creighton Webb, Franklin Weld, Benjamin Ide Wheeler, James M. Whiton, Burt Green Wilder, Walter F. Willcox, Woodrow Wilson, Stephen S. Wise, Serge Wolkonsky, and Stewart L. Woodford.

Unpublished guides available in the library.

481. *White, Andrew Dickson, 1832-1918.*
Papers, 1845-1918.
Addition, 1850-1918. 4 items and 11 reels of microfilm.
In Cornell University Library, Department of Manuscripts and University Archives (Ithaca, New York).
In part, microfilm of originals in the National Archives (Washington, D.C.), the

481. *(Continued)*

New York Public Library, and the American Academy of Arts and Letters (New York City).

Educator and diplomat. Correspondence and dispatches (1878-82) from White during his service as envoy extraordinary and minister plenipotentiary to Germany; diplomatic instructions (1875-87) from the U.S. Department of State to White and other diplomatic representatives; correspondence (1884-1905) from George Frederick William Holls, lawyer and publicist, discussing Holls's successful opposition to the use of public money for religious schools in the New York State Constitutional Convention of 1894, the annexation of Hawaii, the death of the Mugwumps (1898), his work as secretary of the U. S. delegation at the first Hague conference (1899), and state and national Republican politics; and including an interview (1898) between Holls and Arthur James Balfour about American policy toward the Philippine Islands and its relationship to British and German interests in the Far East, and copies of Holls's correspondence with Alfred Thayer Mahan, another delegate to the first Hague conference; correspondence (1902-18) with Robert Underwood Johnson, secretary of the American Academy of Arts and Letters, concerning meetings and elections of the academy and its parent body, the National Institute of Arts and Letters; White's proposal of David Starr Jordan for membership in the institute and academy, and other academy business; and other correspondence with Millard Fillmore, Asahel Clark Kendrick, and Carroll Earll Smith.

A microfilm (149 reels) of the papers has been published by the repository with an accompanying guide entitled "Andrew Dickson White Papers at Cornell University, 1846-1919" (1970).

482. *White, Andrew Dickson, 1832-1918.*

Papers, 1857-1918. 82 items and 8 reels of microfilm.

In University of Michigan, Michigan Historical Collections (Ann Arbor, Michigan).

In part, microfilm made from originals in the Cornell University Library, Collection of Regional History and University Archives.

Educator and diplomat. Eighty-two original letters from White, chiefly to Professor and Mrs. Edward P. Evans, relating to national politics, American colleges and universities, travels in Europe, various scholarly interests, and many other subjects. The microfilm material (1857-65) includes letters to and from White and members of his family, personal accounts, and other papers, many concerning the University of Michigan and Ann Arbor. Correspondents include Charles K. Adams, James B. Angell, Levi Bishop, Charles H. Brigham, Datus C. Brooks, Francis Brunnow, James V. Campbell, Isaac P. Christiancy, Grover Cleveland, Thomas M. Cooley, Elizabeth E. DuBois, Corydon La Ford, Henry S. Frieze, Benjamin Harrison, Erastus O. Haven, Theodore Roosevelt, John Sherman, William Sinclair, William H. Taft, Henry P. Tappan, Moses C. Tyler, James C. Watson, Alexander Winchell, and DeVolson Wood.

Acquired, 1958.

483. *Whitehorn, John Clare, 1894-1973.*
Papers, 1916-73. 37 ft.

In American Psychiatric Association Archives (Washington, D.C.).

Professor of psychiatry and director of the Department of Psychiatry at Johns Hopkins University (Baltimore, Maryland). Correspondence, personal papers, manuscripts of writings, including books, articles, lectures, and speeches; photos, clippings, memorabilia, printed material, and other items. The material relates to Whitehorn's personal and professional life, including biochemical and physiological research at McLean Hospital in Waverly, Massachusetts (under Dr. Otto Folin), teaching at Johns Hopkins and Washington University (St. Louis, Missouri), service on the National Research Council (1932-57), and association with the American Board of Psychiatry and Neurology, the American Psychiatric Association, of which he was president, the American Society for Research in Psychosomatic Problems, and other professional societies. Correspondents include Karl A. Menninger, William C. Menninger, Adolf Meyer, and Merrill Moore.

Unpublished inventory in the repository.

Access restricted.

Information on literary rights available in the repository.

Gift of Joan Whitehorn Boggs, 1973.

484. *Whitman, Sarah Helen (Power), 1803-1878.*
Papers, 1835-   . 417 items.

In Brown University Library (Providence, Rhode Island)

Poetess. Correspondence, notes, articles by Mrs. Whitman and Edgar Allan Poe, and genealogical data. Subjects covered in the correspondence include Edgar Allan Poe, English and American literature, spiritualism, and personal matters. Chief correspondent is John H. Ingram. Other correspondents include William Whitman Baily, Ann Charlotte Botta, Ruth Burbeigh, George Bush, Ellery Channing, William Francis Channing, Maria Poe Clemm, George William Curtis, James Wood Davidson, Horace H. Day, Sarah Gould Day, Julia Deane Freeman, Horace Greeley, Louise I. Greenough, William Fearing Gill, Caleb Fiske Harris, John Hay, Marie L. Houghton, Thomas C. Latto, Stephanie Mallarme, Louise Chandler Moulton, William Douglas O'Connor, Epes Sargent, Rebecca Tillinghast, and Wilkins Updike.

Listed in the manuscript catalog of the library.

Gift.

485. *Wick, Grace, 1888-1958.*
Papers, 1917-58. 8 boxes.

In Oregon Historical Society Library (Portland, Oregon).

Personal correspondence, papers relating to Miss Wick's acting career, and papers concerning the occult sciences and religious groups, and a collection of radical political papers, including correspondence, publications, and ephemera, concerning anti-Semitism, antiwar, antifluoridation, racial prejudice, and similar extremist points of view.

486. *Wickes, Frances (Gillespy), 1875-1967.*
Papers, 1908-68. ca. 2300 items.
In Library of Congress, Manuscript Division (Washington, D.C.).
Psychologist. Correspondence, manuscripts of books, lectures, speeches, and other writings, family papers, notebooks, subject files, dream journals, poems, book reviews, and printed material, chiefly 1939-68, relating primarily to Wickes's study and work in psychology, especially psychoanalysis, child psychology, dreams, and the unconscious. Includes material relating to her work with Carl G. Jung, the Analytical Psychology Club of New York, and Psychology Study Group; and correspondence and writings of Gerhard Adler, Sir Martin and Gay Charteris, Chang Chung-Yuan, Alice Crowley, George Dangerfield, Chauncey Goodrich, Martha Graham, Harriet Jones, Robert Edmond Jones, Carl G. Jung, Rivkah Kluger, Henriette Lehman, Mabel Dodge Luhan, Monica McCall, C. F. Midelfort, Henry A. Murray, Muriel Rukeyser, Helen Thorp, and Eudora Welty.
Unpublished finding-aid in the repository.
Access restricted.
Gift of Mrs. Wickes, Muriel Rukeyser, Monica McCall, C. F. Midelfort, and Mollie Bryan, 1966-71.

487. *Wilder, Burt Green, 1841-1925.*
Papers, 1857-1924. ca. 7 ft.
In Cornell University Library, Department of Manuscripts and University Archives (Ithaca, New York).
Neurologist and university professor. Correspondence relating to the study of neurology, the Wilder quarter-century book, the Wilder brain collection, and activities of the Department of Zoology at Cornell University, and the study of spiders, clippings relating to vivisection; diaries; notes and charts relating to family genealogy; notebooks, pictures, and other material relating to Louis Agassiz; and a copy of Wilder's will. Correspondents include J.F.A. Adams, Elizabeth Agassiz, Louis Agassiz, Harrison Allen, Arthur Bean, Robert Bean, George L. Burr, Andrew Carnegie, John Codman, Anna B. Comstock, John H. Comstock, Eugene Corson, Hiram Corson, George W. Curtis, Margaret Deland, Alice Drew, Charles W. Eliot, Simon Henry Gage, C. L. Herrick, Oliver Wendell Holmes, Henry Holt, William Dean Howells, G. M. Humphrey, T. H. Huxley, David Starr Jordan, John N. Kellogg, D. S. Lamb, Charles Minot, Hugh D. Reed, Jacob G. Schurman, Louis Seaman, Goldwin Smith, Edward A. Spitzer, Henry Van Dyke, and Jeffries Wyman.

488. *Wile, Ira Solomon, 1877-1943.*
Papers, ca. 1894-1943. 21 boxes.
In University of Rochester Library (Rochester, New York).
Pediatrician and psychiatrist of New York City. Correspondence, articles, speeches, and other papers, reflecting Wile's many interests, particularly public health and social medicine. Includes much material on the early birth control movement in the United States, many letters from Margaret Sanger, founder of the American Birth Control League, and papers relating to Wile's extensive study

of left and right handedness and to other aspects of psychology, social and mental hygiene, and pediatrics.

Unpublished finding-aid in the library.

Information on literary rights available in the library.

Gift of Dr. Wile, 1943, and Mrs. Wile, 1944.

489. *Wilson, Robert Patterson Clark, 1876-1953.*

Papers, 1910-39. 2 ft.

In University of Missouri Library, Western Historical Manuscripts Collection (Columbia, Missouri).

Physician and superintendent of the Missouri State School for the Feeble-Minded and Epileptic (Marshall, Missouri). Correspondence and other papers relating to the problems and administration of the school, problems of the epileptic and the mentally ill, the idea of sterilization of the feeble-minded, and Democratic Party politics in Missouri. Correspondents include Wilson's brother, Francis M. Wilson, and B. Park, Lloyd C. Stark, and Harry S. Truman.

Card catalog in the library.

Open to investigators under restrictions accepted by the library.

Information on literary rights available in the library.

Gift of Francis M. Wilson, II, 1958.

490. *Winter, John E.*

Papers, 1906-58. 8 boxes.

In West Virginia University Library (Morgantown, West Virginia).

Head of the psychology department at West Virginia University. College notebooks, lecture notes, class outlines, speeches, reprints, material relating to Winter's study of the cardiopneumosphygmograph, and the psychology of faith healing, mesmerism, and spiritualism, and other office and academic papers.

Gift of J. Lawrence Winter, 1959.

491. *Wolfe, Harry Kirke, 1858-1918.*

Manuscripts, 1889-1918. ca. ½ ft.

In University of Nebraska Archives (Lincoln, Nebraska).

Professor of philosophy and psychology at the University of Nebraska and the University of Montana (Missoula). Manuscripts of writings relating to Christianity, ethics, evolution, philosophy of education, and moral training. Includes a short biography.

Preliminary inventory in the respository.

492. *Women's State Committee of Ohio for Public Welfare, Health and Education.*

Records, 1937-74. 20 items.

In Ohio Historical Society Collections (Columbus, Ohio).

Correspondence, minutes, programs, clippings, and twenty-fifth anniversary material, of an organization of women's club leaders interested in discussion and

492. *(Continued)*

amelioration of state social problems. Topics include prison reform, juvenile institutions, and mental health care.

Information on literary rights available in the repository.

Gift of the committee, 1974.

493. *Women's Suffrage.*

Collection, 1873-1902. ca. 25 items.

In University of Illinois at Chicago Circle Library (Chicago, Illinois).

Correspondence; includes letters from Lucinda B. Chandler in which she writes of her experience with spiritualism and other topics.

Unpublished guide available in the repository.

494. *Wood, Janet Margaret, 1907-   .*

Papers, 1936-53. 3 vols. and 19 items.

In Rutgers University Library (New Brunswick, New Jersey).

Social worker with the American National Red Cross. Collection includes articles on social work, care of crippled children, and the relationship of mental hygiene to public health.

495. *Woodbridge, Frederick James Eugene, 1867-1940.*

Papers, 1884-1940. 317 items.

In Columbia University Libraries (New York, New York).

Professor of philosophy at Columbia University. Correspondence, diaries (1937-40), essays, lecture notes, and notes on Woodbridge's reading, relating to his student days and later relationships with Amherst College, Berlin University, and the University of Minnesota.

496. *Woodworth, Robert Sessions, 1869-1962.*

Papers, 1935-64. ca. 500 items.

In Library of Congress, Manuscript Division (Washington, D.C.).

Professor of psychology at Columbia University. Professional correspondence, a typescript of Woodworth's *Dynamics of Behavior* (1964), notes for class lectures, obituaries and tributes to Woodworth, articles, and photos, chiefly 1948-62, the years of Woodworth's retirement.

Gift of Mary Rose Sheehan, 1970.

Additions to the collection are anticipated.

497. *Wylie, Margaret, 1889-1964.*

Papers, 1927-45. 46 ft.

In Cornell University Library, Department of Manuscripts and University Archives (Ithaca, New York).

Professor of child development and family relationships at Cornell University. Correspondence and work files pertaining to home economics extension work throughout New York State. Includes scripts of a series of radio broadcasts, "The Family Grows Up," and recordings of some of the programs.

498. *Wylie, Margaret, 1889-1964.*

Papers, 1927-45.

Addition, 1926-63. 23 ft.

In Cornell University Library, Department of Manuscripts and University Archives (Ithaca, New York).

Professor of child development and family relationships. These additional papers contain correspondence, reports, and mimeographed and printed matter, concerning various conferences, workshops, and committees pertaining to family life; course outlines (1931-39) and record cards (1933-63) giving dates of meetings, attendance, and topics discussed at Cornell child study clubs throughout the state; report forms from her trips as home demonstration extension specialist; questionnaires, study data, and other records pertaining to the Cornell Twin Study Club of Jamestown, for which Dr. Wylie was advisor; annual reports (1926-50) of the Department of Child Development and Family Relationships Extension Service; correspondence, memoranda, reports, and minutes of the Department of Child Development and Family Relationships; three filmstrips and seventy-five slides concerning extension work in child development and family relationships; and seven photographic records of the White House Conference on Children and Youth (1950). Also, mimeographed letters (1940-42) to friends.

Unpublished guide available at the repository.

499. *Yerkes, Robert Mearns, 1876-1956.*

Papers, 1898-1956. 1275 folders.

In Yale University Library (New Haven, Connecticut).

Correspondence from professional colleagues and incidental writers totaling 1787 correspondents. Files cover Yerkes's service to three universities: Harvard (1901-17), Minnesota (1917-19), and Yale (1924-58). Records cover service in two World Wars, including the organization of Army Mental Testing, service to the American Psychological Association, and his work with the National Research Council. Correspondence includes matters of editing the *Journal of Comparative Neurology and Psychology* and the *Journal of Animal Behavior*, and the founding and development of the Yale Laboratory of Primate Biology. Major correspondents include Carl Akeley, James R. Angell, J. W. Baird, F. A. Beach, Madison Bentley, H. C. Bingham, W. V. Bingham, Edwin G. Boring, Warner Brown, M. W. Calkins, W. B. Cannon, Leonard Carmichael, James McKeen Cattell, J. B. Conant, Wallace Craig, E. A. Culler, Harvey Cushing, C. B. Davenport, Raymond Dodge, E. A. Doll, H. H. Donaldson, Knight Dunlap, C. W. Eliot, R. M. Elliott, H. P. Fairchild, Abraham Flexner, Simon Flexner, L. K. Frank, S. I. Franz, Karl von Frisch, J. F. Fulton, W. H. Gantt, Arnold Gesell, H. H. Goddard, Alan Gregg, G. E. Hale, G. Stanley Hall, G. V. T. Hamilton, H. F. Harlow, William Healey, D. O. Hebb, C. J. Herrick, S. J. Holmes, E. B. Holt, C. L. Hull, W. S. Hunter, Julian Huxley, H. S. Jennings, H. M. Johnson, C. H. Judd, Arthur Keith, Vernon Kellogg, A. C. Kinsey, Heinrich Klüver, Wolfgang Köhler, Z.Y. Kuo, H. S. Langfeld, K. S. Lashley, H. S. Liddell, F. R. Lillie, Walter Lippmann, A. L. Lowell, C. E. McClung, William McDougall, D. G. Marquis, S. O. Mast, M. A. May, J. C. Merriam, Adolf Meyer, W. R. Miles, C. L. Morgan,

499. *(Continued)*

T. H. Morgan, Hugo Münsterberg, Carl Murchison, C. S. Myers, H. W. Nissen, G. H. Parker, I. P. Pavlov, Raymond Pearl, R. B. Perry, G. W. Pierce, Henri Pieron, S. L. Pressey, A. A. Roback, Beardsley Ruml, C. E. Seashore, C. S. Sherrington, E. E. Southard, K. W. Spence, C. P. Stone, W. N. Taliaferro, Lewis M. Terman, E. L. Thorndike, L. L. Thurstone, Niko Tinbergen, Edward B. Titchener, E. C. Tolman, H. A. Wallace, M. F. Washburn, John B. Watson, Earl Waugh, Warren Weaver, W. H. Welch, F. L. Wells, W. M. Wheeler, E. B. Wilson, Clark Wissler, R. S. Woodworth, H. T. Woolley, and C. S. Yoakum.

[This entry is reprinted, with permission, from: Edwin G. Boring, "Psychologists' Letters and Papers," *Isis* 58 (1967): 103-107.]

500. *Yerkes, Robert M., 1876-1956.*
Log, 1930-41.
In Emory University, Yerkes Regional Primate Research Center (Atlanta, Georgia).

501. *Zeller, Adelheid Bertha Marie Zoe, 1892- .*
Papers of Adelheid Bertha Marie Zoe and Cornelia Pauline Hedwig Zeller, 1911-18. 1 ft.
In Cornell University Library, Department of Manuscripts and University Archives (Ithaca, New York).

Notes kept by Cornelia Zeller in bibliography, biology, German, history, philosophy, and psychology classes at Cornell University, taught by Willard Austen (University librarian), Albert B. Faust, Charles Henry Hull, James G. Needham, Frank Thilly, Edward Bradford Titchener, and others; diary (1913-18) of Adelheid Zeller, later Mrs. Ilbert O. Lacy; account book (1912-16) of income and expenses of the Zeller sisters while Cornell undergraduates; and photos, concert and play programs, and memorabilia, pertaining to their student days.

Guide to
Manuscript Repositories

The purpose of this section of the *Guide* is to highlight some of the most important repositories of manuscript material in the history of psychology and related areas; to suggest ways in which researchers might work more effectively, especially outside of the United States; and to publicize some of the important but little-known sources available to the historian. None of the material presented here is based uniquely on the compilers' own research, though their experience has contributed to many of the sections. In fact, many of the essays and listings are based in large part on the work of others. In all cases, citations reveal the articles and books that were used in putting together the material presented. Some descriptions of archival and manuscript repositories include the institutions' own descriptions of their holdings as originally published in: National Historical Publications and Records Commission. *Directory of Archives and Manuscript Repositories in the United States.* Washington: NHPRC, 1978 (hereafter cited as [NHPRC]).

American Philosophical Society Library

The American Philosophical Society traces its origin to several mid-18th-century groups that met in colonial Philadelphia, often in association with Benjamin Franklin. For many years, it was the major scientific society on the North American continent, even after 1776, and its membership today consists of many of the leading scientists and scholars in the United States. The Society issues annual volumes of its *Proceedings*—which often include papers on the history of science—its *Transactions*—which are made up of monograph-length articles on a wide variety of topics—and its *Yearbook*. It also publishes occasional *Memoirs*, which are book-length treatments of important topics. The Society also awards annually many small grants—under $2000—for research in many areas, including the history of science, and in fact it has indicated that it has a special interest in stimulating work in this field.

The Society's Library is one of the largest manuscript repositories for the history of science in America, containing more than 7 million documents. In 1978, the Library described its manuscript holdings as follows:

> 18th and 19th century manuscripts, which consist primarily of correspondence, relate to science in general, including botany, entomology, geology, electricity, evolution, and medicine. 20th century documents, which include correspondence, diaries, laboratory notes, research reports, tape recordings, and photographs, concern chiefly genetics, biochemistry, quantum physics, and medicine. In addition, there are the archives of the Society and several scientific societies, as well as a collection of manuscripts documenting the history, customs, and languages of the American Indian. [NHPRC]

Many of the Library's collections relate to the history of psychology and allied areas; these are described separately in the body of this *Guide*. Useful descriptions of many other of the more important collections in the APS Library may be found in:

> Whitfield J. Bell, Jr., and Murphy D. Smith, compilers. *Guide to the Archives and Manuscript Collections of the American Philosophical Society*. Philadelphia: APS (*Memoirs*, vol. 66), 1966.

> *Mailing Address:* American Philosophical Society Library
> 105 South Fifth Street
> Philadelphia, Pennsylvania 19106
> *Telephone:* (215) 925-9545

American Psychiatric Association Archives

The American Psychiatric Association was founded in 1844 as the Association of the Medical Superintendents of American Asylums for the Insane. In 1892, its name was changed to the American Medico-Psychological Association and it became the American Psychiatric Association in 1921. Its archives reflect the growing interest of psychiatrists in their history from 1940 on and, though limited in scope, form an important source for the history of American psychiatry.

> In 1978, the Archives described its holdings as follows: Official records of the American Psychiatric Association since the early 1940s, in addition to some membership records, correspondence of secretaries, and letters of founders from the mid-1800s to 1940. There are also photographs of psychiatrists, mental hospitals and psychiatric meetings; tapes and tran-

scripts of oral history interviews with more than 50 prominent psychiatrists; record copies of all APA publications; microfilms of records; private papers of important individuals in the history of psychiatry; and memorabilia relating to psychiatry. [NHPRC]

Mailing Address: American Psychiatric Association
1700 18th Street, N.W.
Washington, D.C. 20009
Telephone: (202) 232-7878, ext. 204

American Psychological Association Archives
Library of Congress

Unlike most other archives, this collection has been deposited in a general repository, the Manuscript Division of the U.S. Library of Congress. These records were presented in installments—in 1967, 1968, and 1973. The first two gifts were organized in 1969 as Section I of the collection; the third was arranged in 1974 as a complementary Section II. Access to the APA Archives is unrestricted and single-copy photoreproductions of unpublished materials in the collection may be made without restriction.

Two entries in the body of this *Guide* present relatively brief descriptions of the collection's two Sections. This chapter provides a more detailed look at these papers by presenting a previously unpublished inventory of the collection prepared by the staff of the Manuscript Division and reprinted here with its permission. This inventory describes the collection as it exists in 1981, but it must be stressed that the APA is continually depositing papers at the Library and major additions to the APA Archives are expected in future years. Researchers are therefore urged to check in the Library's Manuscript Reading Room for unpublished descriptions and inventories of new Sections of this collection that will become available after this *Guide* is published.

The Library of Congress also holds as part of the APA Archives tapes of sixty-three oral history interviews conducted by T. S. Krawiec after 1971. These are presently being processed and will be available to the public in the Division of Recorded Sound of the Library of Congress. A list of those interviewed is appended here to the description of the main body of the collections. Additional oral history tapes are expected to be deposited in the future.

Mailing Address: Manuscript Division
U. S. Library of Congress
Washington, D.C. 20540
Telephone: (202)287-5383

BACKGROUND ON THE APA

Founded in 1892 and incorporated in 1925, the American Psychological Association, a professional organization for psychologists, numbered approximately fifty-thousand members in 1980. The primary purpose of the organization is "to advance psychology as a science, as a profession, and as a means of promoting human welfare." To accomplish these objectives, the APA holds annual meetings, publishes twenty-one psychological journals (as of 1980), as well as pamphlets, and books, and strives to improve standards for psychological training and services.

The chief governing body of the APA is the Council of Representatives, whose members include representatives from each of the association's thirty-eight divisions and affiliated state psychological associations. The Board of Directors is the administrative agent of the council and exercises general supervision over the affairs of the association. The board is composed of six council members elected by the council, and six officers of the association (president, past president, president-elect, recording secretary, treasurer, and executive officer). The executive officer, called executive secretary until 1959, generally administers the central office in Washington, D.C., and this office serves as headquarters and coordinating center for all APA activities.

SCOPE AND CONTENTS

As noted, APA records were received by the Library in three parts. The first two installments, totalling approximately fifty-thousand items, span the period 1906-65. They constitute Section I in the Description of Series and Container list in this Register. The third installment, dated 1912-72 and numbering approximately thirty-thousand items, constitutes Section II in this Register.

The collection as a whole spans over six decades, and is divisible into 14 files, or series, with appropriate subdivisions. Section II of the container list is a continuation of the container numbers in Section I, with the addition of two new series—M and N. The bulk of the collection is concentrated in the years 1940-68, with the majority of records consisting of correspondence and other official papers. In addition are reports, memoranda, personal records of various administrators, minutes of meetings, testimonies before congressional hearings, ballots, financial records, informational material, printed matter, and miscellany.

There are few records in the collection prior to 1930. For a succinct and early history of the APA, consult Samuel W. Fernberger's article summarizing the years 1892-1930 in the *Psychological Bulletin,* v. 29, Jan. 1932, pp. 1-89.

Except for Series G, J, K, M, and parts of Series D, which cover the Committee on Training for Clinical Psychology and the ad hoc Committee on Ethical Standards in Psychological Research, the collection is, to a great degree, a history of the association's central office from the files of the executive secretary, and, after 1959, of the executive officer. Largely administrative in nature, the papers reflect problems associated with the organization and management of the boards, committees, and publications under the direction of the executive secretary/officer.

The papers of Willard Olson (Series I), who was secretary of the APA from 1936 to 1945, and of Arthur H. Brayfield, (Series N), executive officer from 1962 to 1968, have been left largely intact, respecting the original arrangements of the files. These papers constitute a microcosm of the entire files for the period these officers served, although Dr. Brayfield's files also include some background material dating back to 1946. The complete files of other executive secretaries or executive officers who served from 1946 to 1962 are not available, but such files as are included in the collection are integrated primarily into the B, C, D, and H Series.

Another file which is left in its original order is that relating to the American Association of Applied Psychologists (AAAP), a separate and autonomous professional psychological society. This file (Series K) deals with the merger of AAAP with APA in 1946. The similarity in structure of the AAAP and the APA is revealed in the arrangement of the numbered series of this file.

Because the APA is the psychologist's spokesman in a wide range of interests, such as governmental and legal matters, evaluation of testing and training programs, and ethical standards, the diversity of subject matter in the collection reflects various specialized disciplines of all member psychologists. The APA maintains cooperative programs with other associations and attempts to coordinate activities which affect the practice of related social sciences and the medical profession. The Subject File and the General Committees Series contain correspondence and reports on topics such as gerontology, mental health, and insurance. Other subjects and areas of interest are the relationship between the APA and numerous governmental agencies, loyalty oaths for teaching psychologists, general ethical standards, civil rights for Negroes (Series A, annual meeting), and topics of current interest such as recognition of women and blacks in the profession.

One interesting file in the General Committees Series is that of the ad hoc Committee on the Ethical Standards in Psychological Research. This committee was charged with the responsibility of writing a code of ethics for the APA. The history of the committee over a four-year period is recorded in its efforts to determine acceptable practices in psychological research with human subjects. Sample surveys in 1968 and 1970 record actual practices and attitudes. of psychologists in research. Topics such as "use of drugs," "deception," and "misuse of research results" probe the entire field, and publication and editing of subsequent drafts of the proposed code elicit and incorporate ideas of psychologists from all over the United States.

Another interesting file is included in the Subject File Series under U.S.S.R. Under an exchange program in 1960-61, a group of psychologists toured Russia for an exchange of ideas and information in their fields. Memos and correspondence from this file report the effectiveness of the program as an exchange effort.

One topic of abiding interest to the APA is legislation which affects psychologists in their work. A researcher who is interested in various legal implications of a subject is referred specifically to Series J and N, and to Subject File topics on mental health, community mental health centers, insurance, congressional committee hearings, forensic matters, and the Jenkins case. Series N details Dr. Brayfield's involvement in legal testimony, legislation, and government agencies. During this period (1962-68), the APA took public stands on medicare, mental health centers, and on the inclusion of psychiatric and psychological services in health insurance programs.

Those psychologists who have a significant amount of correspondence in the collection are Isador Chein, Kenneth Clark, Dorothy Clendenen, John Darley, J. McVicker Hunt, Thelma Hunt, Erasmus Hoch, Fillmore Sanford, Leona Tyler, Dael Wolfle, Robert M. Yerkes, and officers such as George W. Albee, Arthur Brayfield, and Willard Olson. Other possible correspondents can be located by consulting a directory (containers M 17-19) for a list of officers for a specific time period.

DESCRIPTION OF SERIES

Container Nos.	Series
	Section I
A 1-6	Council of Representatives File, 1946-57. 6 containers.
	Letters and memoranda sent and received, reports, and ballots, grouped by type of material and arranged chronologically by month.
B 1-17	Board of Directors File, 1944-60. 17 containers.
	Letters sent and received, telegrams, minutes of meetings, agenda schedules, and ballots, grouped by type of material and by officers of the association. Material within the groups is arranged chronologically by month except for the correspondence of Dael Wolfle which is arranged alphabetically.
C 1-16	Standing Boards and Committees, 1929-65. 16 containers.
	Letters sent and received, minutes of meetings, telegrams, reports, surveys, by-laws, budget and financial statements, and miscellaneous material alphabetically arranged by board or committee and chronologically therein by month.
D 1-35	General Committees, 1920-63. 35 containers.
	Letters sent and received and reports, supplemented by telegrams, statistical data, studies, articles, newspaper clippings, and minutes of meetings, alphabetically arranged by committee and chronologically therein by month, with the exception of the Committee on the Certification of Consulting Psychologists (alphabetically arranged),

Section I *(Continued)*

and the Committee on Training in Clinical Psychology which contains correspondence arranged both chronologically and alphabetically and a subject file.

E 1-4   Representatives File, 1941-62. 4 containers.

Letters sent and received, supplemented by reports, memoranda, bulletins, and miscellaneous material, alphabetically arranged by committee or organization and chronologically therein by month.

F 1-10   Divisions, 1947-62. 10 containers.

Letters sent and received, bylaws, miscellaneous reports, and minutes, grouped by type of material and arranged chronologically under the division number.

G 1-8   Psychology and the Military, 1940-58. 8 containers.

Correspondence, reports, contracts, minutes of meetings, memoranda, studies, and miscellaneous material, arranged alphabetically by subject, committee, or government agency, and chronologically therein by month.

H 1-9   Subject File, 1931-62. 9 containers.

Correspondence, reports, agenda schedules, minutes of meetings, memoranda, printed matter, and other records, arranged alphabetically by subject and chronologically therein by month.

I 1-14   Willard Olson File, 1920-52. 14 containers.

Letters sent and received, memoranda, reports, circulars, telegrams, and other records, chiefly 1930s and 1940s, alphabetically arranged respecting its original order.

J 1-8   Conference of State Psychological Associations, 1942-58. 8 containers.

Correspondence, reports, abstracts, programs, charts, and minutes of meetings, grouped by type of material and arranged chronologically and by subject matter.

K 1-17   American Association of Applied Psychologists, 1935-47. 17 containers.

Correspondence, reports, minutes of meetings, telegrams, lists, account statements, circular letters, newsletters, abstracts, bills and receipts, and printed matter, divided into a numbered and unnumbered series. The numbered series (see Container List) respects the original order of this section of the file. The manuscripts in the unnumbered miscellaneous series are arranged alphabetically by name or subject.

L 1-5   Miscellany, 1906-52. 5 containers.

Monographs, printed matter, reports, speeches, and miscellaneous manuscripts, arranged by type of material.

Section II

A 7   Council of Representatives File, 1956-65. 1 container.

Memos and reports to the council, rules of the council, report of ad hoc committee, and correspondence.

Section II *(Continued)*

B 18-26 Board of Directors File, 1952-70. 9 containers.

Letters sent and received, agenda, proceedings of meetings, ballots, memoranda and reports sent to the board. Correspondence and subject folders for executive officers, particularly John Darley, who served as executive secretary, then executive officer, with inclusive dates of 1958-62.

C 17-22 Standing Boards and Committees, 1947-72. 6 containers.

Correspondence, agenda, minutes, subject files related to Board action, budget, bylaws, and annual reports, arranged chronologically by year, and alphabetically by subject under the board or committee.

D 36-68 General Committees, 1947-72. 33 containers.

Reports, correspondence, publications, studies, research materials, and background materials on committee activities. Arranged alphabetically under commissions, ad hoc committees, and committees, as well as alphabetically under the subject handled by the committee, and chronologically by year and month thereafter. Seventeen containers concern the ad hoc Committee on Ethical Standards in Psychological Standards in Research and include sample population studies and drafts of the final code of ethics of the APA.

E 5-7 Representatives File, 1954-65. 3 containers.

Reports, correspondence, agenda, and informational materials on organizations and committees of organizations in which APA has representatives or delegates. Alphabetically arranged by subject headings.

F 11-24 Divisions, 1945-68. 14 containers.

Arranged numerically by division number and alphabetically therein. Eleven containers are from division 17 and contain committee reports, secretary and treasurer's correspondence, and newsletters from the division.

H 10-20 Subject File, 1945-72. 11 containers.

Correspondence, reports, printed matter, informational materials, background, research results, and miscellaneous material which deals with a specific subject, arranged alphabetically by subject.

J 9-11 Conference of State Psychological Associations, 1952-67. 2 containers.

Correspondence, reports, state forms, and legal requirements, arranged alphabetically by state and chronologically by month within the state file.

K 18 American Association of Applied Psychologists, 1938-44. 1 container.

Notices, memoranda, reports, and correspondence, arranged alphabetically by subject and chronologically by month.

M 1-19 Journals and Publications, 1912-66. 19 containers.

Correspondence, reports, manuscripts, and monographs relating to publications of the APA. The bulk of the material (13 containers) deals with the *Journal of Abnormal and Social Psychology* from 1949-55. Also included are yearbooks of the APA, directories, and reprints of proceedings of annual meetings.

Container
  Nos.

Section II *(Continued)*

N 1-13   Executive Officer File, 1946-68. 13 containers.

Papers of Arthur H. Brayfield: Correspondence, reports, memoranda, and miscellaneous materials arranged by subject, according to the original order of this file. Although the bulk of the file dates from Dr. Brayfield's term of office (1962-68), some background materials predate this term.

ORAL HISTORY TAPES (to be made available in the Division of Recorded Sound)

Adler, Norman	McClelland, David
Ansbacher, Heinz	McConnell, James V.
Ansbacher, Rowena	McGill, William
Arnheim, Rudolph	McGraw, Myrtle
Azrin, Nathan H.	McGuigan, Joseph
Beach, Frank	Matarazzo, Joseph
Berger, Seymour	Milton, Ohmer
Blake, Randolph	Murphy, Gardner
Bugelski, B. R.	Murphy, Lois B.
Burtt, Harold	Neimark, Edith
Campbell, Angus	Newcomb, Theodore
Dollard, John	Ornstein, Peter
Elkind, David	Palmer, Edward
Ellis, Albert	Piotrowski, Zygmunt
Flanagan, John	Pishkin, Vladimir
Geldard, Frank	Pressey, Sidney
Harlow, Harry F.	Rebelsky, Freda
Harrower, Molly	Rhine, J. B.
Hebb, Donald O.	Riggs, Lorrin A.
Irwin, Francis W.	Rodin, Judith
Jacobson, Edmund	Sears, Robert R.
Jones, Edward E.	Seligman, Martin
Katz, Daniel	Shakow, David
Kello, John	Skinner, B. F.
Kristal, Mark	Thompson, Richard F.
Lacey, Beatrice	Thorne, Fred
Lesser, Gerald S.	Turvey, Michael
Ligon, Ernest	Valenstein, Elliot
Little, Kenneth	Vane, Julia
Luchins, Abraham	Webster, Ron
McCall, Ray	Zigler, Edward
McCary, James L.	

Archival Research in Great Britain

Americans accustomed to doing archival research in North American repositories are sometimes bewildered when they begin similar research in British libraries and archives. On the one hand, if they are interested in a person with ties to Oxford or Cambridge, they may find it difficult to sort out the relations among the individual, his or her college, and the university. On the other, they are sometimes surprised at the initial formality of many (but not all) British archival procedures, unmatched by almost any U.S. institution. For example, most British repositories require a formal letter requesting permission to use their materials before they grant admission, and it is not unusual for a researcher arriving at a repository without having done this to be asked to write such a letter on the spot. Sometimes, in fact, American researchers who have not previously written such letters have even been denied access to repositories. Similarly, though less extreme, formal interviews with archival personnel are also not unusual, and researchers are often asked to spell out their plans in some detail. But in almost all cases, once a researcher is granted permission to use archival material, British archivists have a well-deserved reputation for helpfulness, and research in British repositories is often a joy.

One major advantage of this initial formality is that it requires researchers from America to plan their work in Britain before they cross the Atlantic. As they have to write for formal permission to use relevant manuscript material, they have to locate it first, and this step often saves much running around. The first place to check for the papers of an individual psychologist, for example, is, typically, the institution with which he or she was connected. For example, the papers of Frederic Bartlett are in the University of Cambridge Library. But Americans have to keep in mind that Cambridge and Oxford are collections of colleges and that university professors and instructors often have, and had, positions at individual colleges in addition to, and often before, their university appointment. Thus Henry Sidgwick, a major figure in establishing experimental psychology at Cambridge, was Knightsbridge Professor of Moral Philosophy at the University from 1883 until his death in 1900. But Sidgwick always indentified himself more closely with Trinity College, Cambridge, where he was a Fellow from 1859 to 1900, than he did with the University, and his papers are in the Trinity College Library. Consequently, researchers should be careful in tracing an individual's institutional ties.

An individual's institutional affiliation—even one traced laboriously—sometimes does not help to locate his or her papers. For example, the papers of Francis Galton, who after graduating from Trinity College, Cambridge, never had any formal academic ties, are in the archives of University College, London. Similarly, Cyril Burt was linked for many years with the University of London, first as Professor of Educational Psychology at the London Day Training College (later the University's Institute of Education) and then as professor of Psychology at University College. His papers are at the University of Liverpool. In both of these cases, a knowledge of the secondary literature about these psychologists can help the researcher trace the provenance of these collections and locate them today. For example, Galton's first biographer was Karl Pearson, long time Professor at University College, London, and Burt's biography was recently written by Leslie S. Hearnshaw, who taught for many years at Liverpool. These two cases illustrate how important institutional connections are in locating the papers of individuals.

Fortunately, several important British institutions have published guides to their manuscript holdings. Among the most important are:

British Museum (Natural History): *Catalogue of Manuscripts*. London: H. M. Stationery Office, 1971.

Churchill College, Cambridge. *List of Deposited Archives*. Cambridge: Churchill College, 1970.

R. W. Hunt, et al. *A Summary Catalogue of Western Manuscripts in the Bodleian Library at Oxford*. 7 volumes. Oxford: Oxford University Press, 1953.

A.E.B. Owen. *University Library Cambridge: Summary Guide to Accessions of Western Manuscripts (Other than Medieval) since 1857*. Cambridge: Cambridge University Press, 1966.

H. E. Peek and C. P. Hall. *The Archives of the University of Cambridge: An Historical Introduction*. Cambridge: Cambridge University Press, 1962.

D. Ramage. *Durham University: Summary List of Additional Manuscripts Accessioned and Listed Between September 1941 and September 1961*. Newcastle, 1963.

Two national repositories cannot be ignored while doing manuscript research in Britain. These are the British Library and the Public Record Office. The Library was for many years part of the British Museum and it collects manuscripts on almost all topics. Some idea of its holdings can be gained from examining: T. C. Skeat. *British Museum: Catalogues of Manuscript Collections*. London: British Museum, 1962. The Library also regularly issues various publications describing its recent accessions. The most important of these are the *Catalogues of Additions to the Manuscripts of the British Museum*.

The Public Record Office was for many years located in Somerset House in the heart of London. It has since moved to the London suburb of Kew, but all of its collections are still useful for shedding light on the personal and official lives of literally millions of individuals, including most British psychologists. An introduction to its collections and use is available in: Public Record

Office. *Guide to the Contents of the Public Record Office.* 3 volumes. London: P.R.O., 1963-1968.

The Office also regularly publishes additional *Catalogues, Lists, Rolls,* and other guides to its holdings.

Several useful published sources are available to help a researcher trace the manuscript collections that he or she needs. Among the most important are:

Robert Bingham Downs and Elizabeth C. Downs. *British Library Resources: A Bibliographical Guide.* Chicago: American Library Association, 1973.

David Iredale. *Enjoying Archives: What They Are; Where to Find Them: How to Use Them.* Newton Abbott: David and Charles, 1973.

A. Jeffreys, "Locating the Manuscript Sources of Science," *British Journal for the History of Science* 2 (1964): 160.

N. Kurti, et al., "Archives of Twentieth Century Scientists and Technologists," *Aslib Proceedings* 23 (1971): 118-132.

Roy M. MacLeod and James R. Friday. *Archives of British Men of Science.* London: Mansell, 1972.

Roy M. MacLeod and James R. Friday, "The Quest for Archives of British Men of Science," *History of Science* 11 (1973): 8-20.

National Library of Scotland: Catalogue of Manuscripts Acquired since 1925. 3 volumes to date. Edinburgh, 1938-   .

Royal Commission on Historical Manuscripts. *Manuscripts and Men.* London: H. M. Stationery Office, 1969.

Royal Commission on Historical Manuscripts. *Record Repositories in Great Britain.* 4th edition. London: H. M. Stationery Office, 1971.

Finally, there are two institutions that can direct researchers to collections of manuscripts and archival material otherwise unlocatable. One collects information about manuscript material in general, while the other concentrates on scientific collections. They are:

Royal Commission on Historical Manuscripts
Quality House, Quality Court
Chancery Lane
London WC2A IHP
Telephone: 01-242-3205

Contemporary Scientific Archives Centre
10 Keble Road
Oxford OX1 3QC
Telephone: 0865-55174

It should be explicitly noted that the Contemporary Scientific Archives Centre is *not* a repository of manuscript material. Instead, its goals are to locate important collections of scientific papers held privately; to arrange the collections for research; and to deposit the collections in repositories where they can be used for research. In its inquiries, the staff of the Centre has located hundreds of important sets of manuscript material, and the Centre maintains a directory of these collections.

Archival Research in the Federal Republic of Germany And the German Democratic Republic

Many of the same caveats about research in Great Britain can be repeated about research in both the Federal Republic of Germany (the Bundesrepublik Deutschland, or BRD) and the German Democratic Republic (the Deutsche Demokratische Republik, or DDR). In the DDR, in particular, manuscript librarians and archivists tend to follow what has been called "the Soviet approach to archives, according to which all documents are state secrets until declared otherwise." Fortunately, a practical guide presenting formal and informal procedures that work to gain access to manuscript collections has recently been published. All researchers who want to do archival work in the BRD and the DDR, especially in the history of psychology and related areas, should consult Mitchell G. Ash, "Fragments of the Whole: Documents of the History of Gestalt Psychology in the United States, the Federal Republic of Germany, and the German Democratic Republic," in *Historiography of Modern Psychology: Aims, Resources, Approaches.* Edited by Josef Brozek and Ludwig J. Pongratz. Toronto: C. J. Hogrefe, 1980, pp. 187-200. As with Great Britain, researchers should, if at all possible, identify and locate relevant manuscript sources in Germany *before* crossing the Atlantic. The following sources will help scholars do just that:

> Ludwig Denecke, editor. *Die Nachlässe in den Bibliotheken der Bundesrepublik Deutschland.* (Verzeichnis der Schriftlichen Nachlässe in Deutschen Archiven und Bibliotheken, Band 2.) Boppard am Rhein: Harald Boldt, 1969.

> C. Haase. *The Records of German History.* Boppard am Rhein: Harald Boldt, 1975.

> G. O. Kent, "Research Opportunities in West and East German Archives for the Weimer Period and the Third Reich," *Central European History* 12 (1979): 38-67.

> H. Lübling and R. Unger, editors. *Gelehrten-und Schriftsteller-Nachlässe in den Bibliotheken der D.D.R.* 3 volumes. Berlin (D.D.R.), 1959, 1968, 1973.

Minerva. Die Archive im Deutschsprächigen Raum. 2nd edition. 2 volumes. Berlin, 1974.

Wolfgang Momsen, editor. *Die Nächlasse in den Deutschen Archiven (mit Ergänzungen aus anderen Beständen).* (Verzeichnis der Schriftlichen Nächlasse in Deutschen Archiven und Bibliotheken, Band 1.) Boppard am Rhein: Harald Boldt, 1971.

E. Schetlich, et al., editors. *Taschenbuch Archivwesen der DDR.* Berlin, 1971.

Erwin K. Welsch. *Libraries and Archives in Germany.* Pittsburgh: Council for European Studies, 1975.

Archives of Psychiatry, Oscar Diethelm Historical Library

The Oscar Diethelm Historical Library of the Department of Psychiatry at the New York Hospital-Cornell Medical College was established in 1953 and named in honor of its major benefactor in 1962. The Library's Archives of Psychiatry was established informally in the mid-1960s and formally announced in 1975. For more than fifteen years, then, the Archives had a chance to grow and it is now a major repository of important manuscript collections in the history of psychiatry.

None of the Archives' collections have had individual descriptions published. However, a partial listing of individuals and institutions whose papers have been deposited at the Archives includes:

Individuals—
Clifford Beers
David M. Levy
Emily L. Martin
John A. P. Millet

Thomas Salmon
Frankwood Williams
Harold G. Wolff

Institutions—
American Academy of Law and Psychiatry

American Academy of Psychoanalysis (History Committee)

American College of Neuropsychopharmacology

American College of Psychiatrists

American Foundation for Mental Hygiene

American Psychopathological Association

Ittleson Foundation

National Association for Mental Health

New York County District Branch of the American Psychiatric Association

New York Psychiatric Society

New York Society for Clinical Psychiatry

Van Ameringen Foundation

Vidonian Society

William Alanson White Psychiatric Society

World Federation for Mental Health—U. S. Committee

Additional accessions are being made continually, and the importance of the Archives will undoubtedly grow through the 1980s.

Mailing Address: Archives of Psychiatry
Oscar Diethelm Historical Library
Department of Psychiatry
New York Hospital—Cornell Medical College
525 East 68th Street
New York, New York 10021
Telephone: (212) 472-5300

Archives of the History of American Psychology

The Archives of the History of American Psychology (AHAP) was established officially in October 1965 by the Board of Trustees of The University of Akron. It represents the efforts of two of the most important scholars in the history of psychology, John A. Popplestone and Marion White McPherson—Director and Associate Director of the Archives—who worked long and hard to have AHAP founded. Since its foundation, the Archives has grown rapidly to occupy a position of unequalled importance among researchers in the history of psychology and related areas, who typically view AHAP as a useful resource for scholarly work. It is clear that the Archives of the History of American Psychology is by far the most important center for manuscript research in the history of psychology in the United States today.

The breadth of the holdings of the Archives is enormous. The term "American" was included in its title "not on the basis of a nationalistic bias, but out of respect for the need to impose practical limitations. It is interpreted to mean any psychologist who has functioned or does function in the United States, either personally or by virtue of his extensive influence in this country." The collections of the Archives reflect this interpretation.

The materials in the Archives constitute the single largest source anywhere of original documents relating to the development of psychology. More than 550 organizations and individuals have deposited documents. Many of these manuscript collections in the Archives of the History of American Psychology constitute the corpus of the papers of individuals and the complete archives of organizations. In other instances the holdings vary from extensive but incomplete records to documents that deal with only one topic. Whatever the extent, an inventory is made for all items in these collections. In addition, a card file is kept for all collections noting the existence in each collection of letters *by* an individual psychologist, letters *to* an individual psychologist, and documents of any kind that discuss an individual psychologist or his or her work. It is hard to imagine a more useful plan for an index to manuscript collections than this one.

In addition to unpublished documents such as correspondence, lecture notes, and laboratory protocols, the Archives holds more than five hundred pieces of early psychological apparatus. There is also a large collection of standardized tests, audio-tapes (including oral histories), photographs and films. Further, the Archives maintains the records of a number of psychological journals and approximately a dozen of the divisions of the American Psychological Association.

The Child Development Film Archives is an especially important part of the AHAP holdings. It is a collection of approximately 3,500 films, most of which were taken between 1925 and 1975. Most of the films are drawn from two collections: the films brought together at Vassar College by L. Joseph Stone; and the films made by Arnold Gesell, primarily at Yale University. The collection also includes valuable outtakes from the Vassar films, which provide important documentation not otherwise available.

These films, it should be noted, are useful both as historical documents and as sources for contemporary research. That is, they can be used to document older norms of behavior, which can be compared with those studied at a later date. In addition, as the films record a full range of behaviors, they can be used to study many questions formulated long after the filming was completed, without great concern for bias. In all, these films are an important resource that is all too often ignored by historians and others.

In 1980, the Archives took on a new function in acquiring the library of books in psychology and related areas collected for more than thirty years by Josef and Eunice Brozek. This library represents an unmatched resource of published material for the history of psychology, and the Archives expects to add to it in coming years. In all, within a short period, AHAP will probably become *the* center for research in the history of psychology based upon almost any type of primary and secondary sources imaginable.

The collection is much too large to document in this section. However, the lists provided below give partial information on the current holdings. Although these listings are necessarily selective, they nevertheless contain the major holdings of AHAP. The size of the manuscript collections contained in the first list varies greatly from the complete papers of an individual to a small amount of correspondence. Before any trip to the Archives, researchers are strongly advised to write to the Director or Associate Director to inquire about the nature and extent of AHAP's holdings on their topics of interest.

The Archives, in an attempt to see its collections used to the fullest extent, has established a History of Psychology Research Fellowship, which is funded by the AHAP's History of Psychology Foundation. This fellowship, in an amount of up to five hundred dollars is awarded to aid scholars who wish to use the Archives' resources but who otherwise would be unable to do so. The stipend is intended to defray travel expenses to Akron and living expenses while working at AHAP. Further information about this Research Fellowship is available from the Archives.

Mailing Address: Archives of the History of American Psychology
The University of Akron
Akron, Ohio 44325
Telephone: (216) 375-7285

The following is a selective list of psychologists whose papers are deposited, in whole or in part, in the Archives of the History of American Psychology:

Adams, Donald	Ferster, Charles B.
Adkins, Dorothy	Ghiselli, Edwin
Bass, Bernard	Gibson, James J.
Beach, Frank	Goddard, Henry H.
Beck, Samuel	Hall, G. Stanley
Boder, David P.	Halstead, Ward C.
Bradford, Leland	Harrower, Molly R.
Bugental, James	Haslerud, George M.
Burtt, Harold	Hebb, Donald O.
Cartwright, Dorwin	Heider, Grace
Crissey, Marie Skodak	Helson, Harry
Crissey, Orlo	Henle, Mary
Curti, Margaret	Hilgard, Ernest R.
Dashiell, John F.	Hollingworth, Harry L.
Delabarre, Edmund B.	Hollingworth, Leta S.
Diamond, Solomon	Hunt, William A.
Doll, Edgar A.	Hurvich, Dorothea and Leo
Dubois, Philip H.	Ives, Margaret
Dunlap, Knight	Kerlinger, Fred
English, Horace B.	Knapp, Robert H.
Eysenck, Hans J.	Koffka, Kurt
Farnsworth, Paul	Krech, David

Kutner, Bernard
Kepley, William M.
Lewin, Kurt
McClelland, David C.
McKeachie, Wilbert J.
MacLeod, Robert B.
McTeer, Wilson
Maier, Norman R. F.
Maslow, Abraham
Meyer, Mortimer
Moore, Bruce V.
Nutterville, Catherine B.
Ober, Denis
Olson, Willard
Pressey, Sidney
Ratner, Stanley
Razran, Gregory
Rethlingshafer, Dorothy
Riegel, Klaus
Rokeach, Milton
Ryan, Thomas A.
Scheerer, Martin

Schneirla, T. C.
Shaffer, Laurence F.
Shakow, David
Shipley, Walter C.
Smith, M. Brewster
Spence, Kenneth W.
Starr, Henry and Anna
Stogdill, Emily and Ralph
Stone, L. Joseph
Switzer, St. Clair
Taylor, William S.
Teuber, Hans-Lukas
Tolman, Edward C.
Trow, Willard C.
Tyler, Leona
Uhrbrock, Richard
Viteles, Morris
Wechsler, David
Wertheimer, Michael
Wolf, Theta
Young, Paul Thomas

The Archives' holdings of journal records include:

Developmental Psychology

Journal of Animal Behavior

Journal of Applied Behavior Analysis

Journal of Biological Psychology

Journal of Counseling Psychology

Journal of Educational Psychology

Journal of Experimental Psychology: General

Journal of Experimental Psychology: Human Learning and Memory

Journal of Experimental Psychology: Human Perception and Performance

Journal of Marriage and the Family

Journal of the Experimental Analysis of Behavior

Journal of the History of the Behavioral Sciences

Memory and Cognition

Perceptual and Motor Skills

Psychological Record

Psychological Reports

Psychological Review

Association records housed in the Archives include:

American Group Psychotherapy Association

Association for Humanistic Psychology

Case Western Reserve Psychological Research Services Collection

Cheiron: International Society for the Study of the History of the Behavioral and Social Sciences

International Council of Psychologists

International Society for Clinical and Experimental Hypnosis

Midwestern Psychological Association

National Training Laboratory

New York Psychiatric Institution

Ohio Psychological Association

Psychonomic Society

Rocky Mountain Psychological Association

Vineland Research Laboratory

Western Psychological Association

The Archives' holdings of APA division records (by APA division number) include:

6—Physiological and Comparative Psychology
9—Psychological Study of Social Issues
12—Clinical Psychology
14—Industrial and Organizational Psychology
16—School Psychology
22—Rehabilitation Psychology
24—Philosophical Psychology
26—History of Psychology
33—Mental Retardation
35—Psychology of Women
36—Psychologists Interested in Religious Issues

The following oral histories and memoirs are available for scholarly use at the Archives:

Samuel Beck

Harold Burtt and Sidney Pressey
(dialogue)

Paul Farnsworth and
Ernest Hilgard (dialogue)

Frank S. Freeman

Sigmund Freud Memoir
(Pauline Havre, interviewee)

Cora Friedline

Henry H. Goddard Memoir
(Lillian Capell, interviewee)

G. Stanley Hall Memoir
(Evelyn Douglas, interviewee)

Elaine Kinder

Norman R. F. Maier

Emily Stogdill

Lois Hayden Meek Stolz
(interviewed by Ruth Takanishi)

Frederick Thorne

Max Wertheimer Memoirs
(various interviewees)

Gertha Williams

The following articles on the Archives of the History of American Psychology will help researchers who have not used the AHAP before to introduce themselves to its resources:

Mitchell G. Ash, "Fragments of the Whole: Documents of the History of Gestalt Psychology in the United States, the Federal Republic of Germany, and the German Democratic Republic," in *Historiography of Modern Psychology: Aims, Resources, Approaches*. Edited by Josef Brozek and Ludwig J. Pongratz. Toronto: C. J. Hogrefe, 1980, pp. 187-200.

Ludy T. Benjamin, Jr., "Research at the Archives of the History of American Psychology: A Case History," *Ibid.*, pp. 241-251.

Ludy T. Benjamin, Jr. *Teaching the History of Psychology: A Resource Book*. New York: Academic Press, 1981. (This book was especially useful in preparing this appendix.)

Liz Kaplinski, "Preserving the Past: Akron Archives Wins Award," *American Psychological Association Monitor*, January 1980. pp. 3, 41.

John A. Popplestone and Milton L. Kult, "The Archives of the History of American Psychology, August 1965-August 1966," *Journal of the History of the Behavioral Sciences* 3 (1967): 60-63.

John A. Popplestone and Marion White McPherson, "The Archives of the History of American Psychology," *American Archivist* 34 (1971): 13-19.

John A. Popplestone and Marion White McPherson, "The Development of the Archives of the History of American Psychology," *Manuscripts* 21 (1969): 183-188.

John A. Popplestone and Marion White McPherson, "Ten Years at the Archives of the History of American Psychology," *American Psychologist* 31 (1976): 533-534.

Canadian Psychological Association Archives

Though some manuscript material relating to the history of the Canadian Psychological Association has been preserved in the Public Archives of Canada (in Ottawa), the major archival resources relating to the history of the CPA, and to the history of psychology in Canada as a whole, is the tremendous set of oral history interviews collected by C. Roger Myers since 1962. Myers is a long-time member of the University of Toronto Department of Psychology and CPA Archivist and, with the cooperation of the Public Archives of Canada, has made his interviews available for research by others. They may, of course, be consulted at the Public Archives, but researchers may also obtain copies of either the taped interview or its transcript for their own permanent use. To do so, the following formal procedure should be followed:

Anyone wishing access to either tapes or transcripts should address his or her request for access (one at a time) to:

Mailing Addresses: C. Roger Myers, CPA Archivist
Department of Psychology
University of Toronto
Toronto, Ontario
M5S 1A1 Canada

Manuscript Division
Public Archives of Canada
395 Wellington Street
Ottawa, Ontario
K1A ON3 Canada
Telephone: (613) 996-2893

If there are no restrictions on the interview, the Archivist will then authorize the Public Archives of Canada to accede to the request. If there are any restrictions, the Archivist will first require a signed statement to the effect that the requester will adhere strictly to the specified restriction before authorizing release. When authorized for release, re-recorded tapes can be obtained without charge by sending the required number of blank tape cassettes to PAC. Photocopies of the transcript can be obtained from PAC at the current cost of duplication. Following is the list of psychologists currently in the collection. The first number in parentheses indicates the number of sixty-minute tape cassettes required for the original interview. The second number indicates the number of pages in the transcript. The letter that follows indicates the present status of the material according to the following code: A-tape and transcript are available without restriction; R-tape and transcript are restricted; NR-not yet released by the person interviewed; and I-interview incomplete, not yet available:

Ainsworth, Mary Salter (2-55-A)
Amsel, Abram (2-51-R until 1995)
Appley, Mortimer
Arnold, Magda (2-60-NR)
Beach, Ace (1-23-A)
Belanger, David (1-25-I)
Bell, Anne (1-24-A)
Belyea, Ed (4-75-A)
Berlyne, Dan (5-238-R until 1984)
Bindra, Dalbir (1-23-A)
Blair, Buck (4-139-R)
Bott, Ned (2-31-A)
Bredin, Grace Dolmage (2-56-A)
Bridges, Win (1-26-A)
Bromiley, Reg (4-97-R)
Chant, Sperrin (3-49-R)
Clake, John (2-47-A)
Clark, C. A. F. (1-22-A)
Clarke, Stan (2-105-NR)
Cooper, Rod (1-26-A)
Corcoran, Derek (2-47-A)
Davidson, Park (3-82-A)
Decarie, Gouin T. (2-50-NR)
Dörken, Herb (2-68-NR)
Douglas, Virginia (3-133-NR)
Easterbrook, Jim (2-61-R)
Ferguson, George (3-76-A)
Fraser, Allon (2-45-R)
Gaddes, Bill (3-122-NR)
Gibson, David (2-38-A)
Hart, David (3-74-A)

Hebb, Donald O. (2-49-A)
Hewson, Cec (2-94-NR)
Hobson, Gordon (1-33-A)
Hough, Arthur (2-52-A)
Hoyt-Cameron, Ruth (3-83-NR)
Jackson, Doug (2-64-NR)
James, Henry (2-36-A)
Jourard, Sidney (2-69-A)
Kibblewhite, E. J. (2-28-A)
Lambert, Wally (2-52-A)
Little, Brian (3-76-A)
McClelland, Bill (2-76-NR)
MacDonald, Glenn (4-105-A)
MacEachren, John (2-49-A)
MacLeod, Robert (4-85-A)
McMurray, Gordon (2-62-A)
MacPhee, Earle (3-38-A)
Mahoney, Gerry (2-122-A)
Mailloux, Noel (2-35-A)
Malmo, Robert (2-40-R)
Melzack, Ronald (2-117-A)
Mills, John (2-63-A)
Milton, Lex (2-40-A)
Morton, Whit (2-45-A)
Mowat, Sandy (1-23-A)
Myers, Roger (4-131-A)
Neal, Leola (2-56-A
Nelson, Tom (2-72-R until 1990)
Northway, Mary (2-59-A)
Noseworthy, Bill (2-66-NR)
Page, Hilton (1-22-A)

Paivio, Al (3-103-NR)
Philip, Roger (1-29-A)
Pinard, Adrien (2-34-A)
Poser, Ernest (4-178-R)
Potashin, Reva (2-48-A)
Preston, Charles (1-42-I)
Rabinovitch, Sam (3-101-A)
Royce, Joseph (3-88-A)
Runquist, Willie (3-124-A)
Schaub, Ron (2-49-A)
Schonfield, David (3-60-A)
Shephard, Alf (3-63-NR)
Shevenell, Ray (2-51-A)
Signori, Edro (3-58-A)
Skanes, Graham (3-71-A)
Smith, Doug (3-88-A)
Snodgrass, Florence (2-44-R)
Springbett, Bruce (2-41-A)
Stein, Harry (1-30-A)
Stern, Muriel (1-23-A)
Stewart, Jane (2-69-A)
Suedfeld, Peter (2-61-A)
Sullivan, Art (2-52-A)

Taylor, Frank (2-46-A)
Taylor, Gwen Hearle (1-20-A)
Taylor, Tommy (2-56-NR)
Tulving, Endel (3-67-A)
Turner, Gord (3-65-A)
Tyler, Fred (2-47-NR)
Vernon, Dalton (2-95-A)
Vernon, Philip (1-23-R)
Wake, Robert (3-125-A)
Watson, Charles (2-95-NR)
Webster, Ed (2-53-R until 1984)
Weckler, Nora Loeb (2-55-A)
Welch, Louise Thompson (2-44-A)
Wendt, Rusty (2-37-R until 1985)
Weyant, Robert (2-79-A)
Wigdor, Blossom (2-57-A)
Williams, Carl (4-92-A)
Woodsworth, Joseph (A)
Wright, Marion McDonald (1-26-A)
Wright, Mary J. (3-95-R until 1985)
Wright, Morgan (3-67-A)
Zubek, John (2-51-A)

The following articles will help the researcher in using these oral history interviews:

C. Roger Myers, "The Collection, Preservation and Use of Oral History Materials," *Canadian Psychological Review* 16 (1975):130-133.

C. Roger Myers and Robert B. MacLeod, "Talks about Psychology in Canada," *Canadian Psychologist* 15 (1974): 105-111.

Educational Testing Service Archives

Recognizing the importance of testing in modern American life, the Educational Testing Service has recently established an Archives. To date, this repository has not published descriptions of any of its collections, but it hopes to do so soon. Meanwhile, its holding are available to scholars and researchers, preferably through arrangements made in advance of a visit, and preliminary inventories of some record groups are available at the repository.

In 1978, the Archives described its holdings as follows:

Materials pertaining to the educational, research, and testing activities of the Educational Testing Service (1948-   ), and, to a lesser degree, to the earlier testing activities of its founding organizations, the American Council on Education, the Carnegie Foundation for the Advancement of Teaching, and the College Entrance Examination Board. Included are corporate records and papers of staff members; corporate publications and research reports; journal articles and speeches; and photographs, tapes, and other audio-visual material. [NHPRC]

Mailing Address: Educational Testing Service
Princeton, New Jersey 08540
Telephone: (609) 921-9000, ext. 2744

European Archival Material About Wilhelm Wundt

Of all those who have studied psychology since Plato, Wilhelm Wundt has the best claim to be considered as the founder of psychology as a science. Many psychologists and several historians have written about Wundt but only recently have Wundt's own manuscripts been studied by scholars interested in his life and career. Because of his importance and influence, Wundt's papers are undoubtedly of interest to almost anyone doing research in the history of psychology. The following tables provide information about the most important archival collections left by, and relating to, Wundt, and are reprinted here with the very kind permission of their compilers and publisher from: Wolfgang Bringmann and Gustav A. Ungerer, "An Archival Journey in Search of Wilhelm Wundt," in *Historiography of Modern Psychology: Aims, Resources, Approaches*. Edited by Josef Brozek and Ludwig J. Pongratz. Toronto: C. J. Hogrefe, 1980, pp. 201-240. In the following tables, the numbers after the term *Coverage* refer to specific periods in Wundt's life, as indicated at the end of the tables.)

TABLE 1. *Major Repositories of Wundt's Private Papers*

Repository	Description
1. *Wundt Family;* Mannheim (West Germany)	Birth records; books by Wundt; drawings, paintings and sculptures of Wundt and ancestors, memorabilia. (Uncatalogued) *Coverage:* 1, 3, 11. *Provenance:* Estates of Max and Eleonore Wundt.
2. *Library, Bochum University,* Bochum-Querendorf (West Germany)	Many books from Wundt's Library with signatures and notations. (Uncatalogued) *Coverage:* 1-12 (except Philosophy and Folk Psychology). *Provenance:* Estate of Max Wundt.
3. *Wundt Archive, Faculty of Psychology, Karl-Marx-University,* Leipzig (East Germany)	Letters to and from Wundt; notebooks; lecture notes; personnel records; photographs; speeches; newspaper clippings (Partially catalogued) *Coverage:* 1-12 (*Emphasis:* 8-12). *Provenance:* Estates of Eleonore and Max Wundt.

TABLE 1. (Continued)

Repository	Description
4. *Wundt Family*, Tübingen, (West Germany)	Family letters to and from Wundt; diaries of wife; personal documents; genealogical information; photographs. (Cataloguing in process) *Coverage:* 1-12. (*Emphasis:* 6-9). *Provenance:* Max Wundt Estate.
5. *Archive, Tübingen University*, Tübingen (West Germany)	Letters by Wundt to his son Max; 618 typewritten copies of Wundt letters by Eleonore Wundt; copies of Leipzig personnel records; genealogical materials; correspondence with Wundt Archive. (Partially catalogued) *Coverage:* 7-12. *Provenance:* Max Wundt Estate.
6. *Library, Tohoku University*, Sendai (Japan)	Major part of Wundt Library dealing with psychology and related fields. (Catalogued) *Coverage:* 4-11. *Provenance:* Wundt Estate.

TABLE 2. *Additional Primary Sources By and About Wundt in European Archives and Libraries*

Repository	Description
1. *Protestant Parish Office*, Neckarau (West Germany)	Original birth record; photograph of parsonage during 1890s; commemorative tablet. *Coverage:* 1.
2. *Archive, Heidelberg University*, Heidelberg (West Germany)	Academic and personnel records; original of award winning research paper; records of Scientific-Medical Club; diplomas; personnel information about teachers and colleagues Helmholtz, Kussmaul. (Catalogued) *Coverage:* 4, 6.
3. *Library, Heidelberg University*, Heidelberg (West Germany)	Letters by Wundt; records of Workers Educational Association; records of Historical-Philosophical Club. (Catalogued) *Coverage:* 5-11.
4. *City Archive, Heidelberg* (West Germany)	Background information about 19th century Heidelberg; newspapers from Wundt's political period; address books; photographs and other illustrations of "Old" Heidelberg. (Catalogued) *Coverage:* 2.
5. *Administration, Helmholtz School*, Heidelberg (West Germany)	Grade records of Wundt from Heidelberg Lyceum (1846-1851); annual reports of school; biographical information about teachers and classmates. (Uncatalogued) *Coverage:* 2.
6. *General State Archive*, Karlsruhe (West Germany)	Biographical information about Wundt's father and his ecclesiastical career in Neckarau, Leutershausen and Heidelsheim; records of Baden Parliament. (Catalogued) *Coverage:* 1-2, 5.

TABLE 2. *(Continued)*

Repository	Description
7. *Archive, Tübingen University*, Tübingen (West Germany)	Immatriculation and other student records, 1851-1852. (Catalogued) *Coverage:* 3.
8. *Cantonal State Archive*, Zürich (Switzerland)	Personnel records of Wundt 1874-1875; correspondence concerning academic appointments (e.g. Hugo Münsterberg); background information about Zürich University. (Catalogued) *Coverage:* 7, 10.
9. *Central Archive, Academy of Sciences*, Berlin (East Germany)	Letters to and from Wundt re Academy matters. (Catalogued) *Coverage:* 10-11. *Contact:* 1975.
10. *Archive, Karl-Marx-University*, Leipzig (East Germany)	Personnel records of Wundt, assistants and colleagues; partial records of the institute; academic records of doctoral students. (Catalogued) *Coverage:* 8-11.
11. *Dresden State Archive*, Dresden (East Germany)	Personnel records of Wundt; information about call to Leipzig; correspondence about establishment of Institute. (Catalogued) *Coverage:* 8-11.

COVERAGE

(Please note that the dates in brackets are only approximations.)

1. Family and Childhood (1832-1845)
2. School Years (1845-1850)
3. Medical Studies (1850-1855)
4. Early Career (1856-1865)
5. Politics (1859-1869)
6. *The Principles* (1866-1874)
7. Zurich Period (1874-1875)
8. Early Leipzig Years (1875-1879)
9. Origin and Development of Leipzig Laboratory (1879-1883)
10. Expansion of the Leipzig Institute (1884-1897)
11. Students and Colleagues (1883-1917)
12. The Late Years (1897-1920)

FBI and CIA Files as Sources of Information

For many years, the Federal Bureau of Investigation has kept files of information on large numbers of individuals and institutions. The existence of these files raises many questions related to professional ethics and scientific and academic freedom, many of which have been discussed insightfully by other scholars and scientists. Some individuals doing research in the history of psychology and related areas may choose not to make use of the information contained in these files. But historians and other scholars who want to consult them can do so, within certain limits. Under the terms of the Freedom-of-Information Act, researchers can get copies of many items in many of these files, and such information is often quite useful in historical research.

The FBI's files on psychologists and other scientists include the results of security and loyalty investigations, the reports of FBI agents carrying out surveillance of suspected "subversives," the often anonymous reports of self-appointed FBI informants, and sometimes other material. For example, at least some psychologists in the 1930s had their mail opened by the FBI and the Bureau's files contain paraphrases of their correspondence. In other cases, the names of certain psychologists were suggested to the FBI as experts in various scientific fields of interest to the Bureau. (In particular, the FBI was apparently interested in securing a number of expert witnesses on various psychological topics.) In following up these suggestions, FBI agents interviewed other psychologists about the individuals mentioned. The files on these psychologists therefore contain their colleagues' opinions of them and their work.

Several institutions were investigated in great detail by the FBI. For example, in 1953, the FBI followed up a psychologist-informant's report that "during the past ten years it [the American Psychological Association] has been infiltrated and is now controlled by Communists." The resulting investigation included research on the APA itself, all APA officers, all members of its Board of Directors, and the editors of all of its journals. Similarly, the FBI has sometimes investigated the Society for the Psychological Study of Social Issues and, for fifteen years, the Bureau carried out an active surveillance program on The Psychology League of New York, a predecessor of SPSSI. In this investigation, a leader of the group itself played a major part and, as a result, one scholar claims that "the FBI has more League documents than does the APA Archives" in the Library of Congress.

Access to the FBI files on individuals and institutions can be arranged relatively easily, though the process of doing so often involves considerable time and is sometimes expensive. Researchers are asked to write to the FBI's Freedom-of-Information Act Branch, stating the names and death dates of the individuals about whom they seek information, and the names of the institutions in which they are interested. (Under the terms of the Privacy Act, the FBI is not allowed to release any information about a living individual, except to the individual himself, or even to indicate if it has any information about any particular living person.) Each request is acknowledged and assigned a number, which the researcher is urged to use in all correspondence with the Bureau about the request.

Requests are processed as they are received and, sometimes, the FBI asks for additional information relative to a request; e.g., documentation of an individual's death. (Simple citations to a published obituary or to a letter from a relative have proved to be sufficient.) When the search of the FBI files is complete, the researcher is so informed. If the number of pages involved is very small, the Bureau will copy them and send them to the researcher. If many pages are involved, the researcher is asked to pay for photoduplication. In all cases, the Bureau protects its informants by obliterating their names on all copies.

The Central Intelligence Agency is also required by the Freedom-of-Information Act to provide access to its files. The CIA, however, charges researchers for the time its staff members spend in searching its files, and requires extensive documentation about the individuals and institutions with which researchers are concerned. In all, based upon a very limited experience with both agencies, the CIA appears to be a good deal more difficult to work with than the FBI.

The ethical issues of the FBI's surveillance and other activities are discussed in:

N. Blackstock. *Cointelpro: The FBI's Secret War on Political Freedom.* New York: Random House, 1976.

M. Jahoda and S. W. Cook, "Security Measures and Freedom of Thought: An Exploratory Study of the Impact of Loyalty and Security Programs," *Yale Law Journal* 61 (1952): 295-333.

H. C. Kelman, "Apprehension and Academic Freedom," *Public Opinion Quarterly* 23 (1959): 181-188.

Issues concerning the FBI's and CIA's interest in the work of psychologists are discussed in:

P. Greenfield, "CIA's Behavior Caper," *American Psychological Association Monitor,* December 1977, pp. 1, 10-11.

B. Harris, "The FBI's Files on APA and SPSSI: Description and Implications," *American Psychologist* 35 (1930): 1141-1144.

"A Teacher Has No Privacy," *SPSSI Bulletin,* April 1939, pp. 7-10.

Mailing Addresses: Freedom of Information-Privacy Acts Branch
Records Management Division
Federal Bureau of Investigation
Washington, DC 20535

Information and Privacy Coordinator
Central Intelligence Agency
Washington, DC 20505

History of Medicine Division, National Library of Medicine

The National Library of Medicine was founded in 1836 as the Library of the Surgeon General's Office and at first limited its collection to materials on clinical medicine and public health. In 1865, John Shaw Billings became head of the Library and its function and scope soon expanded greatly. In January 1879, it published the first number of *Index Medicus*, a service that the NLM continues today, and in 1880 it began issuing the volumes of the extremely useful series, the *Index-Catalogue of the Library of the Surgeon-General's Office.*

The Library's History of Medicine Division, built in part on the collections that Billings had brought together in the 19th century, is today one of the most important resources in the world for historians of medicine. For the history of psychology and related areas, the Division's most valuable holdings relate to studies of child development. Its manuscript collections include the papers of several important researchers in the area of child development and child behavior and these collections are described in the body of this *Guide.*

The Division also has available two extremely valuable oral history collections on child development and on child guidance, both made up of interviews conducted by Milton J. E. Senn. These collections can be consulted at the Library, and microfilm copies of each can be purchased from the Division. In addition, Senn made use of his interviews to prepare an overview of the topic that is useful to all researchers in the area, and which he published as: Milton J. E. Senn, "Insights on the Child Development Movement in the United States," *Monographs of the Society for Research in Child Development*, vol. 40, nos. 3-4, 1975, 107 pp. Monograph no. 161.

The scope of these oral histories is vast, as can be seen from the following lists of individuals whom Senn interviewed:

CHILD DEVELOPMENT COLLECTION (OH/20)

Aldrich, Robert A.	Bronfenbrenner, U.
Anderson, Harold H.	Clausen, John A.
Assmus, Judy	Cohen, Donald
Bain, Katherine	Comer, James P.
Baldwin, Alfred	Costello, Joan
Barker, Roger G.	Degnan, George
Baumgartner, Leona	Dennis, Wayne
Bayley, Nancy	Edelman, Marian W.
Bergman, Benjamin	Eisenberg, Leon
Biber, Barbara	Eliot, Martha
Boyd, Edith	Elkind, David
Brim, Orville G.	Escalona, Sibylle

Finberg, Barbara
Frank, Lawrence K.
Gershenson, Charles P.
Greulich, William W.
Harmon, Carolyn
Harris, Dale
Hecht, George J.
Hess, Stephen
Hobbs, Nicholas
Hunt, J. McVicker
Hymes, James L.
Jackson, Edith
Jersild, Arthur
Johnson, Sydney
Jones, Mary Cover
Kagan, Jerome
Keniston, Kenneth
Kessen, William
Knapp, Pauline
Lash, Trude
Lesser, Arthur
Levin, Tom
Levy, David M.
Long, C. N. Hugh
Lynd, Helen M.
McCandless, Boyd R.
MacFarlane, Jean
McGraw, Myrtle
Mead, Margaret
Miller, Judy
Mondale, Walter
Moore, Evelyn
Murphy, Gardner
Murphy, Lois B.
Olson, Willard
Perry, Mary Frank

Phillips, Martha
Pierce, William L. °
Polier, Judge Justine
Provence, Sally A.
Quie, Albert
Reid, Joseph
Richmond, Julius
Salk, Lee°
Sapir, Philip
Sauer, Peter
Schmidt, William
Schoellkopf, Judith
Schorr, Lizbeth
Sears, Pauline
Sears, Robert R.
Senn, Milton J. E.
Shakow, David
Smith, William
Solnit, Albert J.
Sontag, Lester W.
Spock, Benjamin
Steiner, Gilbert
Stevenson, Harold W.
Stoddard, George D.
Stolz, Herbert
Stolz, Lois M.
Stone, Joseph
Sugarman, Jule
Thompson, Helen
Washburn, Alfred H.
White, Sheldon
Wickenden, Elizabeth
Yarrow, Leon
Yarrow, Marian R.
Zigler, Edward
Zimiles, Herbert

Also included are two interviews with mothers working in a family day care center and Lola Nash and Elisabeth Campbell discussing their child rearing practices.

°Indicates that restrictions have been placed on the oral history.

178

CHILD GUIDANCE COLLECTION (OH/76)

Ackerly, S. Spafford
Alt, Herschel
Anthony, E. James
Baldwin, Thomas T. (Mrs.)
Beck, Samuel
Beiser, Helen
Bender, Lauretta
Bernard, Viola
Blos, Peter
Boggs, Elizabeth
Borstelman, Lloyd
Bowlby, John
Brazelton, T. Berry
Chess, Stella
Comer, James
Crissey, Marie Skodak
Curran, Frank
Duhl, Leonard
Dybwad, Gunnar
Evans, Robert
Felix, Robert H.
Fisher, Bernard C.
Freud, Anna
Fries, Margaret
Galenson, Eleanor
Gardner, George
Gildëa, Margaret
Ginsburg, Ethel
Goldfarb, William
Goldstein, Joseph
Grossbard, Hyman
Heinicke, C. M.
Hersov, Lionel
Katan, Anny
Kennell, John
Korsch, Barbara
Langer, Marion F.
Laufer, Maurice
Leonard, Charles
Levine, Adeline

Levine, Murray
Lourie, Norman
Lourie, Reginald
Mahler, Margaret
Marsh, Elias
Mason, Molly
Meltzer, Hyman
Midelfort, Frederick
Miller, Jerome G.
Minuchin, Salvadore
Neubauer, Peter
Onesti, Silvio
Parmalee, Arthur
Rexford, Eveoleen
Ridenour, Nina
Robertson, James
Robertson, Joyce
Rodham, Hillary
Ross, Mabel
Sapir, Philip
Sarason, Seymour
Sareyan, Alex
Schlaifer, Charles
Simpson, Esther H.
Sperry, Bessy
Spurlock, Jeanne
Staver, Nancy
Stevenson, George
Stone, Alan
Stubblefield, Robert
Tarjan, George
Visotsky, Harold
Warren, Wilfred
Welsch, Exil
Winnicott, Clare
Witmer, Helen
Work, Henry
Yolles, Stanley
Zimmerman, Kent A.

Mailing Address: History of Medicine Division
National Library of Medicine
Bethesda, Maryland 20014
Telephone: (301) 656-4000

Rockefeller Archive Center

The Rockefeller Archive Center was established in the early 1970s as a repository for the records of the Rockefeller family, The Rockefeller University, and the various Rockefeller philanthropies, most notably The Rockefeller Foundation and its associated agencies. It is located in Hillcrest, a large home on the Rockefeller family estate in Pocantico Hills, in Westchester County, New York. Although permission to use the manuscript collections deposited at the Center is relatively easy to obtain, it is not easy to get to the Center itself without making prior arrangements. The Center's staff is aware of this problem and goes out of its way to help researchers get to the Center, sometimes (whenever possible) by providing transportation from the Tarrytown railroad station. Researchers are therefore urged to make formal arrangements to visit the Center long before they actually arrive in Tarrytown.

For the history of psychology and related areas, the most important collections at the Center are, as noted, those of The Rockefeller Foundation and of the other Rockefeller philanthropies that were gradually merged into it. These include the General Education Board, the Bureau of Social Hygiene, the Laura Spelman Rockefeller Memorial, and the Spelman Fund of New York. These agencies supported a great deal of work in psychology and other closely related areas—especially child development studies—throughout their history, and their papers will do much to allow historians and other researchers to document their influence.

Mailing Address: Rockefeller Archive Center
Hillcrest, Pocantico Hills
North Tarrytown, New York 10591
Telephone: (914) 631-4505

The following articles give additional information about the Center:

Joseph W. Ernst, "The Rockefeller Archive Center," *Bulletin of the History of Medicine* 49 (1975).

Joseph W. Ernst, *"Ut Omnes unum Sint*—The Rockefeller Archives," *American Archivist* 29 (1966).

SRCD *Committee on Preservation of Historical Material in Child Development*

In 1977, the Society for Research in Child Development established a Committee on the Preservation of Historical Material to survey the archival resources available for research on the history of child development. Since that date, it has sponsored a Conference on the Preservation of Historical Materials in Child Development (in 1978, with a grant from the William T. Grant Foundation) and has extended its operations. In 1980, the Committee received a grant from the National Historical Publications and Records Commission "to locate, identify, preserve, and make available the records of individuals and organizations important in the field of child development prior to World War II." Under this grant, the Committee has employed a professional archivist, Lynn Bonfield, and has begun to carry out its charge. In the next few years, it will probably locate and make available for research dozens of collections important for the history of psychology and related areas.

The Committee is chaired by Robert R. Sears, David Starr Jordan Professor of Social Science, Emeritus, Department of Psychology, Stanford University, Stanford, California 94305.

Social Welfare History Archives, *University of Minnesota*

Although this repository does not focus its attention on the history of psychology, its collections are important for research in the field, and, especially, for research in related areas. The following description of the Archives (quoted by permission) is circulated by the SWHA, and gives a good idea of its significance for historians and others.

The Social Welfare History Archives was founded in 1964 through the initiative of history professor Clarke A. Chambers, who has served as its director throughout its existence. The initial collecting policy focused on the records of national voluntary organizations in the social services and the personal papers of their leaders. As a result, the Archives has acquired materials related to a variety of social concerns including recreation, settlement work, child welfare, aging, race relations, community planning, immigration, prostitution, public health, vocational rehabilitation, and voluntarism in American life.

The Archives has intentionally shunned the records of public welfare agencies and programs for the simple reason that by law such records belong to government archives, whether at the national or state level.

Similarly, the Archives chose not to solicit actively the records of private sector social agencies and programs whose services were confined to a local area. This rule has been waived occasionally to accept records of local programs of national significance or other unusual interest (most notably settlement houses in New York City) when another suitable repository could not be found. In recent years, through an agreement with the Minnesota Historical Society, the Social Welfare History Archives has begun to collect the records of social service agencies and organizations in the Minneapolis-St. Paul area. This represents the only systematic effort to acquire other than national-level records and papers.

The Social Welfare History Archives contains more than 3500 linear feet of records and papers. With few exceptions the collections go back no further than the turn of the century, for the reason that few national social welfare associations predate that period. Extensive documentation commences at about the time of World War I. Materials relating to activities of the last five to ten years are very limited, meaning that at present comprehensive coverage for most topics may be expected to concentrate somewhere within the period 1917-1970.

Many of the collections chronicle the development of classic social services offered by professional social workers (including specialists in casework, group work, medical social work, psychiatric social work, school social work, and community organization) and by settlement house workers with the special perspective afforded by their live-in commitment to the neighborhoods they served. Among the groups served are the economically dependent, recent immigrants, migrants and refugees, unwed mothers, abused and abandoned children, the aged, and the mentally and physically handicapped.

Beyond the activities of full-time professionals exist a variety of paid and volunteer efforts involving rank and file labor union members, church leaders, recreational workers, students, housewives, retired persons, journalists, and academicians. The total range of causes and services reflected in the collections include some that might not fit a narrow definition of social welfare: child-rearing advice for parents, recreation programs, music, children's theater, preventive health, and family planning. Certainly not all of the beneficiaries of the activities would think of themselves as social welfare recipients. The common factor is the commitment to improve some aspect of the social environment that affects the quality of humans' lives.

The collections contain a variety of materials, certain types of which recur in many instances: minutes of board and committee meetings, programs and proceedings of conferences and conventions, annual reports, financial records, correspondence, memoranda, newsletters, research reports, and photographs as well as the amalgamation of pamphlets, brochures, clippings, and tear sheets that often accumulate in reference files. The character of the materials changes both quantitatively and qualitatively over time. Early records typically contain extensive correspondence files while more recent files often are characterized by massive amounts of multi-copy regulations, guidelines, directives, and circulars with only an occasional individual-to-individual communication. The contents of personal papers are less consistent or predictable but many of the same patterns may be observed on a smaller scale.

Material in the Archives does not circulate; i.e., it must be used on the premises. The single exception to this policy is that most of the materials on microfilm may be obtained through interlibrary loan. Microfilm material is loaned only to institutions, so the request should be made through the interlibrary loan office of the library where the material will be used.

Permission to use manuscripts normally will be granted to any qualified researcher upon completion of an application form. Advance application to receive permission is not mandatory, but discussion of proposed research prior to the visit will enable the staff to prepare more fully and, perhaps, to suggest preparations that might be made by the researcher.

Inventories of twenty-four collections have been published as University of Minnesota Libraries, *Descriptive Inventories of Collections in the Social Welfare History Archives Center* (Greenwood, 1970). This resource is available in many major research libraries and archives. The recently-issued *Guide to Holdings* contains brief descriptions of all collections held by the Archives. It is available for a cost of one dollar.

Mailing Address: Social Welfare History Archives
University of Minnesota Libraries
Minneapolis, MN 55455
Telephone: (612) 373-4420

Listing of Sources

The compilers consulted many of the following sources in preparing this *Guide* and believe that scholars doing research in the history of psychology and related areas will also find them useful.

Lee Ash. *Subject Collections.* 5th ed. New York: R. R. Bowker, 1978.

Association of Canadian Archivists. *Directory of Canadian Records and Manuscript Repositories.* Ottawa: Bonanza Press, 1977.

Philip C. Brooks. *Research in Archives: The Use of Unpublished Primary Sources.* Chicago: University of Chicago Press, 1969.

Clark A. Elliott. *A Descriptive Guide to the Harvard University Archives.* Cambridge: Harvard University Library, 1974.

Philip M. Hamer. *A Guide to Archives and Manuscripts in the United States.* New Haven: Yale University Press, 1961.

Andrea Hinding. *Women's History Sources: A Guide to Archives and Manuscripts in the United States.* 2 volumes. New York: R. R. Bowker, 1979.

Alan M. Meckler and Ruth McMullin. *Oral History Collections.* New York: R. R. Bowker, 1975.

National Archives and Records Service. *Guide to the National Archives of the United States.* Washington: NARS, 1974.

National Historical Publications and Records Commission. *Directory of Archives and Manuscript Repositories in the United States.* Washington: NHPRC, 1978.

National Union Catalog of Manuscript Collections, 1959-   .

Arthur and Elizabeth Schlesinger Library on the History of Women in America. *The Manuscript Inventories and the Catalogs of Manuscripts, Books and Pictures.* 3 volumes. Boston: G. K. Hall, 1973.

Eugene P. Sheehy. *Guide to Reference Books.* Ninth edition. Chicago: American Library Association, 1976. See also *Supplement, 1980.*

Union List of Manuscripts in Canadian Repositories. Revised edition; 2 volumes. Ottawa: Public Archives of Canada, 1975. See also *Supplement, 1976.*

Margaret L. Young and Harold C. Young. *Directory of Special Libraries and Information Centers.* Fifth edition. Detroit: Gale Research Company, 1979.

LISTING OF SOURCES

In addition, most of the descriptions of repositories in the second section of this *Guide* list books and articles that researchers will find useful in working with the material discussed there.

Indexes

Name and Institution Index

This index lists only those personal names and institutions directly relevant to the history of psychology and related areas which are mentioned in the collection descriptions included in this volume. It does not index all names and institutions mentioned in this *Guide*. Numbers refer to the consecutive entry numbers in the bibliography.

189

Rochlin, Gregory, 353
Rockefeller, John D., 176
Rockefeller, John D., Jr., 176
Rockefeller, John D., III, 63
Rockefeller Institute for Medical
  Research, 288
Roethke, Theodore, 371
Rogers, D. C., 321
Roosevelt, Eleanor, 83
Roosevelt, Franklin D., 63
Root, Elihu, Jr., 73
Root, Elihu, Sr., 73
Rosanoff, Martin Andre, 196
Rose, Wickliffe, 176
Rosenblith, Walter, 372
Ross, Dorothy, 196
Ross, Josephine, 373
Ross, Sherman, 366
Royce, Josiah, 148, 233, 259, 290, 321,
  358, 374, 375, 376, 443, 447, 452
Royster, Hubert Ashley, 377
Rubin, Theodore Isaac, 378
Rucker, William B., 200
Rulon, P. J., 36
Ruml, Beardsley, 36, 73, 379, 421, 499
Rush, Benjamin, 380, 381, 382
Rush, James, 383
Russell, James E., 73
Russell, William F., 73
Russell Sage Foundation, 59
Rutland Corner House, Boston, 384
Ryan, H. H., 428

Sachs, Hans, 33
St. Louis Movement, 204
St. Louis State Hospital, 385
St. Paul Phrenological Society, 386
St. Peter State Hospital, St. Peter,
  Minnesota, 387
Salisbury, Helen, 388
Salt, Henry S., 114
Sanborn, Herbert Charles, 389
Sanford, Edmund C., 184, 447, 448
San Francisco Psychoanalytic Group, 33
Santayana, George, 91, 259, 264, 280
Saperstein, Esther, 391
Sargent, Helen Durham, 391
de Sauze, E. B., 428
Savage, Alexander Duncan, 393
Schaffner, Bertram, 353
Scheerer, Martin, 394
Schiller, Ferdinand, 233

Schilling, Robert, 395
Schleidt, Wolfgang, 1
Schloring, Raleight, 428
Schluderman, Edwin H., 200
Schmalhausen, Samuel Daniel, 143
Scholar, Gustav, 396
Scholle, Howard, 397
Schooland, John B., 1
School and Society, 76
Schroeder, Theodore Albert, 100, 399,
  400, 401
Schurman, Jacob Gould, 402, 487
Schurz, Carl, 290
Science, 76
Science Press, 75
Scott, Walter Dill, 36, 403
Scott Company, 403
Seaman, Louis, 487
Sears, Robert A., 404
Seashore, Carl E., 36, 76, 351, 447, 499
Seashore, Harold, 51
Segal, Arthur, 405
Senn, Milton J. E., 406
Shakleford, Thomas, 233
Shaler, Nathaniel, 208
Shapeley, Harlow, 150, 287
Shattuck, Lemuel, 359
Shaw, Clifford Robe, 82
Shaw, Ruth Faison, 407
Shelton, Mary E., 408
Shelton, Rhoda Amanda, 408
Shelton family, 408
Shepardson, Whitney H., 73
Sheppard, Moses, 409
Sherrington, C. S., 499
Sherwin, Martha May, 410
Shipley, Walter Cleveland, 411
Shipley Institute of Living Scale, 411
Sigmund Freud Archives, Inc., 181
Simmel, Ernst, 33, 167
Sizer, Nelson, 57, 412
Slater-Hammel, A. T., 426
Smith, Adam, 234
Smith, Bunnie Othaniel, 413
Smith, Henry Arthur, 414
Smith, L. W., 428
Smith, Stephen, 35
Snedden, David, 428
Snodgrass, James M., 426
Solomon, Rebecca (Miller), 415
Sommer, Julia K., 149
Sontag, Lester W., 416
Sorley, William Ritchie, 443

Repository Index

The location of each collection, and the collections available at each repository, as listed below, reflect the information available to the compilers as of December 1981. But the user is warned to contact each repository before appearing on its doorstep. Collections are moved from one archive to another, others become unavailable to researchers due to staff shortages and restrictions placed on their use by donors, and still others are withdrawn from use while additional items are interfiled into them. Furthermore, opening and closing hours, conditions of use, restrictions on photoduplication, and the like are constantly in flux. Archivists are always pleased to have the holdings of their repositories used, and are usually more than happy to respond to requests for information.

Subject Index

The classification of any one entry under the headings of this index is clearly arbitrary and, undoubtedly, other subject categories are possible. However, this version reflects the compilers' understanding of the contents of each collection, and it should be serviceable. In any event, many entries have been classified under more than one heading.